D1373958

COUNSELING STRATEGIES
WITH SPECIAL POPULATIONS

Publication Number 965

AMERICAN LECTURE SERIES®

A Publication in

The BANNERSTONE DIVISION *of*

AMERICAN LECTURES IN SOCIAL AND REHABILITATION PSYCHOLOGY

Editors of the Series

JOHN G. CULL, Ph.D.

Director, Regional Counselor Training Program
Department of Rehabilitation Counseling
Virginia Commonwealth University
Fishersville, Virginia

and

RICHARD E. HARDY, Ed.D.

Diplomate in Counseling Psychology (ABPP)
Chairman, Department of Rehabilitation Counseling
Virginia Commonwealth University
Richmond, Virginia

The American Lecture Series in Social and Rehabilitation Psychology offers books which are concerned with man's role in his milieu. Emphasis is placed on how this role can be made more effective in a time of social conflict and a deteriorating physical environment. The books are oriented toward descriptions of what future roles should be and are not concerned exclusively with the delineation and definition of contemporary behavior. Contributors are concerned to a considerable extent with prediction through the use of a functional view of man as opposed to a descriptive, anatomical point of view.

Books in this series are written mainly for the professional practitioner; however, academicians will find them of considerable value in both undergraduate and graduate courses in the helping services.

Counseling Strategies
With Special
Populations

BOWLING GREEN STATE UNIVERSITY · DISCARDED · LIBRARY

John G. Cull

Richard E. Hardy

Diplomate in Counseling Psychology (ABPP)

CHARLES C THOMAS · PUBLISHER
Springfield · Illinois · U.S.A.

BOWLING GREEN STATE UNIVERSITY LIBRARY

Published and Distributed Throughout the World by

CHARLES C THOMAS • PUBLISHER

Bannerstone House

301-327 East Lawrence Avenue, Springfield, Illinois, U.S.A.

This book is protected by copyright. No part of it
may be reproduced in any manner without written
permission from the publisher.

© *1975, by* CHARLES C THOMAS • PUBLISHER

ISBN 0-398-03284-X

Library of Congress Catalog Card Number: 74-12153

*With THOMAS BOOKS careful attention is given to all details of
manufacturing and design. It is the Publisher's desire to present books that are
satisfactory as to their physical qualities and artistic possibilities and
appropriate for their particular use. THOMAS BOOKS will be true to those
laws of quality that assure a good name and good will.*

Printed in the United States of America
C-1

Library of Congress Cataloging in Publication Data

Cull, John G.
    Counseling strategies with special populations.

    (American lecture series, publication no. 965. A
publication in the Bannerstone division of American
lectures in social and rehabilitation psychology)
      1. Rehabilitation counseling. I. Hardy, Richard E.,
joint author. II. Title. [DNLM: 1. Counseling.
2. Handicapped. 3. Social service, Psychiatric.
WM58 C967c]
HD7255.5.C793   361'.06   74-12153
ISBN 0-398-03284-X

361.06
C96c

609510

DEDICATION

This book is dedicated to
DEAN HARLAND W. WESTERMANN, Ph.D.
for his exemplary leadership
and constant support of
rehabilitation efforts

PREFACE

IT IS THE AIM of this book to bring together the results of a great deal of thinking concerning some special problems which counselors face in working with special population groups. Many of the groups and supporting topics described in this book are generally overlooked in the work of the person preparing text and reference handbooks for counselors.

It has been our intention to call attention to these groups and topics and offer useful information to the counselor in his most important work with persons from each special group. While we refer to the rehabilitation counselor on many occasions and in many chapters, we feel the book is not limited to counselors working in rehabilitation settings or to counselors with the job title of rehabilitation counselor. We feel that counselors in most settings have a heavy rehabilitation component in their work. In fact almost all counselors can be considered to be "rehabilitation" counselors to a degree.

While the book is certainly not all-inclusive, it provides a basic pool of information dealing with counseling strategies for some special populations. The counselor of today must be open to a rapid pace of learning and relearning. He must be ready to invest large amounts of energy and a great deal of time in work involvement in order to be effective. In addition, he must have a real body of information about human behavior and the special problems of those with whom he works.

It has been our wish to bring to the reader some of the information which he will need in various counseling settings. We have taken the liberty of selecting certain special populations and disabling situations and offering descriptions of how the counselor can be of service. The counselors reading this book will want to generalize the information to various persons who have similar problems as those described.

This book is the result of our studies, our experiences in counseling, and our philosophy of counseling and human behavior. We are deeply indebted to many persons who have helped us in the development of our view of counseling and particularly our view of the role of the counselor. While we cannot acknowledge the hundreds of clients who have taught us so much about counseling, our many graduate students, and our colleagues along the way who have shared experiences with us, we would like to single out a few who have made a significant impact on our thinking. They include: Dr. Robert P. Anderson, Vernon M. Arrell, Mary K. Bauman, Dr. John M. Cobun, Ben F. Coffman, William T. Coppage, Thorold S. Funk, Dr. Bernard A. Hodinko, William W. Lamprell, Dr. Garris Long, Harriet Naylor, Al Puth, Wendell Taylor, Harry Wellons, and Earl W. Wolfe.

Particular acknowledgement goes to our colleagues who are members of the faculty of the Department of Rehabilitation at the Virginia Commonwealth University: Dr. Paul E. Biles, Professor John D. Hutchinson, Dr. Robert M. Lassiter, Dr. Warren R. Rule, Dr. R. Dean Taylor, Professor Leo A. Thralls and Professor Keith C. Wright and warm and special friends, Kathy and Ted Abernathy of Richmond.

JOHN G. CULL   RICHARD E. HARDY

The following are selected books which have appeared in the
Social and Rehabilitation Psychology Series.

PROBLEMS OF ADOLESCENTS: SOCIAL AND
PSYCHOLOGICAL APPROACHES
    Richard E. Hardy and John G. Cull

REHABILITATION OF THE URBAN DISADVANTAGED
    John G. Cull and Richard E. Hardy

CLIMBING GHETTO WALLS: DISADVANTAGEMENT,
DELINQUENCY AND REHABILITATION
    Richard E. Hardy and John G. Cull

COUNSELING HIGH SCHOOL STUDENTS: SPECIAL
PROBLEMS AND APPROACHES
    John G. Cull and Richard E. Hardy

MEDICAL AND PSYCHOLOGICAL ASPECTS OF
DISABILITY
    A. Beatrix Cobb

THERAPEUTIC NEEDS OF THE FAMILY: PROBLEMS,
DESCRIPTIONS AND THERAPEUTIC APPROACHES
    Richard E. Hardy and John G. Cull

TYPES OF DRUG ABUSERS AND THEIR ABUSES
    John G. Cull and Richard E. Hardy

SPECIAL PROBLEMS IN REHABILITATION
    A. Beatrix Cobb

CAREER GUIDANCE FOR YOUNG WOMEN:
CONSIDERATIONS IN PLANNING PROFESSIONAL
CAREERS
    Richard E. Hardy and John G. Cull

CAREER GUIDANCE FOR BLACK ADOLESCENTS:
A STUDY IN SELECTED PROFESSIONAL OCCUPATIONS
    John G. Cull and Richard E. Hardy

AVOCATIONAL ACTIVITIES FOR THE HANDICAPPED
    Robert P. Overs, Barbara DeMarco, Elizabeth O'Connor

GROUP COUNSELING IN THERAPY TECHNIQUES AND
SPECIAL SETTINGS
    Richard E. Hardy and John G. Cull

CONTENTS

Part Two

COUNSELING STRATEGIES WITH THE PHYSICALLY DISABLED

Part Three

COUNSELING STRATEGIES WITH THE SOCIALLY DISABLED

Part Four
SPECIAL COUNSELING PROBLEM AREAS

COUNSELING STRATEGIES
WITH SPECIAL POPULATIONS

PART ONE

COUNSELING CONCERNS

Developing a Friendly Counseling Relationship
Developing Psychological Services in Social Service Agencies
Placement Advising and Counseling
The Use of Volunteers in Community Service Work

CHAPTER 1

DEVELOPING A FRIENDLY COUNSELING RELATIONSHIP

- Anatomy of the Counseling Session
- Greeting
- Opening the Interview
- Body of the Interview
- Closing the Interview

I**N THE COUNSELING LITERATURE** there is an abundance of information on philosophy, theory, approaches, etc. However, for the new professional worker, little is written on techniques of counseling which helps to insure the success of the counseling relationship. Generally these techniques are learned gradually during many counseling sessions. When discussing these techniques with experienced counselors, it is obvious that many feel such techniques stem from common sense or that everyone knows about them. We beg to differ. We have found in working with new counselors that many who have a good academic grasp of counseling theories still have difficulties in counseling sessions because of a lack of knowledge about how to put the theory and philosophy to work in practice.

ANATOMY OF THE COUNSELING SESSION

Regardless of the theoretical approach a counselor uses, what follows in this chapter holds true. The chapter sections are vehicles by which the counselor's theoretical orientation is implemented. While there may be some minor shifts according to varying theoretical approaches, the basic value and usefulness of

We gratefully acknowledge the substantial contribution of John D. Hutchinson in the development of this chapter.

these techniques remain constant. In rehabilitation counseling, interview sessions fall into three general types. There are interviews in which the goal of the counselor is to provide information to the client; secondly, some sessions are scheduled for the client to provide information to the counselor; and thirdly, the bulk of the counseling contacts may be classified as problem-solving sessions.

In each of these types of counseling sessions integral parts of the session are the same. Generally, in each counseling session regardless of type or purpose the period should be divided into the following parts: greeting, opening, body of the interview, and closing. These parts naturally will be divided unequally, but the counselor should decide before each interview roughly how much time will be spent in each area.

GREETING

Counseling is a directed personal interaction between two individuals. In order to interact effectively, each individual must accept the other. A basis for a warm working relationship must be established. Without this relationship very little, if any, counseling will occur. Instead of counseling sessions, the counselor will engage in conversations with the client. The counselor will gain very little insight into the feelings, motivating forces and reasons for actions of the client. Without the development of this relationship, the counselor often will become frustrated. He will feel thwarted. The client obviously will be motivated to achieve in the vocational rehabilitation process but somehow things just will not seem to click.

The development of this relationship or rapport is a major underlying goal of the early counseling sessions. While the interviews will be scheduled for other purposes (to explain the rehabilitation program, to prepare the client for various evaluative procedures, to obtain basic information, etc.), the counselor pays particular attention to the development of a working relationship with the client. During the first few sessions the counselor should become an individual who cares rather than the representative of an institution. A client can relate to another individual but cannot relate or interact with an institution or program or the representative of an institution or program. Therefore, at this point the counselors is recognizing the humanity of the client and is giving the client the opportunity *used* to do the same with him.

While a concerted effort is required to develop this relationship, once developed little effort is required to continue it. However, some effort is required and this aspect (developing the relationship) of counseling should not be neglected. The remnant of the major effort to establish rapport is the greeting of the client. Each counseling session should be started with a personal greeting. The time spent on this part of the counseling interview is an inverse function of the warmth of the relationship established. After a strong, warm relationship has been established less time is required; however, the greeting never should be overlooked or omitted. We feel a counselor and client must have feelings of friendship for the counseling process to succeed. "Greeting" is the normal activity of friends prior to getting down to more serious business.

If the contacts between counselor and client are relatively frequent, the greeting might be minimal; however, if the counselor and client have not had recent contacts, the counselor should spend more time on this aspect of the interview. This is obvious since it is natural that the longer the period between contacts, the greater the need for renewing the relationship which has been established.

OPENING THE INTERVIEW

After the greeting the counseling session is opened. The object of this next phase is to state the goals of this particular session. The counselor should give the client an evaluation of the progress being made in the rehabilitation process and tell him how the current interview fits into the process. For example:

As you know up to this point we have been gathering some basic information to help us evaluate your abilities and to develop a plan of action. I have received some of the reports we requested. Today, you and I will go over these reports. I will interpret them and next week we will start discussing our plan of action.

If the client does not know or understand the goals of the interview, he is forced to "second guess" the counselor. Each question posed has to be evaluated by the client. His response is directed at achieving his perception of the counselor's goal. If the statement of the goals of the interview is skipped and the counselor begins a counseling session with the question, "How are things going in school?" the answer almost invariably will be "fine," or some other noncommittal answer. Until the client figures out the purpose of this particular counseling session, his answers will remain relatively superficial and meaningless.

We have observed counseling sessions in which the counselor failed to clearly state the goals he wished the client to achieve. In the majority of these sessions the client's simultaneous searching and defensive fending-off of the counselor is quite obvious. The counselor realizes something is wrong, but he is unable to remedy the situation. We have seen some counseling interviews in which, after some time has passed, the client discovered the goals of the counselor. After verifying his perception of the counselor's goals, the client proceeded to repeat the counselor's questions and change or amplify the answers he had given previously.

The answers to almost any question depends upon the reason for the question rather than solely upon the nature of the question. As in the previous example, if the client is asked, "How are things going in school?" without discussing the purpose of the question, the answer will be a noncommittal "fine." This answer will change if prior to asking the question the counselor would say something like the following:

Today, I would like for us to discuss your progress in vocational training since (a) I understand you need some additional help, or (b) I understand you are having some difficulty with some of the other students (or some of the instructors), or (c) I know of a possible job if you and your instructor feel you are "ready," or (d) I understand you have not been attending regularly, or (e) I understand you have lost some of your tools.

After discussing the role of a statement of goals in the counseling session, one wonders why so much attention has been paid to the topic in this chapter since it seems to be such an integral and necessary part of counseling, but it becomes a part of a counselor's technique only after he has gained some experience.

BODY OF THE INTERVIEW

In the body of the interview the goals which were just stated are achieved. There are several factors which determine the degree of success the counselor will enjoy. These factors generally fall into two categories, attitudes of the counselor and actions of the counselor. The two will not be separated below since, as will be seen, the division is obvious.

Acceptance

One of the most important factors affecting the counseling session is the acceptance of the client by the counselor and the acceptance of the counselor by the client. This is an intangible phenomenon, but as the counseling process proceeds it becomes evident. Acceptance is related to rapport but is distinct from it. If the counselor fails to accept the client or the client fails to accept the counselor, an emotional and often rational gap will develop in the relationship. While a warm relationship may exist between the two, without such an acceptance of each other the facility with which mutual counseling goals are achieved will be impaired.

Assurance of the Counselor

The self-assurance of the counselor will determine to a great extent the success of his counseling. If the counselor lacks self-assurance, it is difficult for the client to place his faith and trust in him. The rehabilitation counselor is making a major intervention in the client's life. This intervention may have lifelong ramifications for the client. When the client recognizes a lack of self-assurance on the part of the counselor, he will either reject rehabilitation services or enter into a program of services with less than complete commitment. Either alternative will usually result in the case being "closed—not rehabilitated."

Perhaps the single most effective action a counselor can take to increase his self-assurance and increase the image of assurance he projects to the client is adequate preparation. Prior to each counseling session the counselor should review the case material he has obtained on the client along with what has been recorded in the progress notes. A counselor who has to ask the client what was discussed previously or planned in another session or who forgets events the client feels are of prime importance to his rehabilitation does not instill confidence.

Sincerity

The level of sincerity of the counselor is completely obvious to the client. Much to the surprise of many counselors even most of a counselor's mentally retarded clients are able to discern a lack of sincerity. Regardless of words or obvious actions to the contrary, lack of sincerity "shows through." The counselor should be aware of his actions and comments and evaluate them against the criterion of sincerity. A counselor who does not "level" with his client is courting a counseling failure. A counselor should rarely, if ever, react in a false manner with the client.

Professional Bearing

Even though the counselor establishes a warm working relationship with the client and both share and appreciate the realization of the individuality and humanity of the other, there is a difference between them. The client expects and demands the counselor recognize the difference. Not only does the client demand the recognition of the difference, he demands the difference be sharpened and maintained. The client needs and wants a professional person with whom he can effectively interact. He does not want nor need an equal.

Too often the counselor mistakenly interprets the admonishment to "establish rapport with the client" to mean "get on his level" or "develop a buddy relationship with him." The counselor should maintain his professional posture and be aware of the image he is projecting. Contrary to the beliefs held by many new counselors, a deep rapport can be developed while maintaining this professional distance.

Accuracy of Information

The number of times a counselor will give inaccurate or misleading information in an attempt to keep from having to admit not knowing something is truly surprising. Even with the best case preparation a counselor will have gaps of knowledge. He should have the self-assurance to admit not knowing a point. While this sounds superficial it is important to the counseling relationship. The counselor is not expected to know everything, but he is expected to develop a genuine relationship. As with the other qualities, a lack of genuineness or accuracy of responding will impair the counseling progress.

Verbal Communication

The voice is the prime vehicle for communicating in the counseling process; therefore, the voice plays a vital role in the success of a counseling program with a client. The amplitude of the counselor's voice should be appropriate. It should be maintained at conversational levels except when appropriately raised. Before raising the amplitude of his voice the counselor should have consciously determined it was necessary. Many new counselors and some more experienced counselors almost shout at blind persons. They feel if the client cannot see he cannot hear. Many counselors working with clients whose native language is one other than English tend to raise their voice when the client fails to understand a concept. Often this can be observed also with counselors of the mentally retarded. Rather than explain a concept in simpler terms, the counselor feels he can overpower the barrier to communication by repeating his words louder and louder.

The counselor's voice is a professional tool much as the scalpel is a professional tool of the surgeon. As such the counselor should develop his voice and use it in a fashion which communicates most effectively. Not only should he be aware of the amplitude of his voice (loudness or softness), but he should pay heed to the speed with which he talks and the clarity and tone of his voice. He should speak in a well-regulated voice (not too fast) which is clear. He should be particularly concerned with his enunciation. We feel a new counselor can materially benefit from recording selected counseling sessions to evaluate, among other things, his voice.

Another aspect of verbal communication which must be evaluated for each client is the counselor's vocabulary level. While it is obviously detrimental to the counseling outcomes for a counselor to use a vocabulary which is pitched at a level much higher than the level the client is prepared for, it is equally detrimental for a counselor to use wording which is inappropriately simple. Again, we have observed new counselors in sessions who felt that since the client was physically impaired he must be intellectually impaired. These counselors would attempt to communicate with an intellectually capable client in an insultingly simple fashion. Often the client will attempt to communicate his displeasure by the tone of his responses and more obviously by increasing the vocabulary level of his responses. A sensitive counselor recognizes these cues and modifies his level of approach; however, in many instances the counselor's unconscious stereotype of the relationship between physical impairment and intellectual impairment is so strong that the cues given by the client are ineffectual.

As a part of verbal communication the counselor might choose to use levity. If the time is well chosen and the content of the response impeccable, lightness can be highly effective in a counseling interview. Regrettably, however, these two conditions are not always met. While levity can be highly effective it also can become a devastating influence on the outcome of counseling sessions. A counselor would be wise to sparingly interject lightness into the counseling sessions. Levity misinterpreted by the client can effectively block the establishment of rapport. Generally, people in a dependent status in a relationship tend to have more ideas of self-reference than people playing a more independent role. Therefore, a client easily may feel a counselor is laughing *at* him rather than *with* him.

Nonverbal Communication

While the voice is the prime vehicle for communicating in the counseling session, it is not the only vehicle. Nonverbal communication has a very powerful influence on counseling outcomes. The old adage "actions speak louder than words" is very true in counseling. We communicate many of our feelings and attitudes by our nonverbal behavior. Boredom, lack of patience, disbelief and lack of interest come through all too clearly in our behavior regardless of our words.

One of the most important actions we can take to communicate interest, concern and awareness is to look at the client. Do not read a folder, a report, or a letter when the client is talking with you. Maintain good eye contact. A counselor does not have to adopt an eyeball-to-eyeball posture to communicate interest, but he does have to look at the client. If you feel this is unimportant, turn around the next time a friend or colleague is excitedly describing an event to you. Pay particular attention to his level of excitement or motivation to relate the incident to you. Many counselors feel note-taking during a counseling session is not damaging to the overall result of the interview. We disagree. We feel note-taking and case recording should wait until after the client has left. It takes very little practice for a counselor to develop the ability to record the pertinent points of the interview after the close of the interview.

As a part of eye contact or looking at the client, give him your undivided attention. Nothing seems more fruitless than trying to communicate your feelings or aspirations with someone who is shuffling and stacking papers; playing with a pencil, keys, or coins or constantly cleaning, reaming, filling, and lighting a pipe. While you may be interested and attentive, your nonverbal behavior might not communicate your attention and interest.

A type of client contact with which the rehabilitation counselor should be familiar is voice contact. Without realizing it, a counselor often can reject a client through a type of contact similar to that discussed above. In this case the counselor will ask others to respond for the client, such as a spouse, parent, sibling, attendant, or reader. Often a counselor will ask a sighted spouse to tell the blind client (who is present) that he should go in for a general medical examination or ask the sighted spouse or parent about the client's reaction to an event when the client is completely capable of responding for himself. In restaurants one will repeatedly see a waitress approach a group in which there is a blind customer and ask, "What will he order?" This behavior also occurs among counselors with clients other than blind persons. When this type of contact occurs, many clients are infuriated.

Control of the Interview

The rehabilitation counselor must always control the interview. If the client controls the direction of the interview, counseling ceases. We once observed a student in counseling who turned over control of the interview to the client without realizing what he had done. After asking the client about his vocational plans, the client responded and asked the counselor about rehabilitation counseling (a totally inappropriate field for the client). After the counselor responded, the client continued to elicit responses from the counselor regarding his educational background, his motivation for entering rehabilitation counseling, his hobbies and his vocational plans. It was a beautiful counseling session but the roles were switched. The counselor was totally unaware of the dynamics of the interaction between the two. The client was in complete control of the interview and none of the counseling goals were accomplished.

This counselor listened to the client but did not hear him. In counseling there is a vast difference between listening and hearing. Hearing implies a greater degree of understanding of what is being said than listening implies. A counselor should not only listen to what is being said but should be keenly aware of what the client is communicating on a more basic meaningful level—what he is feeling and what is occurring in the counseling session. The counselor should try to understand not only what the client said but why he said it and what he is trying to accomplish.

In determining the direction of the interview, the counselor also should control the pace of the interview. After setting the goals to be achieved, the counselor should have a relatively clear plan of direction and should pace the interview in such a manner as to achieve the stated goal or goals in the allotted time available. Often a client will gain control, not only of the direction of the interview but also of the pace of the interview. This is done by his going into too much detail in responding to a question or by bringing too much extraneous material into the responses. If the counselor fails to be aware of this type of behavior, he will find he achieves fewer and fewer of his counseling goals. Also he will discover he knows a considerable amount of facts about the client but has developed relatively little insight into the client's feelings.

A third type of control of the interview is that of the sequence of the interview. After the statement of the goals to be achieved, the interview should then proceed in a logical orderly fashion. This sequence should be outlined roughly (at least mentally) prior to meeting with the client.

If something has occurred with the client since the last contact which merits a change in the anticipated goals, the counselor should switch goals, but this switch should be conscious and discussed by the counselor and client. When the goals are not changed, the direction of the session should be obvious to both. If the counselor develops a hit-or-miss illogical sequence, he ends up confusing the client and wondering when he has fully accomplished the goals of the session.

The control of the interview is maintained, among other actions, by the type of questions the counselor asks. When closed questions are put to the client, generally he will answer in the shortest fashion possible. Closed questions do not elicit feelings or elaboration on the part of the client. The following are examples of closed questions:

Do you like school?

Where do you live?

Do you get along well with employers?

Unless a counselor has a highly verbal client, the responses these questions elicit will be relatively useless. More productive questions would have been the following:

Tell me your feelings about school.

Tell me about your home and neighborhood.

What are your feelings about employers and your relations with them?

Another type of nonproductive question counselors often ask is a leading question—one which has a predetermined answer because of the way it is phrased. For example:

You like school, don't you?

You get along well with employers, don't you?

Not only is the type of question important, but the clarity of the question also determines the quality of response. If the client only partially understands a question, he cannot respond to it as fully as the counselor would like. Therefore, care should be taken in phrasing the question or statement to insure it elicits the desired response. A part of the clarity aspect of questions is asking one question at a time. Often a counselor will ask several questions in one statement without realizing it. For example:

> The last few weeks your attendance on the job has been poor, why? Aren't you interested in the job any longer? You have to work regularly to hold a job. What are you going to do?

When a counselor asks a question, he should be sure he has the answer before going on to the next question. First, he should be sure the client answered the question which was asked. Often in a counseling session the answer bears little or no resemblance to the question. The response should be evaluated and discussed or the question repeated. Secondly, the counselor should be patient and allow the client ample opportunity to respond fully before asking the next question or making the next statement.

The last facet of interview control to be covered is the control of the depth of the counseling session. The depth of the interview is controlled by the focus of questions asked and statements made. The more the focus is on feelings of the client, the deeper the session will progress. In many instances the counselor needs to explore the feelings of the client; however, he should be aware of his professional limitations and as such not allow the counseling to proceed to a depth for which the counselor is not prepared professionally to work with. Conversely, if the counselor fails to elicit the feelings of the client their interaction remains on too superficial a level to be of value to the client.

There is a broad band in which vocational counseling is effective. If the counselor allows the sessions to become too deep, they become less vocationally oriented and generally less productive. If the counselor does not take the interview to sufficient depth, he will remain on the conversational level and will discover his "counseling" is rather unproductive.

Atmosphere of the Interview

The client's participation is essential for the success of counseling and his participation is a function of the atmosphere the counselor creates. The counseling atmosphere proceeds on several levels at once. It may be supportive and permissive, authoritarian or threatening, and structured or unstructured. It may be cynical, exacting, warm or possessive. The counselor can best determine the atmosphere he creates by observing the type and quality of participation coming from the client. Also the counselor can get feedback from the client through his reaction to the counselor. Is the client guarded and defensive or is he comfortable and open in his reaction?

CLOSING THE INTERVIEW

The last part of the interview is the closing. Surprisingly, the new counselor often has trouble closing an interview. This is especially true if the client is quite verbal. A natural ending comes and the session continues. The counselor realizes he should terminate the interview but does not know how to go about the task. If he is lucky most of his interviews just naturally wind down and are terminated, not so much by him but more by a tacit mutual agreement. If the counselor has difficulty closing the interview he does not control the interview.

Closing the interview is relatively simple once a pattern is established in the counselor's mind. The pattern for each view should consist of the greeting, the statement of goals, the body of the interview and the closing. The closing consists of a restatement of the goals, a brief review of what was discussed, a brief evaluation of the accomplishment of the goals, a generalized statement of what goals will most likely be accomplished in the next counseling session, an assignment of responsibility for accomplishing tasks before the next session and the assignment of a definite appointment or a statement of the conditions which must occur prior to the assignment of an appointment for the next session. An example of a closing in keeping with the example set in the section on opening the interview follows:

> Now, Mr. Smith, in the few minutes we have remaining let us look at what we have accomplished. We were to discuss the reports we have received on you. We have discussed your General Aptitude Test Battery scores, the results of the interest test you took, and have evaluated your past jobs and hobbies in light of these scores. We have discussed your interest in a particular vocation. Next week, we will explore this vocation in some depth. Prior to our next meeting on Friday at 11:00, you go to the vocational training school and talk to Mr. Jones about this particular vocation and I will contact some employers in this field to obtain some information regarding current demands, entry salary range, and advancement potential.

This is a quite natural closing for a counseling session. Some counselors get to this point and then almost compulsively ask the client some related question. This results in confusion for the client (is the interview over or not) and frustration for the counselor (after having closed the interview how do you go about closing it again).

SUGGESTED READINGS

Brammer, Lawrence M. and Shostrom, Everett L.: *Therapeutic Psychology.* Englewood Cliffs, Prentice-Hall, 1968.

Carkhuff, Robert R.: *Helping and Human Relations.* New York, Holt, Rinehart and Winston, 1969, vol. I.

———: *Helping and Human Relations.* New York, Holt, Rinehart and Winston, 1969, vol. 2.

Cull, John G. and Hardy, Richard E.: *Counseling High School Students: Special Problems and Approaches.* Springfield, Thomas, 1974.

Hardy, Richard E. and Cull, John G.: *Group Counseling and Therapy Techniques in Special Settings.* Springfield, Thomas, 1974.

Ivey, Allen E.: *Microcounseling.* Springfield, Thomas, 1971.

Mitchell, Calvin M., Bozarth, J. D., and Craft, C. C.: *Antecedents to psychotherapeutic outcome.* Arkansas Rehabilitation Research and Training Center, University of Arkansas, NIMH, Final Report, March 1973 #MHI2306.

Shertzer, Bruce and Stone, Shelly S.: *Fundamentals of Counseling.* Boston, Houghton, Mifflin Co., 1968.

CHAPTER 2

DEVELOPING PSYCHOLOGICAL SERVICES IN SOCIAL SERVICE AGENCIES .

- Developing and Using Psychological and Related Services
- Indications for Psychological Evaluations
- Contraindication for Psychological Evaluation
- Referral for Psychological Services
- Selection of a Psychologist
- The Psychologist's Report
- Use of Psychological Evaluation
- Developing Models of Psychological Services for State Rehabilitation Agencies
- State Rehabilitation Administrators' Views on Psychological Evaluation

---

DEVELOPING AND USING PSYCHOLOGICAL AND RELATED SERVICES

THIS CHAPTER WILL INCLUDE various concepts concerning the development of psychological services in socially and vocationally oriented settings. The number of persons being served through social agencies has skyrocketed. Psychological services must be expanded and improved, and this is a priority consideration in serving clients.

The counselor has been called the key to effective rehabilitation work and rightly so since he is the center of activity, the coordinator, and often the developer of services to his clients. The responsibility for the success of various steps in the rehabilitation process rests upon the counselor's shoulders—psychological and related services are no exception.

19

Psychologists are engaged in a wide variety of activities, many of which relate directly to the goals of the individual client's needs. The counselor must develop professional psychological resources in much the same way that he develops community resources. Of the wide array of services offered by psychologists, three in which the counselor will be particularly interested include the following:

1. General psychological evaluations—relatively superficial but broad spectrum screening evaluation.

2. Speciality psychological evaluations—narrow in-depth evaluations (diagnosis of learning disabilities, determination of abilities, aptitudes and interests, and description of personality patterns of handicapped clients).

3. Individual and group adjustment counseling.

Counselors are becoming increasingly aware of the need for making the most effective use of psychological services during the counseling process. Therefore, the new counselor should acquaint himself thoroughly with the services provided by the psychologist and the role each of these services plays in the counseling process. He can then provide the most needed services to his client at the appropriate time in the professionally appropriate manner.

INDICATIONS FOR PSYCHOLOGICAL EVALUATIONS

Quite often the new counselor is in a quandary concerning when he should obtain additional psychological data. He feels, as a counselor, it is his responsibility to evaluate his client in order to counsel him. While he can agree on the necessity for psychological evaluation in the counseling process, he needs some rather specific guidelines relative to securing such evaluation. The most obvious response to this question is, "The counselor should secure a psychological evaluation when he has a specific question regarding his client's personality or personal attributes which he (the counselor) cannot answer." More specifically, the counselor should obtain a psychological evaluation when he is developing a counseling plan which will be of long-term duration. If a long-term plan or counseling strategy is developed, some basic assumptions are made relative to mental ability, interests, aptitudes and emotional stability. These assumptions should be checked out early in order to help insure the ultimate success of the plan. If the assumptions are not verified by means of a psychological evaluation but are found erroneous, a great deal of the client's time and energies can be wasted.

Many psychological evaluations are obtained at the beginning of the counseling process during the diagnostic phase when the individual's basic problems are being established. A psychological evaluation should be made in cases in which need for counseling services is based upon mental retardation, functional retardation and behavioral disorders.

In developing the counseling plan, the counselor needs to have a fairly complete understanding of the client's functional educational level, mental ability, aptitudes, and interests. If this needed information is missing, it should be obtained. If part of the information the counselor has is unclear, ambiguous, or contradictory, the counselor should clear up the confusion with a psychological evaluation. For example, if the client has a reported educational achievement level or reported level of intellectual ability substantially lower than that required on a job the client performed successfully, the counselor should clarify the obvious contradictions by psychological testing.

If the counselor suspects important talents, capacities, abilities or disabilities which are unreported but have a bearing on the probable vocational objective, a psychological evaluation should be purchased to delineate these attributes. Also an evaluation should be obtained if the client has certain disabilities which later on materially affect his capacities, abilities, skills or personality. For example, a client who is experiencing mild anesthesia in his hands and fingers should be tested for manual dexterity prior to settling on a vocational objective calling for a manipulative ability. A client interested in electronics assembly work should be tested for color blindness.

Lastly, a psychological evaluation should be obtained if the client is exhibiting or has exhibited behavior the counselor does not understand. If the client's current behavior patterns are not predictable and are difficult to understand, the counselor should enlist the aid of the psychologist to explain the client's personality structure. If the client's past history is filled with events or actions the counselor can not reconcile, such as unexplained job changes, frequent moves from one community to another, a lack of organization to the client's vocational history and so forth, a psychological evaluation is in order to describe the client's personality structure in an effort to explain his behavior pattern.

CONTRAINDICATION FOR PSYCHOLOGICAL EVALUATION

Perhaps looking at cases when psychological evaluation is unnecessary would be meaningful. An obvious case in which a psychological evaluation is unnecessary is when the client recently has been successfully employed and intends to return to his particular vocation following the physical restoration and other rehabilitation services he will receive.

If the client has been successfully employed but is now unable to find similar work because of employer prejudice toward the client, it is necessary for the counselor to use his counseling and vocational placement skills to convince the employers of the client's ability. In this case it would not be appropriate to obtain a psychological evaluation in an effort to change the client's vocational objective.

Psychological testing is not needed when a client has been successfully employed and the new vocational objective constitutes only a minor shift or the new job is directly related to his prior work. There is no need for testing when the client has developed a long and rich background of information regarding a particular industry or job family; and his new vocational objective, though not previously performed by him, is sufficiently related for the counselor and client to be safe in assuming he can meet the demands of the job. A separate but related case concerns the client having a long and rich background of educational information and experience, and the client plans to study or work in areas related to his background. Evaluation is not needed in this case.

Summary   In essence, a psychological evaluation is needed when the client's behavior is to be predicted over a long period or his behavior is difficult to predict over a short period of time. An evaluation is not needed when the client's behavior is understandable and predictable or if he has established a related pattern of vocational growth over an extended period of time.

At times, counselors will threaten to deny services if a client refuses to submit to the testing and interviewing of a psychologist. In many instances, if the client continues to refuse, the case is closed—"The client is not motivated." Even though this occurs much less frequently than it has in the past, it is appropriate to discuss. As counselors become more professional and more aware of the needs of clients, they will be more attuned to the motivating factors operating in the client. If the client refuses services which the counselor offers, the counselor should seek to understand and modify behavior through counseling rather than being threatened and defensive himself and reacting in a punitive manner toward the client.

REFERRAL FOR PSYCHOLOGICAL SERVICES

When securing psychological services, the counselor should ask himself some basic questions: What specific knowledge can be obtained from the psychologist which will be of value in the counseling process? What data can he (the counselor) obtain and what data should he request from the psychologist? When these questions have been asked and answered, the counselor is better prepared to make an intelligent referral to the psychologist. As mentioned above, there are numerous types of psychological evaluations; therefore, it is inadequate for a counselor to merely refer a client for a "psychological evaluation." If he is expecting highly specific definitive information from the psychologist, the rehabilitation counselor must set definite limits for the psychologist and provide him with the appropriate background information. Gandy's referral form, if used, will tend to increase materially the quality of psychological reports the counselor receives. This referral form should constitute the minimum information forwarded to the psychologist; however, generally little more than a request for an evaluation is sent.

Much of the information called for on the form is already in the case folder so it is easily accessible to the counselor. In order to select the appropriate instruments and interpret them, the psychologist needs the social-vocational-medical background information. Therefore, to facilitate the work of the psychologist and relieve the client of having to answer the same questions repeatedly and to increase the effectiveness of the psychological interview, the counselor should make a concerted effort to supply the psychologist all pertinent information.

REFERRAL FOR PSYCHOLOGICAL-VOCATIONAL EVALUATION

FROM: .... DATE: ....

TO: ....

IDENTIFICATION:

Name of Client ....

Social Security No. ....

Address ....

Sex .... Age .... Race .... Marital Status ....

No. Dependents ....

SOCIAL-VOCATIONAL-MEDICAL:

Economic Stratum ....

Family Environment ....

Formal Education ....

Usual Occupation ....

Vocational Success ....

Leisure Activities ....

Physical or Mental Impairments ....

General Health ....

BEHAVIORAL OBSERVATIONS:

General Observations (appearance, mannerisms, communication, attitude, motivation):

....
....
....

REASON FOR REFERRAL:

Statement of Problem ....
....

Specific Questions ....
....
....

Enclosures: ....
....

This form was taken from Gandy, J.: The psychological-vocational referral in rehabilitation. Unpublished Master's Thesis, University of South Carolina, 1968.

An individual's economic status, home situation, the degree of vocational success he has experienced and the physical or mental impairments he has will have a direct and major bearing on his behavior and personality. Test responses and results have to be evaluated in comparison with the above factors. If this information is not provided to the psychologist, he will have to interview the client at some length. The more time he spends in this duplicative effort, the less time he has to evaluate the client.

The counselor generally has had several contacts with the client before the client is referred to the psychologist. Also, the counselor is a professional who is skilled in observations; therefore, it is of particular value to the psychologist to have access to the observations the counselor has made. These observations can be quite meaningful since the counselor sees the client under a variety of conditions and the psychologist sees the client only in the testing and interview situation on one occasion.

Perhaps the most important information the psychologist should receive is usually not given to him. This is a statement of the problem which prompted the counselor to refer the client to the psychologist. In order to specifically meet the needs of the counselor, the psychologist should have this statement since it will, in many cases, determine the particular instruments the psychologist will use. In conjunction with this statement of the problem, the counselor should outline the specific questions he wants answered by the psychologist. By considering these questions, the psychologist can further tailor his evaluation to the specific needs of the counselor.

Lastly, a good referral should include other reports, evaluations and examinations which have a direct bearing upon the psychological evaluation. These would include other psychological evaluations, social evaluations and reports, psychiatric data, the general medical examination report and some medical examinations by specialists.

SELECTION OF A PSYCHOLOGIST

After deciding upon what information the counselor himself will obtain and what information will be expected from the psychologist, the counselor has to select a psychologist. The counselor can obtain psychological data himself or he may rely upon a psychometrist (an individual skilled in the administration and interpretation of psychological, vocational and educational tests; an individual trained at a lower level than that of a psychologist), a psychologist in private practice outside the agency, a staff psychologist or a consulting psychologist (these latter two will be discussed later). Generally, if he selects either the psychometrist, the staff psychologist, or the consulting psychologist, the agency will describe the mechanics of referral in a policy manual or procedure manual. Therefore, here we will concern ourselves only with using the psychologist in private practice.

When the counselor is attempting to do part of the psychological study himself, it is very important for him to recognize his limitations in the field of evaluation. Certainly few counselors are skilled in psychological evaluation to the degree that they are able to use a wide variety of instruments. All counselors, however, should be able to use skillfully a small number of tests comprising a specific battery. When the counselor is inexperienced in the type of testing which he feels should be done, he must be able to secure the services of a qualified psychologist.

When obtaining the services of a psychologist in private practice, the counselor should have at hand a list of psychologists who are well known for their competency and who are experienced in working with handicapped persons. It is generally felt that psychologists who belong to the division of clinical psychology, the division of counseling psychology, or the division of psychological aspects of disability of the American Psychological Association will be interested in the field of rehabilitation and will be most helpful to the counselor. However, the counselor must recognize that psychologists, like other professionals, have areas of special interest. A psychologist who is knowledgeable concerning the emotionally disturbed or the mentally retarded may be relatively inexperienced in testing the physically handicapped.

When the client is sent to the psychologist, he is referred on an individual basis just as he is for a general or speciality medical examination. The payment is made according to a fee schedule developed by the agency and usually the state or local psychological associations. As with a new physician, a psychologist in private practice who is being utilized for the first time should be contacted. The counselor should discuss the vocational rehabilitation program, its goals, its procedures for referral, reporting, payment and the agency's fee schedule.

THE PSYCHOLOGIST'S REPORT

After the referral of the client, the counselor has every reason to expect and should demand speedy service for his client. This speedy service entails both a prompt appointment to see the client and a written report of the finding submitted. While the report should be received within ten days of the client's appointment, quite often it takes longer; however, if it routinely takes longer and at times exceeds three weeks, the counselor should discuss the problem with the psychologist so that he may receive better service or change psychologists. When the counselor receives the psychological report, it should cover five basic areas:

1. Clinical observations of the psychologist
2. Tests administered
3. Results and interpretation of results
4. Specific recommendations
5. Summary

The observations of the psychologist are important since they provide the flavor of the evaluation and, without them the evaluation would be quite sterile. These observations will comment on the client's emotional behavior, appearance, motivation, reaction to the testing and so forth.

The tests which were administered should be spelled out for two reasons; first, most fee schedules are based upon the number and type of tests administered; but, more importantly, the counselor needs to know upon what data the psychologist is basing assumptions and making recommendations. In the reporting and interpreting of results, the counselor should find the results of all the tests given with an explanation of their importance. This section is highly technical, however, it should be very logical since this is where the psychologist builds his case. If some of the test results are not noteworthy or are not used in the diagnosis and recommendations, this fact should be mentioned and explained in the interpretation section. Essentially this is where the psychologist logically bridges the gap between his clinical observations, the test results, the diagnosis, and the recommendations he will make. Above all the sections should be very sensible and understandable.

In the recommendations section, the psychologist should make a number of suggestions which are addressed to the specific referral problem and the questions the counselor asked on referral of the client. Recommendations should be stated clearly and concisely. If the counselor does not understand them, he should never hesitate to call the psychologist for clarification. The summary is a short, clear summation of the evaluation stated in nontechnical terms.

USE OF PSYCHOLOGICAL EVALUATION

After receiving the report, the counselor is confronted with how to use the evaluation. The use of the data will be easier if psychological evaluations are viewed as an integral part of counseling and closely related to all other rehabilitation services and not as an isolated event or service. The evaluation can be used in counseling sessions to aid the client in better understanding himself and in identifying his major problem areas. Additionally, the counselor can use the psychological evaluation as a counseling tool to aid the client in developing insights specifically related to his relative strengths and limitations and in helping him in making reasonable plans and decisions.

In interpreting the test results to the client, the counselor should develop short, clear, concise methods of describing to the client the purpose of the tests he took and the meaning of the results; but, by all means, the counselor should communicate only on the level at which the client is fully "with" the counselor. A most effective means of interpreting test results is relating test data in meaningful terms to the client's behavior. A trap to avoid is becoming overly identified with the client's test scores. They should be presented in a manner that will allow him to question, reject, accept or modify the presentation and interpretation without having to reject the counselor. The counselor should not project his own subjective feelings into the results he is using.

CAUTIONS IN USING PSYCHOLOGICAL TEST SCORES

While psychological testing plays a vital role in the counseling process, there are some cautions which need to be exercised in their use. It should be remembered that test scores are just that— only test scores. The indications are a product of the interpretation of the scores. Tests are only an aid to the counselor; they should never become the prime reason for a program of action. They are too fallible. They are too susceptible to human error to be relied upon completely. While scores are valuable in indicating vocational areas which merit consideration, the counselor should remember that tests are rather weak in industrial validation. But most importantly, it should be remembered that the individual can adjust to several occupations. Inherent in testing philosophy is the concept that an individual is "predestined" to only one occupation.

DEVELOPING MODELS OF PSYCHOLOGICAL SERVICES FOR STATE REHABILITATION AGENCIES

As the scope and commitment of vocational rehabilitation has expanded to include services to the culturally disadvantaged and those with behavioral disorders, so has the reliance on and need for psychologists in rehabilitation work. Psychologists who are trained at the doctoral level and who are aware of rehabilitation objectives and procedures are needed urgently.

The number of psychologists employed in vocational rehabilitation is limited. In order to obtain psychological services on a statewide basis, many vocational rehabilitation departments have generally taken one of three approaches in developing models of psychological services. The approaches might be labeled as (a) the consultation model, (b) the strict panel model and (c) the supervising psychologist model.

Description of Models

The *consultation model* is relatively simple in structure. The department of rehabilitation must develop cooperative relationships with psychologists who are employed by institutions or who are in private practice. Usually rehabilitation area office supervisors contact these individuals and ask that they serve as consultants in psychology to the vocational rehabilitation program.

There are some problems with this approach. Many counselors and other rehabilitation workers are not knowledgeable about the selection of qualified psychologists, and many psychologists are unaware of the objectives of rehabilitation. Unless there is considerable effort on the part of rehabilitation personnel and psychologists to develop understanding, the relationship between the rehabilitation department and consulting psychologists can be strained. This type of working relationship results in complaints from rehabilitation personnel that they are not getting the type of information they really need from psychologists. In addition, psychologists may not become fully involved and committed to the objectives of the rehabilitation programs. In addition, there is often confusion about fees and the selection of psychologists for various types of work such as psychotherapy and psychological evaluation of clients with catastrophic disabilities.

The *strict panel model* is the second approach which is used by some departments of rehabilitation. In this model, a part-time state consultant in psychology is usually hired. The state consultant in psychology and the rehabilitation department, in cooperation with the state psychological association, selects a panel of psychologists who represent various phases of professional psychology. The panel rules on the qualifications of psychologists who apply to perform various service functions for the vocational rehabilitation department and specifies areas of competency of individual psychologists. The state psychological consultant for the vocational rehabilitation department usually chairs the panel. Panel members develop a list of psychologists and describe services psychologists are qualified to offer to the vocational rehabilitation department.

This approach can be criticized as duplicated effort if the state has a certification or licensing board. Such boards examine the credentials of psychologists and determine areas of competency. The state licensing or certification board also is concerned with violations of ethical standards. The strict panel model can be very useful in states where no state board of examiners has been appointed.

The *supervising psychologist model* is a third approach which is used by departments of rehabilitation. This model requires the employment of a full-time psychologist who serves as state supervisor of psychological services. The supervising psychologist has statewide responsibility for developing effective working relationships with other psychologists employed on either a full-time or part-time basis. He recommends psychologists for work with the rehabilitation department. He may also act as chairman of a panel of psychologists which meets to consider special psychological problems in vocational rehabilitation. The panel can also help in developing cooperative relationships between the rehabilitation department and consulting psychologists.

The supervising psychologist helps rehabilitation staff members develop understanding of concepts that will be of value to them in their work in vocational rehabilitation. He should participate actively in in-service training activities for professional rehabilitation staff members. He visits area offices and facilities in order to work with consulting psychologists and rehabilitation personnel.

In addition, the supervising psychologist assures that psychologists working for the rehabilitation department maintain standards of practice in accordance with the laws of the state and with standards established by the American Psychological Association. He may also plan training programs for them in order that they may develop improved understanding of the complexities of vocational rehabilitation work.

These models and general variations of them have been used by most state rehabilitation departments, although some departments have not yet developed psychological services on a statewide basis.

Of the three described models, the supervising psychologist approach seems most effective, mainly because it allows an individual who is a psychologist to devote a substantial portion of his time to psychological services within the department of rehabili-

32   *Counseling Strategies With Special Populations*

tation. A supervising psychologist should hold a doctoral degree in psychology or a closely related field. He must be carefully selected. He has crucial responsibility for the effectiveness of psychological services in an important statewide social service program.

STATE REHABILITATION ADMINISTRATORS' VIEWS ON PSYCHOLOGICAL EVALUATION

The rehabilitation process relies, of course, upon a thorough understanding of the rehabilitated client. Counselors develop this understanding by careful evaluation and study of medical, social, psychological and vocational components.

According to Hardy and Cull (1969), the widening range of rehabilitation services, along with the increasing complexity of disabilities with which rehabilitation has become involved, heightens the need for more comprehensive evaluation services in the rehabilitation process. Even though a high level of evaluation is essential to providing adequate services to the rehabilitation client, obtaining pertinent and topical psychological information has been a continued source of frustration to the rehabilitation counselor. Not only does obtaining psychological information present a problem to counselors who have difficulty locating psychologists to evaluate their clients, but the psychological evaluation of clients presents a challenge to the rehabilitation administrators who must plan budgetarily for the provision of psychological evaluation.

CONSIDERATIONS IN OBTAINING PSYCHOLOGICAL EVALUATIONS

The dilemma of handling psychological evaluations is a topic of frequent discussion by counselors and administrators. A basic question seems to be how the rehabilitation counselor can obtain an adequate psychological evaluation of his client without paying prohibitively large amounts in psychological fees for the increasing numbers of clients who need this type of evaluation.

Rehabilitation counselors and administrators generally acknowledge that from their experience, psychological examinations are extremely important in overall planning in the rehabilitation process. A study by Sindberg, Roberts and Pfeifer (1968) has confirmed this acknowledgment by indicating that, in terms of the usage of recommendations of psychologists, reports are definitely useful in the rehabilitation process. More than half of the recommendations of psychologists were followed completely or were followed to a large extent by rehabilitation counselors involved with the cases in the rehabilitation process.

Administrators Sampled

This study (Cull and Hardy, 1970) is concerned with reactions of state rehabilitation agency directors relative to satisfaction with psychological services obtained from psychologists in private practice and the use of rehabilitation counselors in obtaining psychological information. All state vocational rehabilitation agencies were surveyed during the summer of 1969; of the ninety-one questionnaires sent out, fifty-five or approximately 60 percent were returned. Thirty-two of the fifty-five questionnaires which were returned indicated that state agency administrators do not believe that rehabilitation counselors should be prepared to administer a basic battery of psychological tests. Of the administrators responding to the questionnaire, 49 percent (or 27) did believe that rehabilitation counselors should be trained to administer interest tests, 47 percent (or 26) felt they should learn to give aptitude tests, and 44 percent (or 24) believed that they could administer intelligence tests with training.

Results

All fifty-five administrators who participated in this study stated that private psychologists are their primary source of psychological evaluations. Almost half of those persons returning questionnaires indicated that their state agency had hired psychologists on a full-time basis. Forty-three of the fifty-five agency administrators indicated that they were generally satisfied with the adequacy of reporting and professional services offered by outside psychologists. The most often expressed reason for dissatisfaction by the twelve agency administrators who were not satisfied with outside consulting psychologists were (a) reporting was not sufficient for rehabilitation purposes and (b) there was an unacceptable time lag in getting material from the psychologists. Agency administrators concerned with programs serving blind individuals stated that psychologists in private practice often were not trained to evaluate blind persons. This observation apparently supports Allan's (1968) statement that less than 3 percent of all psychologists work in the area of mental deficiency and only 2.5 percent are engaged in programs for the physically handicapped.

A majority of the administrators (58%) indicated that rehabilitation counselors should not attempt to administer a basic battery of tests because counselors lack an understanding of the principles of testing and evaluation. Additionally, thirty stated that in their opinion counselors lacked the time necessary to achieve effective testing and evaluation.

In states that recommend that the counselor have a counselor's test kit for his personal use in evaluation of clients, the following tests were most often recommended:

1. Tests of Intellectual Functioning
   Peabody Picture Vocabulary Tests
   Wechsler Adult Intelligence Scale
2. Tests of Academic Achievement
   Wide Range Achievement Tests
3. Tests of Vocational Interest
   Kuder Performance Record-Vocational
4. Tests of Motor Dexterity
   Purdue Peg Board
5. Tests of Vocational Aptitude
   General Clerical Test
   Test of Mechanical Comprehension

In some states, the Otis Self-Administering Test of Mental Ability and the Revised Beta Examination are being used in lieu of the Wechsler Adult Intelligence Scale and the Wechsler Intelligence Scale for Children. The following comment from a state director on the Eastern seaboard indicates the general thinking of state administrators concerning the use of a counselor test kit, "We feel very strongly that counselors should be able to administer basic pencil-and-paper tests requiring level B competency and preparation. We strongly urge that they not become involved with projective techniques and complex personality inventories."

Results of this survey seem to indicate that about 42 percent of the state agencies are moving toward having counselors use tests to make initial screening judgments of their clients relative to some of his basic needs and toward gaining an understanding of the client. Also, it appears that these screening procedures being utilized by rehabilitation counselors are helpful to them in making decisions which concern whether the client should have further evaluation by psychologists or should be involved in extended evaluation. Since fees for psychological services represent a substantial portion of the case service budget in the state agencies' overall budget, it seems practical to screen many of these clients through the use of a counselor's testing kit along with evaluating other data from the social and medical areas which may be available in order to make basic decisions regarding the rehabilitation process for individual clients. After such screening, the number of clients referred to psychologists for in-depth psychological testing and evaluation can be substantially reduced. This procedure would seem to allow for improved services to all clients since much of the money expended for psychological evaluation could be spent on other case services and comprehensive psychological testing could be completed only when, in the counselor's opinion, it would be necessary for the rehabilitation of the client. As a result of this study, it is the opinion of the authors that agency administrators have confidence in their counselors and generally believe that they can depend upon them to make the complex decisions which are required regarding the variety of types of psychological evaluation needed.

In summary, it was found that almost half of the state agency administrators felt counselors should be equipped to administer interest tests, aptitude tests and intelligence tests; however, a majority felt administration time requirements precluded counselors' routine administration of a basic battery of tests. While over half of the agencies have employed full-time psychologists, the major source of psychological evaluations in all cases was from psychologists in private practice. Although a large majority of state directors were satisfied with this arrangement, the main dissatisfactions concerned the relevancy of evaluations to vocational rehabilitation and the time lag in getting reports from psychologists.

Effective rehabilitation work requires comprehensive evaluation of clients. Psychologists offer invaluable information to the total vocational evaluation effort. The fullest and most effective use of their services by state social and rehabilitation service departments is of high priority.

REFERENCES AND SELECTED READINGS

Allan, W. S.: *Rehabilitation: A Community Challenge.* New York, John Wiley & Sons, 1968.

American Psychological Association: *Ethical Standards of Psychologists.* Washington, 1953.

Cull, J. G., and Hardy, R. E.: State agency administrator's views of psychological testing. *Rehabilitation Literature, 32* (3) :78-79, 1971.

Cull, J. G., and Wright, K. C.: Psychological testing in the rehabilitation setting. *Insight,* 1970.

DiMichael, G.: *Psychological Services in Vocational Rehabilitation.* Washington, D. C., U. S. Government Printing Office.

Hardy, R. E., and Cull, J. G.: Standards in evaluation. *Vocational Evaluation and Work Adjustment Bulletin, 2* (1) , 1969.

Lerner, J.: The role of the psychologist in the disability evaluation of emotional and intellectual impairments under the Social Security Act. *Am Psychol, 18* (5) , 1963.

Sindberg, R. M., Roberts, A., and Pfeifer, E. J.: The usefulness of psychological evaluations to vocational rehabilitation counselors. *Rehabilitation Literature, 29* (10) , 1968.

University of Arkansas: *Psychological Evaluation in the Vocational Process.* Fayetteville, Arkansas, In-service counselor training project for vocational rehabilitation counselors in Arkansas, 1957. Monograph 3.

CHAPTER 3

PLACEMENT ADVISING
AND COUNSELING

———— ———— ———— ———— ———— ———— ———— ———— ———— ————

- A Science of Vocational Behavior
- Client-Centered Placement
- Developing an Employment Program
- Five Questions Counselors Must Be Able to Answer
- Some Guidelines and Tools in Locating Employment
  Opportunities
- Professional Placement
- Getting the Client Ready for Employment
- Eight Common Misconceptions About Vocational Placement
- Job Analysis
- Relating Psychological Data to Job Analysis Information in
  Vocational Placement
- Follow-Up After Placement

———— ———— ———— ———— ———— ———— ———— ———— ———— ————

ONE OF THE MOST SUBSTANTIAL contributions a rehabilitation counselor can make which affects his client's overall mental and physical adjustment is the placement of the individual on a job that is well suited to his abilities and interests. Vocational placement is underrated by many rehabilitation counselors and others who do not understand the full effects of its outcome. Helping the client find employment is often relegated to scanning newspaper want ads in search of opportunities or responding to a call from an employer who happens to have a job available. Certainly, occupational opportunities can be located through these means; however, the matching of the individual and the job is a complicated process which requires careful study and evaluation through interrelating all casework data on the in-

37

dividual with all information that can be secured relating to job requirements and job setting.

A SCIENCE OF VOCATIONAL BEHAVIOR

Loftquist and Davis (1969) discussed a "science of vocational behavior" which they see as essentially vocational psychology. Whether one agrees or not that the "science of vocational behavior" is actually vocational psychology, the necessity for the full development of vocational behavior study as a science cannot be overstressed. The substantial growth during recent years of interest in the Vocational Evaluation and Work Adjustment Division of the National Rehabilitation Association and the subsequent publication of the *Vocational Evaluation and Work Adjustment Bulletin* have done a great deal to stimulate thinking and research on vocational behavior and practical problems of the individual and groups in the world of work. Certainly, in the future, vocational adjustment studies and work evaluation will take an even more prominent place in the rehabilitation counselor's work and in rehabilitation counselor education within the university settings.

Above all, the rehabilitation counselor must be able to understand the "work personality" of his client. The "work personality profile" consists of such factors as vocational and avocational interests, abilities, needs, work habits, psychological maturity and interaction with on-the-job factors including job hierarchies, communication and health factors.

The rehabilitation counselor interested in developing expertise in placement should become familiar with available research on work adjustment. Studies done in vocational rehabilitation at the University of Minnesota since 1957 offer a great deal of useful information.

CLIENT-CENTERED PLACEMENT

Rehabilitationists have heard much about "client-centered counseling" over the years. Because placement is an important part of the rehabilitation process, counselors should think of "client-centered placement." Job placement is a major client service which has helped rehabilitation agencies in getting substantial amounts of federal and state funds for program operations.

The goal of work is one of the unique characteristics of rehabilitation. The placement of individuals on jobs through which they can find methods to maintain themselves is the concept which has allowed rehabilitation counseling to gain in stature as a social service profession with a substantial contribution to make to the individual and to society. In fact, most laymen would probably say that the location of appropriate jobs for clients is the main function of the rehabilitation counselor. It is interesting that rehabilitation counselors downplay the importance of placement in their jobs when they describe their activities to their friends and colleagues. Counselors might reflect more seriously upon their placement responsibilities if clients were thought of as consumers of their services and were given an opportunity to actually evaluate the jobs which they have obtained with the help of the counselor.

In fact, the use of the phrase "PLACE in employment" is one which misleads the rehabilitation counselor trainee and others concerning the method which should be used. The client and counselor must work together in order for the client to reach a decision concerning the type of job he wishes to have. After this decision is made and the rehabilitation counselor helps the client secure information about various jobs that exist in the geographical area where he wants to be employed, the client himself should take some initiative whenever possible to get employment with the assistance of the counselor. Once a feasible job is located, the client should be given the opportunity to evaluate it as the source of his future livelihood.

Quite often, when considering placement, the counselor is confronted with the dilemma of determining to whom he owes basic loyalty—the client or the employer—that is, should he be protective of the client when dealing with an employer or protective of the employer. How much of the client's problems and disability should the counselor relate to the employer? Should he obscure the client's disability in discussions with the employer?

If the professional relationship were bilateral and concerned only the client and counselor the answer to the dilemma would be immediately obvious; however, the relationship is trilateral.

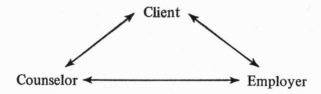

As such, the counselor owes equal professional responsibility to both the client and prospective employer. Therefore, the counselor should communicate with the employer in a basic, forthright manner. The counselor is professionally obligated to be honest in his dealings with the employer.

If the counselor fails to be completely honest and forthright with the employer, he not only jeopardizes his professional relationship with this employer thereby obviating any possibility of placing clients in this area in the future, but he also takes a great chance of jeopardizing the client-employer relationship later when the employer becomes more aware of the client's attributes which the counselor chose to hide or misrepresent. Consequently, the authors feel rather strongly that the counselor should discuss with the client what he is planning to relate to the employer. If the client refuses to allow the counselor to discuss his assets, liabilities and disability with the employer, the counselor should modify his role in the placement process. His role should be one of providing placement information to the client, but he should not enter actively into the placement process with the client.

There are two limits to this interchange between the counselor and employer relative to the client:

1. The counselor and employer should discuss thoroughly those aspects and only those aspects of the client's background which have a direct relation with the job.
2. The counselor should communicate with the employer on a level at which both are comfortable in the exchange of information.

Quite often a counselor approaches a prospective employer regarding a specific client and as the conversation progresses the counselor finds himself relating information which, while highly pertinent in the rehabilitation process, has little to do with the client as an employee. In each instance in which the counselor makes an employer contact for placement purposes, the counselor should have summarized previously all material in the case folder which is directly related to the client's proficiency in a particular position—both his assets and liabilities. After reviewing this summary the counselor should refrain from relating any other information he may have derived from counseling sessions, training evaluations or diagnostic work-ups. A mark of professionalism is the ability to communicate the essential factors relating to the client and still respect the client's fundamental right to confidentiality of case material.

The second limitation to communication between the counselor and employer requires the counselor to assess the sophistication of the employer and communicate with him on that level. As a general rule the counselor should avoid using terminology which, though descriptive, is highly laden with emotional connotations. The most effective approach the counselor can take in discussing the client's assets and liabilities is to describe behavior rather than categorizing it with diagnostic labels. For example: This person experienced learning difficulties in the academic areas rather early and is slow in learning new procedures. He is ineffective in dealing with abstract concepts and carrying out complex, oral instructions and should not be placed in a situation requiring independent judgments in changing conditions; however, he is very adept in performing concrete tasks and is capable of making routine, repetitive judgments. This description means more to the employer than the term "mental retardate."

DEVELOPING AN EMPLOYMENT PROGRAM

Counselors who are involved with placement should be familiar with information offered in the publication, *Workers Worth Their Hire* (American Mutual Insurance Alliance), which is available through the President's Committee on Employment of the Physically Handicapped. Myths concerning employment of the handicapped are dispelled by information given in this publication. Counselors will find that discussions of the excellent record of handicapped persons in such areas as safety, absentee-ism, production and motivation to work are of considerable help to them in their discussions with employers, union leaders and work supervisors. The counselor should be certain that he not only talks about these factors with top agency employment offi-cials but also that he manages, at the appropriate time, to men-tion these subjects to supervisors within the work area. The de-gree of acceptance which supervisors give to handicapped clients is often highly influential in not only helping them "get off to a good start" but also in maintaining their work at a level com-mensurate with the supervisor's expectations.

Some rehabilitation counselors have felt that the counselor should not have a specific client in mind when talking with an employer, but that he should sell the concept of hiring the hand-icapped to the employer and later get into the work setting in or-der to locate the types of jobs which would be available to handi-capped individuals. This concept can be extremely useful and can help open many doors to handicapped employees; however, after convincing the employer of the value of hiring handi-capped persons, the counselor often will be asked to refer a pro-spective employee immediately if a particular opening exists in the work setting. If a counselor is unable to meet this request, his public relations and sales program can be substantially damaged in terms of future placements with the employer.

Each rehabilitation counselor should constantly evaluate his efforts in placement to make certain that he is moving clients to-ward jobs in line with their overall adjustment and ability. One of the key sources of learning about job opportunities for any client is often the client's past experiences and previous job re-sponsibilities. In many cases, clients will wish to return to the type of employment held prior to the onset of the employment handicap. In fact, many former employers will feel a responsi-bility for injured employees and wish again to offer then employ-ment after they have received rehabilitation services. The client will offer many insights about himself to the counselor who then has the responsibility to match abilities, needs and interests of the client with requirements and offerings of the job. One of the primary sources, then, of information about types of employment for the client is the client himself. This information can be gained by a study of his background and from interest inventories and interviews with him and his family.

The counselor will also wish to use the services of the state employment agency which maintains local offices throughout the United States. Many prospective employers inform the employment service of job openings. This agency also offers counseling, placement and evaluation services for handicapped job applicants. The Vocational Rehabilitation Act, Public Law 89-565, stipulates that the vocational rehabilitation state plan shall "provide for entering into cooperative agreements with the system of public employment offices in the state and the maximum utilization of the job placement and employment counseling services and other services and facilities of such offices."

FIVE QUESTIONS COUNSELORS
MUST BE ABLE TO ANSWER

Of course, many different problem areas can arise when the counselor is discussing hiring handicapped workers with an employer. Questions range from, "How will the person get to the place of employment?" to "What will he do in case of fire?" Incidentally, these two questions usually can be answered with the same responses which any employee would give—in the first case, "By bus or car," and in the second, "Get the hell out like everyone else."

The first basic question which usually arises is that of increased insurance rates if handicapped workers are employed. This is most often an honest employer reaction to the question concerning employment of handicapped workers. Insurance rates would rise if individuals were employed in an agency which tended to have more accidents; however, handicapped workers have been proven to be as safe in the performance of their duties as other workers. In fact, some handicapped persons such as the blind have actually shown better records of safety than nonhandicapped workers. American Mutual Insurance Alliance has published materials relevant to the fact that handicapped workers are as safe or safer than nonhandicapped workers. The counselor should have this information readily available and indicate to the prospective employer that indeed workmen's compensation insurance rates are determined, in part, according to the relative hazards of the work done by the industry in question. Yearly rates also are determined according to the industry's record of accidents and insurance claims. These are good reasons for hiring handicapped workers. If an employer persists in believing that his insurance rates will increase, the counselor should ask him to contact his insurance agent or read again his insurance contract.

A second question which often arises is this: Why should I hire a handicapped individual when I can employ "normal" persons whom I can count on for employment without difficulty? The counselor will have to answer this question according to his own philosophy and training. Some helpful responses might include the following:

1. Ask why he should not employ individuals whose employment records have been proven and who are well known and highly recommended by rehabilitation and employment specialists.

2. Describe the medical, social and psychiatric evaluations completed on all clients (not being specific or violating confidentiality). In other words, why not hire an individual who comes to the employer, in a sense, "certified" as ready for employment?

3. Remind him that by doing so he is actually supporting what he, as a taxpayer, has already invested some money in—an employment program for the handicapped which has proven to be highly successful.

Another question which frequently is raised in employment interviews concerns the firing or dismissal of the employee and the employer's reluctance to treat the rehabilitant in the same manner he would treat other employees. The counselor again will have to rely on his own resources; however, an analogy may be helpful here.

Indicate that if you, as a salesman, were selling refrigerators and the employer bought one which later malfunctioned, you would stand by your product and attempt to get it in good working order. The counselor could briefly discuss follow-up procedures with the employer at this time. He might also indicate that once the handicapped employee has worked for the employer for a time, the employer will feel that he is a fully functioning, well-adjusted employee who should be treated just as all other employees are. Assure the employer of your confidence in the client.

A fourth question which counselors must be ready to answer concerns architectural barriers and physical limitations of the work setting. Counselors should be frank in their responses to questions concerning limitations of the client and restrictions imposed by the work setting. The counselor should be the first to indicate that certain jobs are infeasible for many of his clients. He should be certain to get across to the employer that he is not going to place a client on an unsafe job or on a job which he cannot handle.

A fifth question which often arises concerning employment of the handicapped is that of the "second injury" which might result in total disability and effect the workman's compensation payments made by the employer. In a vast majority of states and the District of Columbia and Puerto Rico, "second injury" funds or equivalent arrangements have been established. In these localities, the employer is responsible only for the last injury and the employee is compensated for the disability which results from combined injuries.

SOME GUIDELINES AND TOOLS IN LOCATING EMPLOYMENT OPPORTUNITIES

1. The counselor should be aware of industrial developments within the area that he serves and in adjacent areas.

2. The three volumes of the *Dictionary of Occupational Titles* (1965) offer a wealth of useful information for rehabilitation counselors. Much emphasis is given to descriptions of physical and personality requirements for various jobs. In addition, these volumes can help expand the counselor's concepts about various types of jobs which are related to the general interest area of the rehabilitation client.

3. Employers with whom former clients have been placed can be important sources of information.

4. Previously rehabilitated clients can offer many sound ideas about existing employment opportunities.

5. Local Chambers of Commerce usually provide an industrial index which lists types of work available in most communities. Counselors also should coordinate their efforts with those of the state employment service since the mutual sharing of job information can be valuable to both employment service counselors and rehabilitation counselors.

6. When placing persons on jobs in rural areas, the worker should consider enlisting the support of local community leaders such as doctors, city councilmen, postmasters and religious leaders as well as Rotary, Kiwanis, Ruritan and other civic groups.

7. If the counselor is interested in assisting individuals in becoming small business managers and operators, he should get in touch with the Small Business Administration office serving his local area.

PROFESSIONAL PLACEMENT

In rehabilitation jargon, "professional placement" generally means developing client employment opportunities which require at least a college education. Bauman and Yoder (1962) offer excellent coverage of this area of placement as it pertains to work for the blind. Professional placement is "facilitative" work for the counselor. The counselor can help his client in terms of giving advice and information; however, he must be certain not to take the place of the client in securing actual jobs. The client must be ready to meet without the counselor with the employer to discuss his professional qualifications for work. When he has a particular problem, the counselor should be able to assist him with information which could be helpful during the employer interview. For example, he should be coached on how to present himself most favorably. The counselor might help his client develop a resume or portfolio which would outline his training and give examples of any previous work done in the job field in which he wants employment. Other procedures usually followed in placement may or may not be appropriate according to the judgment of the counselor.

A worker in charge of professional placement may want to organize precollege orientation groups for clients. It will be necessary also for the counselor who is dealing with persons in training to inform them about services available while they are in training and away from their home area. If, for instance, clients are attending college, the rehabilitation counselor should help them become acquainted with college counseling center services at the institution they attend.

Effective professional placement requires long-range planning on the part of both counselor and client. Two years before placement (in training cases) is not too early for the client to begin planning with his counselor in order to solve problems related to his securing the type of employment he wants. The counselor will need to prepare by knowing who the prospective employers are and the requirements of the job.

GETTING THE CLIENT READY FOR EMPLOYMENT

Planning for placement does not begin once the client has had vocational training and ready "skillwise" for employment, but when the counselor first reads the client's rehabilitation referral form. The rehabilitation worker must constantly learn about his client in order to effectively help him secure the type of employment he needs. Jeffrey (1969) has developed a job readiness test which helps in the evaluation of job preparedness of clients. While the total instrument is not applicable to all rehabilitation clients, certain questions are quite helpful with most rehabilitation clients.

Role playing is an excellent method to use in preparing a client for employment interviews. After going through a mock interview which includes a variety of questions, the counselor can give suggestions concerning how the client might improve the impression he makes with the employer. In role playing, it is helpful for the counselor as well as the client to play the role of the employer. Once this is tried, counselors will immediately realize the usefulness of this procedure. The client should realize that getting a job is not an easy task and that he, to the best of his ability, should participate in the job-securing aspects of placement. In some cases, it is an indicator of effective rehabilitation procedures when the client is able to, in fact, "get his own job," assuming of course that he is ready for employment. The ability with which the client will be able to do this will vary with his motivation and the severity of his social, mental or physical handicap.

The rehabilitation counselor must stress "training" as a partial answer to many of the problems of the handicapped worker. Overtraining a worker for a job which will affect his personal and family adjustment for many years to come is seldom done. In each case, the counselor must take an individual approach to helping his client. In the case of those who are educationally or socially retarded, various remedial programs may be necessary before actual work training programs can begin. In each case, the counselor must exercise considerable judgment concerning what his client needs in order to be totally ready for employment.

On-the-job training can be a very effective arrangement for client training. In many of these cases, the state rehabilitation agency will make "tuition" payments to the employer-trainer in order that the rehabilitation counselor may get the employer interested in training a client and evaluating his work. It may be necessary for the counselor to help the employer arrange the appropriate payment schedule for the client since he is not a trained employee and would not receive an amount equal to a regularly salaried employee.

Bridges (1946) offered four major factors which are involved in successful employment of handicapped workers. These remain as highly important considerations for the counselor:

1. The worker should have the ability to accomplish the task efficiently—that is, to be able to meet the physical demands of the job.

2. The worker should not be a hazard to himself.

3. The worker must not jeopardize the safety of others.

4. The job should not aggravate the disability or handicap of the worker.

EIGHT COMMON MISCONCEPTIONS ABOUT VOCATIONAL PLACEMENT

1. Because placement occurs toward the end of the rehabilitation process, the counselor's responsibility to the client diminishes.

2. Placement is an activity which requires no counselor training and is a matter of matching an available client with an available job.

3. Client location of his job or "self-placement" cannot be effective rehabilitation work.

4. When a client is ready for vocational placement, the information in his case folder is no longer of value to his counselor since the client has been, in a sense, readied for employment.

5. Follow-up after placement always can be handled easily by phone or mail communications with the employer or client.

6. Labor market trends and job information and analysis are the responsibilities of placement specialists and employment service counselors, not of general rehabilitation counselors.

7. An employer will notify the counselor and the rehabilitation agency when he is dissatisfied with a client placement.

8. An employer will automatically call upon the rehabilitation agency to furnish him with additional employees when he needs them.

Rehabilitation counselors should be certain that their clients understand that it is not necessarily bad to be turned down for a job. Counselors should understand that experience has shown that nine or ten employer contacts often must be made before the counselor makes a placement.

JOB ANALYSIS

Every rehabilitation counselor should be thoroughly familiar with the techniques of job analysis for use in selective placement. The rehabilitation counselor has to be able to match the prospective worker's social, mental and physical qualifications with requirements of the job. Factors such as judgment, initiative, alertness and general health and capability must always be taken into consideration as well as the individual's social and economic background.

Job analysis should answer certain questions concerning the job. *What* does the worker do in terms of physical and mental effort that go into the work situation? How is the work done? In other words, does this job involve the use of equipment and mathematics, or does it require travel. *Why* does the worker perform the job? This component of the job analysis answers the question concerning the overall purpose or the sum total of the task and is the reason for doing the job. The worker also should understand the relationship of his task to other tasks that make up the total job.

Generally, the rehabilitation counselor should attempt to place clients on jobs which they can "handle" and which do not require modification. In some cases, however, minor modifications can be made with little or no reengineering effort. The counselor will have to be careful in suggesting reengineering of a job, since this can be a costly undertaking in many instances. The major objective should be that of helping handicapped workers integrate effectively into the total work force without major modification or change in the work situation.

The following outline can be used in evaluating a job which is to be performed by a handicapped worker:

A. Name Used for Position Surveyed
    1. *D.O.T.* title
    2. Alternate titles
    3. *D.O.T.* definitions
    4. Items worked on in plant surveyed
B. Usual Operator
    1. Sex
    2. General characteristics
C. Physical and Psychological Demands
    1. Activities
    2. Working conditions
    3. Skill required
    4. Intelligence
    5. Temperament
    6. Other
D. Description of Physical Activities
E. Description of Working Conditions
F. Description of Hazards
G. Steps Required to Accomplish the Goal of the Work
H. Equipment Found in the Particular Plant Surveyed
    1. Identification
    2. Set-up and maintenance

3. Modification (if required for the handicapped persons)
I. Equipment Variations Which May Be Found in Other Plants
J. Preemployment Training Required
K. Training Procedure
L. Production
   1. Full production definition
   2. Time to reach normal efficiency
M. Interrelation with Preceding and Succeeding Jobs

RELATING PSYCHOLOGICAL DATA TO JOB ANALYSIS INFORMATION IN VOCATIONAL PLACEMENT

As a first step in getting to know clients well, the counselor should make arrangements to secure appropriate psychological information about them. He should either complete job analyses or use available job evaluation data to make decisions about types of information which will be of value to his clients in the job selection and placement procedure. In many instances, however, the counselor fails to synthesize information obtained from two of his most important sources: the psychological evaluation and the job analysis.

The counselor should take five basic steps, as described by Hardy (1969), in developing a successful procedure for interrelating and using important information. He should:

1. Study the needs of the client and the types of satisfaction meaningful to him.
2. Make certain that valid psychological and job analysis data have been gathered.
3. Review the requirements of the job and evaluate the individual traits needed to meet job requirements.
4. Consider the environmental pressures with which the individual must interact.
5. Discuss the job analysis and psychological evaluation with the client so that he will understand what the work will require of him and what it will offer.

Both client and counselor need to have an understanding of the job requirements in order to make realistic decisions. One important move should be structuring a set of goals—a guide to help the client avoid useless floundering that gets him nowhere. What satisfactions is he seeking? What is important to him in the long run and what types of work or work settings will provide these satisfactions? These are questions which the counselor must help the client answer.

Maslow (1954) has suggested a hierarchy of the individual needs which the counselor must understand in order to evaluate a client's psychological status—his satisfactions and frustrations. In the usual order of prepotency these needs are for (a) physiological satisfaction; (b) safety; (c) belongingness and love; (d) importance, respect, self-esteem and independence; (e) information; (f) understanding; (g) beauty; and (h) self-actualization.

In our society, there is no single situation which is potentially more capable of giving satisfaction at all levels of these needs as a person's work, and it is the responsibility of the counselor to help his client plan for future happiness through adjustment on the job.

The worker needs to help his client become fully aware of the social pressures of the job because these are as important to the individual as the actual job pressures. A client's ability to adapt to the social interactions of the work environment will directly affect his job performance.

The counselor always must ask himself what the requirements of the job are. This question can be answered superficially or in considerable detail. A lay job analysis can give superficial requirements, but the responsibility for an in-depth job description belongs to the expert—the counselor who will often have to give direct advice to the client.

Effective placement requires effective planning. Planning cannot be really useful unless appropriate information has been obtained, interrelated and skillfully utilized so that the client and the counselor have a clear understanding of possible problems and possible solutions.

FOLLOW-ALONG AFTER PLACEMENT

A rehabilitation counselor often is tempted to consider his job completed when the client is placed on a job which appears suitable for him; however, the phase of rehabilitation which begins immediately after the person has been placed in employment is one of the most complex. Follow-along involves the counselor's ability to work as a middleman between employer and client in order to help the client solve problems related to his handicap which may arise after being hired. The counselor must be diplomatic and resourceful in maintaining the employer's confidence in his client's ability to do the job. At the same time, he must let the client know that he has full faith in him. The counselor, however, must somehow evaluate how his client is performing on the job and make certain that he is available to help if problems arise which the client cannot solve.

In addition to the worker's service to the client during follow-along, this period can offer real public relations opportunities for the counselor, especially when the employer notes the interest with which the counselor "follows" his client. The frequency of follow-along varies according to the counselor's judgment of the client's job ability and adjustment.

Agency regulations usually require that a final follow-along be done after thirty days in order to make certain that placement is successful before a "case" can be closed as rehabilitated. Counselors should also consider follow-along periods of sixty to eighty days after placement. Again, this helps reassure the client of the interest of the agency and the counselor in his success and can be of value to the counselor in further developing employment opportunities for handicapped persons.

In follow-along after professional placement, however, the counselor must forget the sixty- to ninety-day period which is usually adequate in the placement of clients in nonprofessional jobs. A longer period will be necessary and this period will vary with job complications and severity of the client's handicap. Bauman and Yoder (1962) have recommended six months to a year for follow-up for most cases of blind persons placed in professional work.

Counselors will probably wish to schedule specific days for follow-along in the field. Generally, the period of follow-along is a time when the counselor sees the efforts of the entire rehabilitation process coming to fruition. If the job has been well analyzed and the client well evaluated and placed, follow-along will be a pleasurable experience for the counselor.

Summary

The counselor's responsibility in vocational placement must not be underrated. The decision made at this stage in the rehabilitation process not only affects the client's immediate feelings of satisfaction and achievement but also, of course, his long-term physical and mental health. The counselor has a real responsibility to "ready" the client for employment by giving him the type of information that he needs about the job and about holding employment once it is achieved. Placement should be "client-centered" with strong emphasis given to the client's opinions about work and how it will affect him and his family. Counselors must be ready to answer the questions that employers will ask about hiring handicapped persons and about the rehabilitation program. Vocational placement is high level public relations work.

The counselor must be knowledgeable about job analysis and must interrelate all medical, psychological and social data with job analysis information in order to be successful in client-centered placement. Once placement has been achieved, the counselor must "follow" the client in order to make certain that he is doing well on the job. The client should have an opportunity to evaluate his job and also the efforts of his counselor in helping him decide on and obtain the job. Effective placement requires effective planning and counselors must constantly evaluate their knowledge of the world of work and their ability to interrelate information in order to assure real placement success.

REFERENCES AND SELECTED READINGS

American Mutual Insurance Alliance: *Workers Worth Their Hire.* Chicago, 1970.

Bauman, M. K. and Yoder, N. M.: *Placing the Blind and Visually Handicapped in Professional Occupations.* Washington, D. C., Office of Vocational Rehabilitation, Department of Health, Education and Welfare, 1962.

Bridges, C. C.: *Job Placement of the Physically Handicapped.* New York, McGraw-Hill, 1946.

Cull, J. G. and Hardy, R. E.: *Adjustment to Work*. Springfield, Thomas, 1973.

Cull, J. G. and Hardy, R. E.: *Vocational Rehabilitation: Profession and Process*. Springfield, Thomas, 1972.

Department of Veterans' Benefits, Veterans' Administration: *They Return to Work*. Washington, D. C., U. S. Government Printing Office, 1963.

Hardy, R. E.: Counseling physically handicapped college students. *The New Outlook for the Blind, 59* (5) :182-183, 1965.

————: Relating psychological data to job analysis information in vocational counseling. *The New Outlook for the Blind, 63* (7) :202-204, 1969.

Hardy, R. E. and Cull, J. G.: *Vocational Evaluation for Rehabilitation Services*. Springfield, Thomas, 1973.

International Society for the Welfare of Cripples: *Selective Placement of the Handicapped*. New York, 1955.

Jeffrey, David L.: *Pertinent Points on Placement*. Clearing House, Oklahoma State University, November, 1969.

Lofquist, L. H., and Davis, R. V.: *Adjustment to Work—A Psychological View of Man's Problems in Work-Oriented Society*. New York, Appleton-Century-Crofts, 1969.

McGowan, J. F., and Porter, T. L.: *An Introduction to the Vocational Rehabilitation Process*. Washington, D. C., Rehabilitation Services Administration, 1967.

McNamee, H. T., and Jeffrey, R. P.: *Service to the Handicapped 1960*. Phoenix, Arizona State Employment Service, 1960.

Maslow, A. H.: A theory of human motivation. *Psychol Rev, 50:*370-396, 1954.

Office of Vocational Rehabilitation: *Training Personnel for the State Vocational Rehabilitation Programs—A Guide for Administrators*. Washington, D. C., U. S. Government Printing Office, 1957.

Sinick, D.: *Placement Training Handbook*. Washington, D. C., Office of Vocational Rehabilitation, 1962.

Stalnaker, W. O., Wright, K. C. and Johnston, L. T.: *Small Business Enterprises in Vocational Rehabilitation*. Washington, D. C., U. S. Department of Health, Education and Welfare, Vocational Rehabilitation Administration, Rehabilitation Services Series No. 63-47, 1963.

Thomason, B. and Barrett, A.: *The Placement Process in Vocational Rehabilitation Counseling*. Washington, D. C., U. S. Department of Health, Education and Welfare, Office of Vocational Rehabilitation, GTP Bull. No. 2, Rehabilitation Service Series No. 545, 1960.

U. S. Employment Service: *Dictionary of Occupational Titles*. Washington, D. C., U. S. Government Printing Office, 1965.

————: *Selected Placement for the Handicapped* (Rev. Ed.) . Washington, D. C.: U. S. Government Printing Office, 1945.

Weiss, D. J., Davis, R. V., Lofquist, L. H. and England, G. W.: *Minnesota Studies in Vocational Rehabilitation*. University of Minnesota, Industrial Relations Center, 1968.

CHAPTER 4

THE USE OF VOLUNTEERS
IN COMMUNITY SERVICE WORK

- Origin and Types of Volunteer Activity
- Use of the Volunteer
- Types of Volunteers

COUNSELORS IN MANY DISCIPLINES (rehabilitation, psychology, guidance, employment, etc.) are becoming increasingly aware that no one agency or professional can meet all the needs or solve all the problems of any individual; therefore, information referral and tracking systems are becoming more obvious in our priority systems for community development. It is becoming more important for a counselor regardless of his disciplinary affiliation to become aware of community activities and make intelligent referrals for the needs of his client. Also gaining in importance is voluntary action groups. Volunteer groups are becoming the *sine qua non* of social services. A comprehensive counseling paradigm will include the intelligent use of voluntary action organizations.

Voluntary action has grown to the point of an emerging profession. The work of volunteers has existed for many decades, but recently this work has changed from an avocation to a permanent, established vocation. Part of the growth is the result of the large manpower pool of healthy, retired persons; the need for more manpower due to the emphasis on social welfare services; and lastly, federal legislation which facilitates the growth and development of volunteer service agencies. Volunteers appear by the thousands —these are idealistically motivated persons who want to devote some portion of their lives to serving their fellowman. They come not for pay, though some may receive a token amount.

They come not with expectation of a career, though some may eventually enter a helping profession.

There are many names for volunteers. They are called aides, indigenous workers, community workers, candy stripers, gray ladies, etc.; however, they all have one thing in common—they give their services for the satisfaction of helping people. The most significant change in the functions of volunteers is the result of our becoming more people-oriented. A few decades ago, we had a federally sponsored, massive voluntary action effort in the Civilian Conservation Corps. This organization was a materialistically-oriented operation. Today, we have comparable federally supported voluntary action programs; however, they are focused on people. These programs include the Volunteers in Service to America (VISTA), the Peace Corps, the Retired Senior Volunteer Programs (RSVP), etc. Our focus is on people helping people. Our needs for people to minister to the social, psychological, and vocational needs of others is so great that voluntary action is evolving to its rightful role in social welfare.

ORIGIN AND TYPES OF VOLUNTEER ACTIVITY

Marris and Rein (1967) have indicated that in order for a person who wishes to bring about reform in the American society to be effective he must: (1) recruit a coalition of power sufficient for his purposes; (2) respect the democratic tradition which expects every citizen not merely to be represented but to play an autonomous part in the determination of his own affairs, and (3) be rational in his policy. These principles provide a basis for an individual to gain acceptance for those ideas which he feels are needed in order that he may be successful in changing some of those things in the society which he feels should be changed. These principles are of utmost importance in gaining the support of other citizens in order to bring about change.

Volunteerism has as one of its basic objectives the elimination of problematic situations through individual and group action. The organizing of individual groups for effective social service and reform is a major problem in that individuals who wish to be involved in volunteer work are often out of touch with the people who have need for their services. In addition, once volunteers or groups of volunteers begin to work, they may be highly ineffective due to the lack of proper coordination and supervision of their efforts.

Volunteer work is a tradition in America. Volunteers are involved in health services, education, corrections, rehabilitation and the various phases of community service work. Volunteerism particularly has been focused recently in the area of education because of an increased awareness of the inequalities of educational opportunities. Persons are now volunteering by the thousands to do various types of work and volunteerism seems to be stable and ongoing in nature. Many persons have been working as much as three years and expect to continue. Persons working with volunteer associations are participating because they choose to do so. They are free to participate as long as they wish or to stop whenever they choose. Volunteer activities drastically affect health, educational, recreational, and social programs.

Title I of the Higher Education Act of 1965 offers the means for state educational authorities to administer the development of community leadership projects under the auspices of institutions of higher education. The Economic Opportunity Act has a similar provision. These actions by Congress represent the first offering of such resources for the training of volunteer leaders subsidized through federal funds.

Early Developments

The Judeo-Christian ethic has helped move man forward toward a constant improvement of his voluntary organizations for the social welfare of his fellowman. In general, the conditions within society, the healthiness or unhealthiness of the economy, the political climate, and cultural forces have given most of the meaning and direction to the development of voluntary work.

Many people felt that governmental services were insufficient to handle the many problems of those who needed help. In addition, special interest in certain subgroups of the population gave great emphasis to volunteer activities as did the interest of many religious groups in providing social services in line with their doctrine. Industrialization and urbanization at the last half of the nineteenth century gave great impetus to voluntary efforts. Some of the problems and early concerns were those relating to migration, child labor, rehabilitation of those injured in industrial accidents and immigration to the United States.

There are probably more than 115,000 voluntary health and welfare organizations that receive contributions from the general public. A similar number of civic and veterans organizations, health and welfare groups plus many of the churches of the country are offering their services (Cull & Hardy, 1973). There are national voluntary agencies, various foundations, state and local agencies, and religious groups which could be considered either local, state, or national. On a national level organizations often do a great deal of planning and development and give direction to local efforts. These national programs also often offer some training to persons on a local level and develop general guidelines for ethical procedures and practice within their area of concern.

Local organizations and agencies are often the source of funding for national organizations. There is a great deal of autonomy within local programs. In recent years there has been an increased emphasis on joint collaboration and cooperation among the local and national organizations.

Also in the areas of health and education, private foundations have offered a great deal to the field of voluntary activities through various grants. Most states have various conferences concerning problems in education, health, and social welfare. All states have a conference on social welfare which usually directs itself toward certain social action that should be taken in order to improve various conditions within the state. A number of states have what has been called state planning organizations which do planning and offer different types of information on social action and legislation and coordinate with local communities. Almost all communities now have a planning council concerned with health and welfare.

One of the first recorded observations on volunteer efforts in the United States was made by Alexis de Tocqueville (1961) after a visit in 1931. He stated as follows:

Americans of all ages, all conditions, and all dispositions, constantly form associations. They have not only commercial and manufacturing companies in which all take part but associations of a thousand other kinds—religious, moral, serious, futile, extensive or restrictive, enormous, diminutive. The Americans make associations to give entertainment, to fund establishments for education, to build inns, to construct churches, to defuse books, to send missionaries to the antipodes; and in this manner they found hospitals, prisons, and schools.

The answers to how varied voluntary organizations and agencies began are many, for there are many different types of voluntary organizations. A number are old and well established and others have been developed more recently. There, of course, will be new ones continuing to develop.

Some of the early concerns in volunteerism were related directly to health. There were those organizations which were concerned with specific diseases such as poliomyelitis, cancer, tuberculosis, diabetes, and sexual problems. There were those which were concerned with the health and welfare of special groups of the society such as mothers (planned parenthood or child spacing) and the mentally ill (mental hygiene). There were those which were directed toward disorders of certain special organs such as the eye, heart, and skeletal frame.

A good example of an important health organization is the National Tuberculosis Association which was organized between 1892 and 1904. When this organization was established, twenty-three associations were formed on state and local levels (Knoph, 1922). Cancer was a major concern for all and continues to be. European countries organized in order to fight cancer in the late 1800's. The first organized attempt was the League Against Cancer in France. A campaign in the United States was begun in 1913 under the stimulus of Dr. Thomas D. Cullen, a Baltimore surgeon.

The London Society for the Prevention of Blindness and the Improvement of the Physique of the Blind was organized in the late 1800's. Doctors Roff and Dudgen were early pioneers in this volunteer activity. Work in the area of prevention of blindness started in the United States in New York State around 1905 when the national committee for the prevention of blindness was formed. This was later called the Society for the Prevention of Blindness. Various other organizations such as The League for the Hard of Hearing were organized. This one was for persons who were too poor to pay for lipreading instruction. This early work began in New York in the first ten years of the twentieth century (Hardy & Cull, 1973).

The establishment of a division of child hygiene in New York City's Department of Health in 1908 was one of the first moves in the area of volunteer health organizations concerned with problems affecting health and welfare of the society in general. This organization was followed by the conference on the prevention of health mortality which was organized through the American Academy of Medicine in Connecticut around 1909.

Clifford W. Beers in his epochal book, *A Mind That Found Itself* was instrumental in moving the nation toward more effective volunteer work in the area of mental hygiene. This book was published in 1908 when Mr. Beers also formed the Connecticut Society for Mental Hygiene. The organization (Beers, 1908) was "to improve conditions among those actually insane and confined and for the general purpose of protection of the mental hygiene of the public at large."

There are a number of other voluntary organizations and these could easily require a book to cover adequately. A very important one which should be mentioned is Planned Parenthood which was the outgrowth of the monumental efforts of Margaret Sanger who was most concerned with the needs of poor women for birth control information. She was able to gain substantial public attention and support in 1914 by openingly breaking some laws through the dissemination of informational literature concerning birth control clinics. She called the first National Birth Control Congress in 1921 and from this was formed the American Birth Control League.

One of the most substantial developments in volunteerism occurred in the late 1930's. This act was the establishment of the National Foundation for Infantile Paralysis. In a very short period of time, this organization's effect was felt all over the entire nation. It grew as rapidly as any national foundation has and received wide support from all quarters.

A substantial period of work in voluntary activity was during the depression in the 1930's. Various volunteer organizations and agencies were set up in localities throughout the country and voluteers were in particular demand in hospitals, civic and church groups, and recreational programs (Cull & Hardy, 1973).

The National Advisory Committee on Citizen Participation was established in 1945. This committee was sponsored by Community Chests and Councils in the National Social Welfare Assembly until 1951. One of the most important pieces of work which it did was a study on how to hold the interest of many volunteers who became very active during World War I and World War II. As a result of some of this work, the Association of Volunteer Bureaus was established. The association did a great deal of work in terms of developing professional expertise in volunteerism through developing materials, holding workshops and other activities (Cull & Hardy, 1973).

It was really during the Second World War that the potential value of volunteer activities was clearly demonstrated. During this period, many volunteer offices were responsible for meeting the needs of various persons including women, youth, the handicapped, and others whose relatives and loved ones were heavily concerned in the war effort.

Probably the most heavily emphasized volunteer activity to take place in recent years was the establishment of the Peace Corps (in 1961) which by the summer of 1963 had recruited some 9,000 volunteers for work in more than fifty nations of the world. Other significant developments included the 1962 amendments to the Social Security Act which provide for 75 percent matching through federal grants in aid to states in support of approved state plans for volunteer services. There are various other programs such as those concerned with urban renewal, housing, juvenile delinquency, etc. which encourage persons in the community to become involved and have local communities rewarded through their involvement by grants of federal funds to the local community (Hardy & Cull, 1973).

USE OF THE VOLUNTEER

Volunteers are not a free source of help, either professional or paraprofessional. The cost in terms of recruitment, training, and supervision is substantial. The volunteers are in many respects equivalent to employees of the organization in that they require job descriptions, in-service training programs, supervision, and well-planned rewards for meritorious service.

The volunteer is misused and is done an injustice when he is selected indiscriminately and immediately assigned a task. He should be provided the same personnel management services as other employees if his services are to be of maximum benefit to himself and to the organization. The purpose of the volunteer is to provide a diversity of interaction with the members of the organization (a service based on a different experiential background), and to allow for a richer level of contact than would be allowed if the organization were forced to rely exclusively on paid staff. However, the facility should not solicit volunteers exclusively for the economic benefits inherent in a volunteer program.

TYPES OF VOLUNTEERS

There are volunteers in almost every type of human endeavor. Whenever man has needed help, there has been a volunteer to assist in his need. As volunteers have become more numerous, volunteerism has become more structured. In this chapter, we will present some of the more prevalent types of situations in which volunteers operate. This discussion is by no means exhaustive but is presented only to exemplify the diversity of the emerging profession, volunteerism.

Volunteers in the Rehabilitation Setting

Traditionally, rehabilitation has been an individualized program to provide services to individuals who are handicapped as a result of disabling conditions. These conditions may be physical, mental or emotional. Since the approach is individualized, the personnel needs are of an overwhelming magnitude; therefore, rehabilitation is a natural area for the spontaneous development of volunteerism.

Perhaps the first disability group which benefited from volunteers was the blind and visually impaired. This group had and continues to have very obvious needs which require extraordinary concentrations of manpower such as readers who will spend time reading to the blind to keep them abreast of the current events, for amusement purposes, and for educational purposes. The blind need volunteers as travel companions, for teaching mobility, arts and crafts, homemaking skills and many other activities. The next group in historical order to utilize volunteers to provide services in rehabilitation settings was the deaf and those with impaired hearing. The specific needs of the deaf in relation to volunteers are quite similar to the visually handicapped.

According to Levin (1973), approximately 300,000 volunteers participated in volunteer programs in rehabilitation facilities in 1969. In this study, 72.9 percent of the facilities reported the volunteers were involved in recreational activities for the handicapped; 76.7 percent reported volunteers assist in professional services such as counseling, testing, and supervising rehabilitation clients; 55.7 percent reported volunteers' activities included fund raising; secretarial and clerical activities ranked fourth with 55.6 percent of the facilities reporting this type of activity; and public relations ranked fifth with 46 percent.

Volunteers in the Welfare Setting

Concerned citizens have long been interested in improving the quality of life for the indigent in our society. Many citizens have mobilized and organized to help this segment of our population. Some of the outstanding examples of these types of organizations include the Salvation Army, the Volunteers of America and various church outreach groups.

There are two types of volunteers in this area. The first volunteers were the more affluent who were working to improve the lot of the less fortunate or were attempting to lessen the burden of poverty. These volunteers are still in great demand. They provide many functions such as fund raising and gathering food, clothing, and household supplies. They "adopt" children for special events such as birthdays, Christmas, etc. These volunteers provide counseling services in family planning, budgeting, and family interaction. They provide needed transportation to medical and social services and, at times, shopping. There is a need to provide tutoring services for families which can be met through volunteers.

The second type of volunteerism in the welfare setting has evolved recently. This is the indigenous volunteer, the disadvantaged individual who is working to assist the other disadvantaged in his area. These volunteers serve the most important function of interpreting disadvantagement and its effects on others to professionals, community leaders, legislators and concerned citizens. They become members of citizen action groups to bring attention and needed services to the individuals trapped in the pockets of poverty in both the urban and rural settings across the country. They serve to facilitate communication between those who provide services, legislate provisions for services, budget funds for services and recipients of the services. These volunteers work not only to interpret the needs and describe the conditions and impact of poverty but also identify and locate those in need of additional services.

Another facet of their responsibility is communicating with the disadvantaged by describing and putting into perspective the various agencies' goals. Often the socially and culturally disadvantaged are not as highly motivated or eager to accept services as many middle and upper socioeconomic classed individuals—both professional and nonprofessional—might assume. As a result of previous unfortunate experiences with social welfare type agencies these individuals are reluctant to become involved. They do not wish to raise their hopes to have them dashed as they have been in the past. The indigenous volunteer can play a vital role in this area of public welfare.

Volunteers in Health Agencies

Health agencies in the United States have had a long and rich history. These health agencies have made the general population aware of the needs and medical aspects of various diseases or disability categories. These agencies generally are organized around one specific group; for example, the National Multiple Sclerosis Society, the Cystic Fibrosis Foundation, the American Cancer Society, the National Tuberculosis and Respiratory Disease Association, the National Association for Retarded Children, and many others. Volunteers are essential to the function of these agencies. Characteristically, these agencies create an awareness in the general population relative to a specific health problem. They sponsor education programs regarding the disease or disability, its prevention or treatment; they support medical research in the cause, prevention and treatment of the disease; and they provide support for local services and develop informational and referral systems. They represent a strong lobbying force to influence federal legislation.

According to Lowry (1973), there are two kinds of volunteers in health agencies—professional volunteers and lay volunteers. The professional volunteers perform the myriad of tasks which require professional training and which are so necessary for the functioning of the agency. These professionals include physicians, dentists, nurses, physical therapists, occupational therapists, speech therapists, psychologists, accountants, lawyers, social workers, and many others. They advise the disposition of research and professional education grants. They convey the messages of the agency to their own professional societies. They see to it that the agency's financial reports are properly made, that legal requirements are met, that professional ethics are not violated, and that public and professional education materials and information are accurate and consonant with the interests of the patients being represented. They identify existing community resources of potential service to patients, create receptivity to dealing effectively with their problems within those agencies and arrange appropriate referrals. These services are of inestimable value and are too often not understood by the public.

While professional volunteers' work is oriented toward the health agency organization and its functioning, the lay volunteer is oriented more toward the people with whom the health agency is concerned. They provide the manpower to increase the human services. They provide the warmth and concern which is so necessary for someone when he is in a condition of poor health. According to Lowry (1972) they visit patients in the hospitals or at home, performing tasks the patients cannot do alone. They do everything from letter writing and cooking to providing transportation to clinics and recreational activities. They prepare medical supplies, do clerical work, distribute literature, show films, man exhibits, make speeches, operate "loan closets" of medical equipment and supplies. For the individual interested in this kind of activity, there are ample opportunities to serve his community through volunteer action with health agencies.

University Students as Volunteers

As our cultural structure becomes more complicated and as the lines dividing academic disciplines become hazy, universities have increasingly seen the need for some type of intensive laboratory experience in order to communicate adequately many of the basic tenets of some of our disciplines. The general format of the voluntary action in the university setting differs from university to university; however, generally, in the upper levels of undergraduate work an opportunity is afforded the student to take a three, six- or nine-semester-hour course which involves his working in the community in some area related to his major area of emphasis. This is a unique opportunity for the students who attempt to solve problems outside the academic setting by principles they have learned in the academic setting. This experience can be a very humbling one, and from the experience many universities have had, it is felt that it is a motivating influence for students in their last year in the university, for these types of experiences communicate very readily how inadequate many of his concepts really are.

In this type of university program which encourages voluntary action, the students are placed in a setting related to their academic discipline. They are supervised by a faculty member, and also are supervised by an administrator in that particular work setting. The students are generally required to submit various types of reports remarking on their progress, on the type of insight which they have developed and generally are required to have periodic conferences with a university representative. There are many departments which develop programs such as this in the community. Some of the most obvious include departments of education with programs such as elementary education, educational administration, educational psychology, guidance counseling, etc.; participating departments of psychology, economics, urban and regional planning, geography, business management, personnel management, psychology, sociology, social work, rehabilitation and others. There are many opportunities in the urban setting for these types of university students to volunteer. The activities in which they engage include such things as family counseling, tutorial work in various settings, economic counseling, and family planning; many work as teachers' aides; and some provide social welfare services. There are opportunities to provide basic remedial instruction to people at all educational levels and in various social situations. These types of students work in psychiatric wards of general hospitals and in psychiatric institutions to assist in nursing care and various aspects of rehabilitative therapy. Under supervision, many of these students provide behavior modification experiences to retarded and severely culturally deprived individuals in various settings. Some of these university volunteers work in rehabilitation centers and in sheltered workshops assisting in the provision of work adjustment training, vocational and psychological evaluations, in remedial and vocational education and perform some skills in placing individuals in competitive employment. Many of these university volunteers work in information and referral programs within the urban setting. They track down social agencies to provide a wide variety of services to many of the clients with whom they work. They provide outreach services to take the service to the ghetto or the innercity or the area in which the concentration of clients reside. They function as an advocate for these individuals in interpreting their needs to the service agency.

One such program is called Project SUMMON. This program was an academic program founded to do two things at the same time. One was to give students and faculty of the University of Miami an education in reality. The other was to provide competent and regular assistance to those in the community who need it and want it. Its aims and philosophy are simple. Simple, too, is the one crowning point of the program that makes it worthwhile—it works!

Because what the students do is considered an educational experience, they receive three credits for a semester's work at the University of Miami. The granting of academic credit accomplishes two purposes. First, the volunteer agency can be guaranteed each student will work a minimum of six hours per week on a regularly scheduled basis for the course of the semester. Second, because credit is involved and the faculty have to safeguard that investment, professors monitor students on a regular basis, thereby making them not only regular in their performance of their duties, but somewhat competent as well. The students take the program on a pass-fail basis. The student passes if he lasts the semester, doing his work regularly and performing well. The type of things the students learn (respect and humanistic enlightment) cannot be graded.

According to Manasa (1973), professors monitor students on roughly a one-to-ten ratio. Their job is not to program as they do in the classroom, but to listen to the experiences the students have and translate that experience into terms of their discipline. They also offer the students professional insight into how they might do their work better. The students act as direct multiplying agents of the professor's expertise in the community. In this teacher-student relationship, the student is no longer the passive partner, but the active one—he who experiences while the professor becomes what his role meant him to be: a guide.

The program accomplishes five basic purposes. They are listed here.

1. The program gives students of the university an education in reality. The program provides the vehicle by which people might learn by doing. The program is a humanities laboratory composed of the elements of real life.
2. The program reforms the traditional professor-student relationship. The student is made an active partner in this relationship.
3. The program revolutionizes the university curriculum and changes it from its current situation of being an intellectu-

al endeavor to a place where its views of life have some basis in reality.

4. The program "humanizes" the university. Because of their huge size and factory-like atmosphere and because there is no longer any common ground where people learn their need for one another, universities have become places where the most pronounced thing they can teach is academia. This volunteer project attempts to use the community as a new common ground where through common efforts, failure, and success, the university participants might come to know one another again and the relationships and needs for various disciplines.

5. The program provides competent, compassionate and consistent help to the people in the community who need it and want it. This cannot happen without the successful attainment of the above goals.

Volunteers in Service Programs for the Blind

Presently there is a critical shortage of trained personnel in the field of health, recreation, education, and social welfare. According to Pogorelc (1973), at the present time more than 400 volunteer agencies and organizations provide direct services to blind persons through the use of professionally trained and qualified mobility instructors, braille and typing teachers, home economists, occupational therapists, psychologists, social workers, counselors, work evaluators, etc. In addition, many of these agencies also utilize volunteers for reading, friendly visiting, shopping trips, social, cultural, and recreational trips, etc. on behalf of the blind person. Volunteers also serve, as in health agencies, on Board of Directors, Advisory Committees, and as administrators and supervisors in these agencies and organizations.

Notable examples of volunteer utilization within agencies for the blind can be found in every part of the country. At the Braille Institute of America in Los Angeles, 1,445 volunteers have given over 104,000 hours of service in eleven different service categories. The New York Jewish Guild for the Blind has over 300 volunteer workers serving in every area in which professional staff are engaged. These individuals are serving in accordance with their individual skills and interests.

The Phoenix Arizona Center for the Blind is heavily dependent upon its 350 volunteers who donated 25,000 hours of their time on over 8,500 separate assignments during a period of a year. At the minimum wage, this represents a value of $35,000 which would double their present budget.

The Hadley School for the Blind in Winnetka, Illinois, utilizes over 150 volunteers without whom the program would be severely handicapped since the contribution of manpower which volunteers represent is considered beyond estimate. The four locations of the Massachusetts Association for the Blind received the services of over 500 volunteers who assisted clients with tasks for which there is no substitute for sight.

In addition, national organizations utilized the services of volunteers across the country for specific programs. The National Society for the Prevention of Blindness has over 17,000 volunteers, mostly young mothers providing preschool visual screening as well as those services as officers and directors of its state affiliates and national organization (Hardy & Cull, 1973).

The National Braille Association has more than 2,100 members who are for the most part dedicated to volunteer braillists from all parts of the United States. A unique group of volunteers is the "Telephone Pioneers" who as veteran employees of the Bell Telephone System throughout the country volunteer to repair Talking Book machines in their respective localities. This group numbers in excess of 3,600.

These are just a few examples of volunteer utilization gleaned from comments and reports submitted to the Office for the Blind and Visually Handicapped, Rehabilitation Services Administration, and U. S. Department of Health, Education and Welfare in response to a recent survey.

The need for increased services to blind individuals far surpasses the supply of trained professional staff. In order to reduce the impact of this problem, both professional workers for the blind and the public in general must be made aware of, and accept the fact that, volunteers are making, and can make, significant contributions to this field. In addition, the application of sound personnel policies and practices, plus the development of ways to recruit and utilize these volunteers can lead to the provision of more and better services to the blind within the limits of present financial and manpower resources.

REFERENCES AND SELECTED READINGS

Beers, Clifford W.: *A Mind That Found Itself*. Garden City, Doubleday, 1908.

Cull, J. G. and Hardy, R. E.: *Volunteerism: An Emerging Profession*. Springfield, Thomas, 1973.

de Tocqueville, Alexis: *Democracy in America*. New York, Schocken Books, 1961, vol. II, pp. 128-129.

Gunn, Selskar M. and Platt, Phillip S.: *Voluntary Health Agencies*. New York, Ronald Press, 1945.

Hardy, R. E. and Cull, J. G.: *Applied Volunteerism in Community Development*. Springfield, Thomas, 1973.

Janowitz, Gail: *Helping Hands*. Chicago, University of Chicago Press, 1965.

Knoph, S. A.: *History of National Tuberculosis Association—The Anti-Tuberculosis Movement in the United States*. New York, National Tuberculosis Association, 1922.

Lawry, S.: Functions and values of voluntary health agencies. In Hardy, R. E. and Cull, J. G.: *Applied Volunteerism in Community Development*. Springfield, Thomas, 1973, pp. 30-45.

Levin, S.: Volunteers in rehabilitation. In Hardy, R. E. and Cull, J. G.: *Applied Volunteerism in Community Development*. Springfield, Thomas, 1973, pp. 115-129.

Manasa, N.: College students as volunteers. In Hardy, R. E. and Cull, J. G.: *Applied Volunteerism in Community Development*. Springfield, Thomas, 1973, pp. 48-67.

Marris, Peter and Rein, Martin: *Dilemmas of Social Reform*. New York, Atherton Press, 1967, p. 7.

Naylor, Harriet H.: *Volunteers Today—Finding, Training, and Working With Them*. New York, Association Press, 1967.

Stenzel, Ann K. and Feeny, Helen M.: *Volunteer Training and Development*. New York, Seabury Press, 1968.

PART TWO

COUNSELING STRATEGIES WITH THE PHYSICALLY DISABLED

Counseling With Severely Disabled Persons
Special Considerations in Counseling Blind and Severely Visually
    Impaired Persons
Counseling With the Critically Ill
Counseling With Physically Handicapped College Students

CHAPTER 5

COUNSELING WITH SEVERELY DISABLED PERSONS

- Characteristic Ingredients Necessary for Effective Counseling and Therapy
- Idiosyncratic Intervention Strategies
- Special Roles of the Psychologist
- Psychosexual Readjustment
- The Role of Defense Mechanisms and Psychoanalytic Concepts in Adjustment
- Postadjustment Life-Styles of the Disabled
- General Implications for Professionals Working With the Cord Injured Individuals

Introduction

IN THIS CHAPTER material is offered which will be helpful in counseling severely disabled persons. The area of spinal cord injury has been chosen as an example of severe disability. The principles suggested here can be applied in work with various individuals who are severely handicapped.

The fact that our clients are much more similar to us than they are dissimilar is a truism, but they differ in one major respect. They have suffered the psychological impact of disability and have adjusted or are in the process of adjusting to this impact. In the case of the spinal cord injured individual, adjustment problems are severe in that emotional recovery or adjustment for the traumatically injured person is torturous. The counselor or therapist serving the spinal cord injured individual should recognize that his client will not necessarily show a severe disintegrative personality crisis that always requires in-depth therapeutic involvement at an immediate period after injury, but the client may fall into an emotional depression over everyday problems of routine personal management and interpersonal relationships. Severe crisis can come about from so-called lower level problems (cues to client feelings are exaggerated demands on his part, refusal to cooperate in medical treatment procedures, and the development of psychosocial or psychoneurotic reactions). The point to be made here then is that treatment staff should be very much "tuned in" to various cues that may signal severe emotional distress. These cues are not necessarily indicative of severe personality disintegration but may be more indicative of an emotional adjustment crisis.

CHARACTERISTIC INGREDIENTS NECESSARY FOR EFFECTIVE COUNSELING AND THERAPY

There are three central ingredients of a "helping relationship" which have been identified after extensive research and which are necessary interpersonal skills no matter what counseling or therapeutic approach is used by the counselor. These ingredients have been defined by Truax and Carkhuff (1967), and Truax and Mitchell (1971, pp. 11) as follows:

1. An effective counselor or therapist is nonphony, nondefensive, and authentic, or *genuine* in his helping or therapeutic encounters;
2. An effective counselor is able to provide a nonthreatening, safe, trusting, or secure atmosphere through his own acceptance, positive regard, love, valuing, or *non-possessive* warmth, for the client; and
3. An effective counselor is able to understand, "be with," "grasp the meaning of," or have a high degree of *accurate empathic understanding* of the client on a moment-by-moment basis.

These ingredients are required but not necessarily sufficient conditions in order for the therapist or counselor to bring about successful behavior change. In addition to accurate empathic understanding, warmth, genuineness, experiencing, and self-exploration, we must add the necessary and sufficient conditions for the successful intervention of a counselor or therapist in dealing with a particular client or helpee who has a special problem at this definite or particular time in his life (Mitchell et al., 1973).

IDIOSYNCRATIC INTERVENTION STRATEGIES

Knowledgeable researchers have experienced considerable difficulty in determining specific antecedents to psychotherapy and counseling outcome. Research has generally indicated that the ingredients listed earlier must be evident in order for any level of successful therapeutic outcome to be achieved. These ingredients must be offered by the therapist in all counseling situations with various clients in various idiosyncratic conditions. Even the length of time in psychotherapeutic treatment in terms of its relationship to outcome is now in dispute (Luborsky et al., 1971 and Mitchell et al., 1973).

The same two reports have shown differences in terms of the seriousness of diagnosis as this is associated with improvement as a result of counseling. The Luborsky (1971) study showed less improvement with serious diagnosis and the Mitchell et al. (1973) study indicated that the more seriously diagnosed clients were associated with more improvement. The helping person will wish to explore various relationship elements with the client such as the quantity of verbal interaction (is the client doing more listening then talking or more talking than listening). The helping person will also wish to concern himself with the content of the verbal interaction of the helpee or client (is the person dealing mainly with external reality or interfeelings; is the helping person offering support mainly or is he doing selective interpretation).

Certainly the helping person must realize that immediately after the traumatic spinal cord injury is sustained the client is almost completely helpless and few demands should be made on him. The counselor must deal with him in a direct manner and the helpee's questions must be answered realistically and objectively.

As the client begins to stabilize, he may be helped more actively by the counselor or therapist. It is at this time that some elementary concepts in rehabilitation may be introduced. In terms of his idiosyncratic condition, he should be permitted to have some time in order to realize that he is out of impending danger. After a short period the counselor may increase the amount of challenging stimulation which the client experiences.

The client will actively attempt to deny his injury and may withdraw into a passive dependent adjustment pattern. A helping person must constantly stay "on top of" these changing situational concerns. In other words as severe regression evolves, so does the counselor need to change his perception of the client's situation.

The client must be helped in realizing that he has changed in physical capacity and while this change may be indicative of a lessened physical capability it does not mean that the person as an individual has lessened in value. While he may be different, he is not inherently useless or bad. After the client's feelings of dispair related to a changed body and sense of self have been accepted, the helping person may begin aiding the client in understanding his feelings concerning helplessness. It is important for the counselor to offer support, encouragement, acceptance as well as information which is useful in exploring emotional realities.

In a disability involving no damage to brain tissue, the physical limitations imposed by the disability may cause excessive frustration and in turn result in behavioral disorders. For example, an active "outdoors man" and nature lover may experience a greater psychological impact upon becoming severely disabled than an individual who leads a more restricted and physically limited life.

It is obvious that the restrictions imposed by the disability demand a greater change in the basic life style of the "outdoors man." Therefore, it is important to note in the predisability (pre-morbid) personality of the individual that factors directly associated with the actual limitations of the disability as well as the individual's life-style have an important bearing on the individual's reaction to the disability.

The helping person must explore the individual's attitude toward the spinal cord injury as a particular disability. The individual's adjustment to his injury is dependent upon, to some degree, the attitudes he held prior to his disability. If his attitudes toward other spinal cord injured persons and the disabled in general were quite negative and strong, he will naturally have a greater adjustment problem than an individual with a neutral or positive attitude toward disability and disabled people. A part of this attitude formulation prior to the onset of disability is dependent upon the experiences the client has had with other disabled persons and the stereotypes he has developed. If psychoanalytic theory is applied to stigma, we can hypothesize that a nondisabled person who is prejudiced toward disabled people is a relatively immature individual with unexpressed hostilities and a need to feel psychologically superior (English, 1974). If one then wishes to take the psychoanalytic view, he can determine much about the individual's reaction to his disability by his attitude toward disabled persons prior to becoming disabled.

The amount of fear a client expresses or emotion he expends during the onset or duration of an illness or accident leading up to a disability also helps determine the psychological impact of the disability. Generally, the greater amount of emotion expended during onset, the better the psychological adjustment to the disability. If an individual is suddenly injured in a car accident, for instance, his psychological reaction to the disability is much greater than if a great deal of emotion has been expended during the process of becoming spinal cord injured.

In addition, the more information an individual has relating to his spinal cord injury, the less impact the disability will have. If a newly disabled individual is told about his disability in a simple and direct manner, he will have an easier time accepting and adjusting to the disability than if it remained shrouded in a cloak of ignorance and mystery. Any strangeness or unpredictable aspect of our body associated with its function immediately creates anxiety. And if not clarified, this anxiety can rapidly be totally debilitating; therefore, it is important for psychological adjustment to a disability that the individual have communicated to him, in terms that he can understand, the medical aspects of his disability as soon after onset as he is able, as indicated earlier, to undertake such discussion.

When we are in strange or uncomfortable surroundings our social perceptiveness becomes keener. Social cues which are below threshold or not noticed in comfortable surroundings become highly significant to all of us in a strange, new or uncomfortable environment. Upon the onset of a spinal cord injury, the client will develop a heightened perceptiveness relative to how he is being treated by family members, friends, and professional persons. If others start treating him in a condescending manner and relegate him to a position of less importance, his reaction to the psychological impact of cord injury will be poor. Professional helping persons can react to the client from an anatomical orientation (what is missing) or a functional orientation (what is left to use). The anatomical orientation is efficient for classification purposes but is completely dehumanizing. The functional orientation is completely individualistic and as such enhances a client's adjustment to his disability.

Perhaps a key factor in the adjustment process is evaluation of the future and the individual's role in the future. In many physical medicine rehabilitation centers, a rehabilitation counselor is the first professional worker to see the patient or client after the medical crisis has passed. The purpose of this approach is to facilitate the patient's psychological adjustment. If the client feels there is potential for his regaining independence and security his reaction to cord injury will be improved. While the counselor cannot engage in specific vocational planning with the client at this time, he can discuss in depth the available vocational rehabilitation programs, and through these preliminary informational sessions the counselor can help the newly disabled person evaluate his future.

The last factor which determines the adjustment process and helps the counselor understand the idiosyncratic situation of the client is based upon the individual's view of the purpose of his body and the relationship this view has with the type and extent of disability. Body image theory is a neopsychoanalytic system which has been used by many professional persons in explaining adjustment to disability. The concept of body image has been closely related to that of self-concept although these are not equivalent concepts in the minds of those who advocate body image theory (Wapner and Warner, 1965). It is generally felt however that body perceptions accurately reflect generalized feelings of self.

The views individuals have of their bodies may be characterized as falling somewhere along a continuum. At one end of the continuum is the view that the body is a tool to accomplish work; it is a productive machine. At the other end is the view that the body is an esthetic stimulus to be enjoyed and provide pleasure for others. This later concept is much the same as that which we have for sculpture and harks back to the philosophy of the ancient Greeks. Everyone falls somewhere on this continuum. To adequately predict the impact of a spinal cord injury upon an individual, one has to locate the individual along this continuum; then evaluate the disability in light of the individual's view of the function of his body.

The most obvious conclusion to be drawn from the information given is that the degree of psychological impact is not highly correlated with the degree of disability. This statement is contrary to popular opinion; however, disability and its psychological impact is a highly personalized event. Many helping persons fall into the trap of equating degree of disability with degree of psychological impact. It should be remembered that relatively superficial disabilities may have devastating psychological effects. The psychological impact of cord injury is not necessarily greater than the psychological impact of disabilities which are less severe.

SPECIAL ROLES OF THE PSYCHOLOGIST

One of the most important roles which the psychologist has in dealing with the spinal cord client is that of evaluation. Many clients are paraplegic or quadraplegic because of the dramatic traumatic injury such as falls, automobile and diving accidents. The psychologist must rule out the possibility of organic brain damage. Various tests are used for this purpose including the Bender-Gestalt, Graham-Kendall, and the Hooper.

The psychologist should be particularly aware of one characteristic that is associated with the sudden onset of disability— that of deep depression. When such a trauma occurs with resulting disability in terms of paraplegia or quadraplegia, the absence of the grief response indicates pathologic concerns. The meaning of the absence of grief is generally that the patient is denying the extent or permanence of the injury.

The psychologist works with the rehabilitation counselor and others and often is more concerned with organized group counseling and therapy than is the rehabilitation counselor, although functions overlap according to level of training of individual team members. As the client progresses and time nears for his leaving the rehabilitation setting, he will become somewhat anxious concerning the fact that he is now to leave his protected environment. This reaction can be extreme and at times can reach panic proportions. Psychologists should work with other team members in order to expose the client gradually to the outside world. The family should be heavily involved in helping the patient make the transition from rehabilitation center or hospital to home. The psychologist often may wish to suggest weekend passes in order to aid the client in this adjustment.

PSYCHOSEXUAL READJUSTMENT

We should like to preface our remarks with several statements of caution. A counselor or therapist should never exceed his professional competency in the name of providing services which he is not qualified to offer to his client. In the area of sexual counseling, for instance, the counselor must be certain that he is the individual to do the job. This can be done only by evaluating his own credentials in comparison with those of other counselors who are specializing in the field of marital and sexual problems. In serving spinal cord injured individuals, rehabilitation counselors, psychologists, and others generally are not doing the job which should be done in terms of providing useful information and meaningful relationships during so-called sexual counseling.

Many rehabilitation counselors and psychologists are not qualified to do in-depth therapy. The counselor and psychologist must evaluate whether or not the client is receiving the necessary services. If the client is not receiving such services because professional personnel are in short supply, then the rehabilitation counselor and/or psychologist must take it upon himself to develop expertise under the guidance and supervision of highly trained persons in order that he may meet the needs which his clients constantly exhibit.

It is interesting that the psychosexual readjustment of the cord injured individual is a subject of such concern not only to clients but to professional staff members as well that films have been recently developed for the primary purpose of desensitization of staff members who are working with cord injured persons (Coles, 1971). In other words, personal inhibitions are so strong among professional staff persons that desensitization is necessary in order for them to openly discuss sexual relations in counseling with clients. The foregoing statements are good indication of the level of difficulty cord injured persons themselves may have in dealing with their problems.

Generally speaking, cord injured persons "cry out" for advice, information and counseling related to altered sexual functioning. Rehabilitation center and other staff persons have not been thoroughly informing themselves concerning sexual functionability of cord injured persons. Social role theory holds that related to successful role enactment is the concept of role reciprocity (Sarbin, 1954). In other words, every role is closely interwoven with one or more others. The spinal cord injured person is expected by others in terms of role set or attitudes or expectations to enact the "sick role." This expectation is constantly enforced by many persons including medical and therapeutic staff, family members and others who should be supporting an attitude of exploration in order to determine an actual role rather than a sick role. In other words, is the individual exempt from certain routine duties of life? Is he not accountable for his actions? Is he exempt from social responsibility? Must he always comply with medical advice and cooperate with medical experts? And, must he always view health as necessary for optimal performance of the most important life tasks including sexual give and take? These ideas are applied to spinal cord injured persons by the authors using original concepts of Parsons (1951).

A factor which probably influences the effectiveness of staff persons in dealing with sexual problems of spinal cord injured persons is that of generation. Persons who are not members of the younger generation are quite accustomed to repressing sex-

BOWLING GREEN STATE UNIVERSITY LIBRARY

uality as a part of their general mores or ways of life. Persons of the present younger generation appear to have many less inhibitions and fewer needs for repression of sexual thought and feelings. This fact in and of itself may lead to improved psychosexual readjustment of cord injured individuals.

Of course the helping person must keep in mind that many factors influence sexual functioning. These include religious orientation and other psychological, social, and emotional concerns. Hohmann (1972, pp. 108-109) has offered the following in reference to defining sexual relationships:

> Sexual relationship may be defined in many ways, only a few of which are mentioned here to point out that sexuality is indeed a "many splendored thing." It can be (1) a massive buildup of autonomic and striated activity culminating in orgasm; (2) a biological process serving the purpose of procreation of the race; (3) a means of bolstering the faltering ego and attendant self-esteem of the participants; (4) a means of manipulation and controlling another important individual involved in the patient's life; and (5) a means of expression of two individual personalities and of merging them in symbolic and physical feelings of tenderness, respect, and concern for each other and their pleasure.

We have already described some of the characteristics which counselors need in order for them to be effective. With great particularity these concepts must be present in order for a sexual counselor dealing with cord injured clients to be successful. In other words he must develop a relationship with the client which is conducive of good mental health. Inherent in an effective counseling relationship is the absence of threat. The counselor must remove threat if the client is to grow and be able to solve his problems in an uninhibited manner. Counseling as a relationship is also typified by the types of feelings that many of us have for our closest friends. True close friendships are characterized by honest caring, genuine interest, and a high level of concern about helping a person in need. Real friendships often require that one person put aside his own selfish needs in order to listen long enough and with enough empathy so that a friend's problem may begin to work itself out in a natural and constructive manner.

The counselor working with the cord injured client should recognize that no matter what particular school of counseling he accepts as a practitioner, the most important factor determining outcome of counseling effectiveness is his own personality. In other words, whether he counts himself as Rogerian, Ellisonian, or eclectic, his personality will come through in the counseling sessions and affect the outcome to a degree which will determine whether or not the counseling session is effective. Just as teachers can bring about enormous growth and changes in students by modifying their attitudes toward various subject matters, the counselor can bring about substantial changes in his client for better or worse. The counselor who is helping the client deal with spinal cord injury must have accurate physiological, psychological and neurological information at hand.

In working with the spinal cord injured client in the area of sexual concerns, the counselor must evaluate his own personality in terms of attitudes, "hang-ups," religious feelings, moral values, etc., in order to ascertain whether or not he is free in the degree of openness which may be needed to help the client adjust to his disability. Stories are legion concerning exploitation of clients by unknowing and knowing counselors as counselor needs are met instead of client needs. Examples include the frigid female counselor who may threaten a client by being seductive as she assumes that the client will be unable to even make a "pass" at her and the male counselor who may use the client as he explores his own masculinity and psychosexual maturity.

In terms of a knowledge of the psychology of sexual relationships, it is most important for counselors to be highly sophisticated. Counselors should have an in-depth understanding of the differences between typical males and females in terms of their needs, attitudes, desires, etc. Women for instance may be intensely more interested in love relationships and companionship than in orgastic potency.

Generally speaking the counselor working with cord injured clients should assume that some sexuality may be possible until experience and careful neurological workups demonstrate that actual intercourse is not possible. Comarr (1970) has shown that in upper motor neuron complete lesions, between 8 and 43 percent of cord injured males had been unsuccessful in attempting coitus. Of those with incomplete lesions who attempted coitus there was one group (thoracic lesions between 7 and 12) in which unsuccessful attempts were at 20 percent. The counselor must always consider that the male client may be able to experience genital relationships through the use of reflexogenic or even psychogenic erections. According to Hohmann (1972) the range of functions is from those with incomplete lesions who may have normal genital sexual functions to those spinal cord injured males with complete upper motor neuron lesions who are able to perform sexual genital acts with reliability and endurance in terms of reflexogenic behavior. In addition, many who are free of various sexual hang-ups and inhibitions may derive substantial pleasure for themselves and their spouses through various types of foreplay. This includes for both male and female various types of touching and caressing of both the primary and secondary erogenous zones, cunnilingus, fellatio, digital stimulation, and the use of prosthetic phallic devices. The counselor must be very certain that the client understands that such activities must be mutually pleasing to both parties and that attitudes in reference to sexual behavior will need to be explored gingerly by the counselor with either male or female client or both and through mutual discussions between spouses.

The counselor may find a review of *Individual Psychology* as offered by Alfred Adler (1927) of help. The most important of Adler's theoretical constructs that may relate here deal with the stigmatization of the physically disabled in terms of "striving for superiority," "inferiority," "compensation," and the general idea of the "life-style." Dr. Adler has written that all people possess an innate drive to strive for superiority. This particular drive evolves into a pattern or life-style from early childhood. This striving for superiority seems to be motivated by an eagerness to compensate for certain innate feelings of inferiority. We can see from this pattern of reasoning then that the chances for unrealistic striving for superiority among cord injured individuals are greatly increased over those of the non-cord injured. The point for the counselor to keep in mind is that there are substantial changes for occurrence of greater emotional difficulties among disabled people than among the nondisabled (this is especially true during adjustment phases) although the emotional stability of the disabled has compared favorably overall with the nondisabled (Wright, 1960, English, 1968, McDaniel, 1969).

The importance of body image theory has been mentioned earlier (Schilder, 1950). In this particular theory, body attitudes are felt to be the result and reflection of interpersonal relationships. In 1960, Cleveland reported that body attitudes appear to change during psychotherapy and after later research he observed that body feelings are often correlated with personality adjustment test results. There are other research studies which have been reported in the literature dealing with this subject and it is not the purpose of this paper to reflect all these studies here. The point is simply that research has been done to indicate that attitudes toward the body are often the result of relationships among persons, and we know that these body attitudes can be particularly affected by sexual partners and especially if one is partially disabled in function.

We cannot overemphasize the importance of the establishment and maintenance of a successful meaningful relationship between the spinal cord injured person and spouse. This can do more for the improvement of the self-concept than any other one factor.

The counselor should make every effort to encourage open willingness on the part of both spouses to enter into mutual discussions among themselves concerning various problems related to sexual relationships. Central tenets should always be genuine concern and mutual respect as well as a gentleness in approaching conversations concerning new topics and problems. The client should realize that discussions on the topics of sexuality can take place along a continuum and that all problems will not be solved this year or the next. The topic of sexuality should be one which can be raised whenever the client wishes. The counselor should never force the client to talk about his sexual problems until the client is willing to do so. This will come about as the relationship between the client and counselor develops and as the client feels the need to discuss the subject.

The counselor should encourage group activity on the part of the spinal cord injured individual. In other words he should when possible join groups of other cord injured individuals in order to gain information concerning his sexual functionability as well as other data helpful to adjustment. Spouses of cord injured persons can also meet in groups including the injured or only the noninjured parties. A great deal of very helpful information can be conveyed through such meetings, and these meetings should continue as long as individuals are receiving help from them (for an excellent description of group work among severally disabled persons, see Poor, 1974).

It will be important for the counselor to meet with the spouse of the cord injured individual in order to discuss his or her attitudes in reference to sexuality and care of the injured person. Hohmann (1972) has stated there is a possibility of destroying the libidinous interest of the noninjured wife especially when she is caring for a severely disabled quadriplegic husband. Wives have reported that it has been nearly impossible for them to take care of routine bowel care, feeding, etc. for their husbands and still retain an interest in them as sexual objects. Hohmann has indicated that the wise counselor will quickly sense this problem and encourage outside resources such as visiting nurses and part-time attendants for these anesthetic chores.

Generally speaking female spinal cord injured persons are in better condition sexually than males in terms of sexual functionality. Irrespective of the level of the cord injury, females if they are in the childbearing period of their life have the potential to give birth. And, since females generally place a high value on the interpersonal relationship, they can often achieve a quite satisfactory sexual adjustment when a warm and genuine personal relationship exists with the noninjured spouse.

THE ROLE OF DEFENSE MECHANISMS AND PSYCHOANALYTIC CONCEPTS IN ADJUSTMENT

The human mind has been described by Gunther (1969) as resembling an iceberg, eight tenths being below surface (the unconscious). According to Gunther all overt, objectively observable behavior, including that which appears inexplicable or irrational, has both unconscious as well as conscious origins and meanings to the individual. The counselor needs to understand the unconscious origin of any behavior if that behavior is to be fully understood and dealt with by both counselor and client.

Barker, Wright and Gonick (1946) and Wright (1955) have offered information concerning adjustment to disability which relates to what has been called "the requirement of mourning." The mourning requirement when interpreted through Social Role Theory by English (1974) has to do with the concept that there is an expectational demand made on any disabled person that he act sick whether or not he wishes to or not for a time determined by society following disablement. According to English's interpretation of Social Role Theory, the expectation to be depressed over the loss of functionality and to brood or mourn is universally imposed upon disabled persons. Mourning is almost always observed after disablement along with such related affective dimensions as self-devaluation and generalization of dysfunctional anxiety. Some have interpreted this as a period of body image death as well as reintegration and a process of almost being reborn as a new individual. This has been particularly applied by Carroll (1961) in reference to blindness.

The cord injured individual goes through various stages in terms of his reaction to traumatic disability. The first stage is one of shock and may last for several hours or days. A person during this period is generally considerably slowed down in his thought processes, his feelings are rather flat, and he appears confused and out of touch. At this period of time he has not realized fully what has happened to him.

After the shock period begins to subside, the client will enter a period of partial recognition of his problem, and as might be expected he becomes more responsive, less confused. He will experience substantial anxiety. He will at this time attempt to protect himself from his actual feelings concerning what has happened to him and he will give very little thought to the future. In a third stage which has been called initial stabilization by

Gunther (1969), he has become superficially reconciled to his disability. This stage may last for months or years. The client may become more cheerful and cooperative and appear more stable. At this time his outward behavior may be quite deceiving in that he has not come to full dealing with his feelings about his injury.

Denial

This state of regression may last for many months in the spinal cord injured patient. It is an unconscious rejection of the obvious fact of the injury which is too disruptive of the personality or too emotionally painful to accept; therefore, in order to soften reality, the obvious fact is denied. Immediately upon onset of disability the individual denies it happened. He denies his disability. Then as the fact of the disability becomes so overwhelming to him that its existence can no longer be denied, there is a denial of permanency of the disability. The newly cord injured individual, while utilizing the defense of denial, will adamantly maintain that he shall be whole again. There will be a miraculous cure or new surgical technique to save him.

When the staff puts pressure on him in order that he be involved in a treatment program he may balk and fall back on primitive pathological attitudes. He may project responsibility for his illness and its cure and accuse personnel of various errors in treatments, etc. He may later even become openly hostile and paranoid.

While there are few steadfast rules in human behavior, one is that rehabilitation at best can be only marginally successful at this point. Rehabilitation cannot proceed adequately until the client accepts the permanency of his disability and is ready to cope with the condition. This is what is meant by many professional persons when they say a client must accept his cord injury. Denial is the front line of psychological defense, but it may outlast all other defenses.

Regression

Regression is the defense mechanism which reduces strain by avoiding it. The individual psychologically returns to an earlier chronological age period that was more pleasant to him. He adopts the type of behavior that was attractive at that age but now has been outgrown.

As the newly cord injured individual withdraws, becomes egocentric and hypochrondrical, he may regress to an earlier age which was more satisfactory. This regression may be manifested in two manners. First he may, in his regression, adopt the dress, mannerisms, speech, etc. of contemporaries at the age level to which he is regressing. Secondly, he may adopt the outmoded dress, mannerisms, speech, etc. of the earlier time in his life to which he regressed. The second manifestation of regression is considerably more maladaptive since it holds the individual out to more ridicule which at this point in his adjustment to disability, quite possibly will result in more emphasis on the defense mechanism of withdrawal. This could be regressive as far as adjustment process is concerned.

As the cord injured person becomes fully aware of his altered body and begins to think about his future, he experiences many agonizing feelings.

Repression

Repression is selective forgetting. It is contrasted with suppression which is conscious voluntary forgetting. Repression is unconscious. Events are repressed because they are psychologically traumatic. As mentioned earlier, the attitudes of the client relative to his cord injury and to another cord injured and disabled person has a major bearing upon his adjustment. If these attitudes are highly negative, the client will have to repress them at this point if his adjustment is to progress. Until he represses them he will be unable to accept the required new body image.

Reaction Formation

When an individual has an attitude which creates a great deal of guilt, tension or anxiety and he unconsciously adopts behavior typical of the opposite attitude, he has developed a reaction formation. In order to inhibit a tendency to flee in terror, a boy will express his nonchalance by whistling in the dark. Some timid persons, who feel anxious in relating with others, hide behind a facade of gruffness and assume an attitude of hostility to protect themselves from fear. A third and last example is that of a mother who feels guilty about her rejection of a newborn child and may adopt an attitude of extreme overprotectiveness to reduce the anxiety produced by her feelings of guilt. This example is seen more often in cases of parents with handicapped children.

In this new dependent role which the cord injured person finds himself, he will feel a varying degree of hostility and resentment toward those upon whom he is so dependent—wife, children, relatives and others. Since these feelings are unacceptable he may develop a reaction formation. The manifest behavior will be marked by concern, love, affection, closeness, etc.—all to an excessive degree.

Fantasy

Fantasy is daydreaming. It is the imaginary representative of satisfactions that are not attained in real experience. This defense mechanism quite often accompanies withdrawal. As the client starts to adjust to his new body image and a new role in life, he will develop a rich, overactive fantasy life. In this dream world he will place himself in many different situations to see how well he fits.

Rationalization

Rationalization is giving socially acceptable reasons for behavior and decisions. There are four types of rationalizations that are generally accepted. The first is called blaming an incidental cause—the child who stumbles blames the stool by kicking it; the poor or sloppy workman blames his tools. "Sour grapes" rationalization is called into play when an individual is thwarted. A goal to which the individual aspires is blocked to him; therefore, he devalues the goal by saying he did not really want to reach his goal so much anyway. The opposite type of rationalization is called "sweet lemons." When something the individual does not want is forced upon him, he will modify his attitude by saying it was really a very desirable goal and he feels quite positive about the new condition. The fourth and last type of rationalization is called the doctrine of balances. In this type of rationalization, we balance positive attributes in others with perceived negative qualities. Conversely, we balance negative attributes with positive qualities. For example, beautiful women are assumed to be dumb; bright boys are assumed to be weak and asthenic; and the poor are happier than the rich.

The cord injured individual will have to rationalize his disability to assist him in accepting the permanence of the disability. One rationalization may be that he had nothing to do with his current condition; something over which he had no control caused the disability. Another dynamic which might be observed is the adherence to the belief on the part of the client that as a result of the disability there will be compensating factors (for example, he might have more time to read and develop special competencies since he no longer has to work). We once worked with a paraplegic client whose rationalization for his disability was somewhat as follows: All of the men in his family had been highly active outdoor types. They had all died prematurely with coronaries. The client was a highly active outdoor type; however, now that he was severely disabled he would be considerably restricted in his activities. Therefore, he would not die prematurely. The logic resulted in the conclusion that the disability was positive and he was pleased to have become disabled. Granted, rationalization is seldom carried to this extreme in the adjustment process, but this case is illustrative of a type of thinking which must occur for good adjustment.

Projection

A person who perceives traits or qualities in himself which are unacceptable may deny these traits and project them to others. In doing so he is using the defense mechanism of projection. A person who is quite stingy sees others as trying to steal from him. A person who feels inferior rejects this idea and instead projects it to others—that is, he is capable but others will not give him a chance because they doubt his ability. These are examples of projection. With the cord injured person many of the feelings that he has of himself are unacceptable. Therefore, in order to adjust adequately he projects these feelings to society in general. "They" feel he is inadequate. "They" feel he is not capable. "They" feel he is inferior and to be devalued. This type of thinking, usually, leads directly into identification and compensation which are in reality the natural exits from the mental maze in which he has been wandering.

Identification

The defense mechanism of identification is used to reduce an individual's conflicts through the achievements of another person or group of people. Identification can be with material possessions as well as with people. A person may derive feelings of social and psychological adequacy through his clothes ("The clothes make the man"), his sports car, his hi-fi stereophonic paraphernalia and so forth. People identify with larger groups in order to take on their power, prestige and the respect attributed to that organization ("our team won"). The larger group may be a social club, lodge, garden club, college, or professional group.

In adjusting to disability, the spinal cord injured client will identify with a larger group. It may be a group of persons with his particular disability, an occupational group, a men's lodge, a veteran's group, etc. But at this point in the adjustment process, he will identify with some group in order to offset some of the feelings he has as a result of the projection in which he is engaging. If successful, the identification obviates the need to employ the mechanisms of denial, withdrawal and regression.

Compensation

If an individual's path to a set of goals is blocked and he finds other routes to achieve that set of goals, he is using the defense mechanism of compensation. A teenager is seeking recognition and acceptance from his peers. He decides to gain this recognition through sports; however, after a spinal cord injury he is unable to make the team and decides to become a scholar. This is an example of compensation. Compensation brings success; therefore, it diverts attention from shortcomings and defects, thereby eliminating expressed or implied criticism. This defense mechanism is most often used to reduce self-criticism rather than external criticism. As the individual experiences successes he will become less preoccupied with anxieties relating to his disability and his lack of productivity.

Identification and compensation usually go together in the adjustment process. When the cord injured individual starts using these two defenses he is at a point where he may adequately adjust to the new body image and his new role in life.

As will be noted from the above description of the adjustment process, there are four phases through which the individual passes in achieving adjustment. This is correlated with Siller's (1969) work with the cord injured. Siller discussed four behavioral patterns in the adjustment to traumatization. These are passivity, dependency, aggression, and compensation.

In the above paradigm the newly traumatized individual exhibits a strong element of passivity. At this point he begins employing the defense mechanisms of denial and withdrawal. By doing so he is escaping from the demands of the environment. According to Siller (1969), passivity has been defined as a mode of adaptation to one's environment that involves going back from it. This is exactly what we feel is occurring in the initial phases of adjustment.

Next the individual enters a dependency period. When he is employing the next series of defense mechanisms as we have outlined above the patient is adjusting by adopting a dependent status. This allows him to evaluate the extent and ramifications of his disability in relation to his life in the future. When this evaluation is complete and has been internalized or accepted, the patient enters the next broad phase of adjustment—aggression. At this point in the adjustment process, the individual starts fighting back at the environment. He aggressively reaches out and interacts with those around him. He becomes action-oriented in his adjustment to the disability.

As he enters this period of aggressively dealing with the environment he is becoming prepared for the next and final phase of adjustment—compensation. It is compensation which allows the patient to compete on somewhat of an equal footing with others in his social and vocational environments.

POST-ADJUSTMENT LIFE-STYLES OF THE DISABLED

Allport (1954) outlined several traits which are defenses due to victimization. These traits include obsessive concern, denial of membership, withdrawal and passivity, clowning, strengthening in group ties, slyness and cunning, self-hate through identification with the dominant group, aggression against one's own group, prejudice against outgroups, sympathy, militantly fighting back, enhanced striving, symbolic status striving, neuroticism and the self-fulfilling prophecy. While he applied these specifically to conditions which were highly ladened with prejudicial evaluations of other people, his description of many of these traits hold especially true for the reactions of the disabled and most especially for disability groups which have a high degree of visibility such as the spinal cord injured, blind, neuromuscularly impaired, etc.

The first of these which Allport discusses is *obsessive concern*. In this type of reaction the individual who is the object of the prejudice or stigmatization, the handicapped individual, expresses an obsessive concern for his condition. He is excessively sensitive about his condition. It is almost as if he is waiting for expressions of hostility, denegation, etc. from others. Each time a handicapped person is looked down upon or rejected or relegated to second class citizenhood his feelings of inferiority and inadequacy increase which additionally increases and supports the rationale and validity of his obsessive concern for rejection by others. As an example of his overconcern Allport relates the following:

> One day in the late thirties a recently arrived refugee couple went shopping in a village grocery store in New England. The husband ordered some oranges.
> "For juice?" inquired the clerk.
> "Did you hear that," the woman whispered to her husband, "For Jews?" "You see, it's beginning here too."

This type of hypersensitivity is often observed in disabled individuals as a result of their disabling conditions. Many handicapped individuals are so sensitive to prejudice or the stigmatization they encounter they often will reject any outward sign of the disability. For example, often blind people, as a result of this obsessive concern, refuse to use the guides and rehabilitative aids which are available to them. As such many blind people refuse the use of the white cane since they feel it symbolizes blindness and they do not want to be identified as being blind. Many amputees will reject the use of artificial limbs and would rather have an empty sleeve than an artificial limb since they feel this obsessive concern for the disability.

A particularly interesting reaction on the part of disabled people is the *denial of membership in a group.* As we mentioned earlier, one of the first ego defense reactions to disabling conditions is the denial of the presence of the disability, and then as the fact of the disability becomes so obvious it can no longer be denied, there is a denial of the permanence of the effects of the disability. Then as the adjustment process proceeds the need for employing this ego defense mechanism will fade. Related to this denial of the disability is denial of membership in various groups (that is, the individual not only will deny his disability but he will deny there is any similarity between himself and others with this disability). Eventually after he adjusts to his disabling condition to the extent that he can admit he is disabled he may continue to deny membership in this group because denial of membership is maintaining perhaps his last vestige of resistance to the disability. In an individual who is expressing this denial of membership there is an underlying theme of rejection of disabled persons themselves; however, in denial of membership in a group, the individual will suffer a neurotic-like guilt for he unconsciously is aware of the fact that he belongs to this group and by denying membership in the group he is to an extent denying the reality of his own circumstances. As Allport quoted: "A Jewish student confessed with remorse that in order not to be known as Jewish he would sometimes 'insert in my conversation delicate criticisms pertaining to Jewishness which, while not actually vicious, conveyed a total impression of gentile malice.' "

As you will note in the above quotation, the individual felt remorse and guilt at rejecting his heritage but still was compelled to deny his membership in the Jewish population. This reaction is most obvious with the more severely impaired individual such as the spinal cord injured client.

Withdrawal and passivity are very powerful tools which the severely disabled individual has at his disposal. He uses them to mask his true feelings and prevent much of the hostility and strong emotionality from rising to the surface and being directed toward those upon whom he is dependent and toward those who are critical and prejudicial. Many severely impaired individuals feel that this degree of passivity is the only way in which they can survive the prejudice of the nonhandicapped directed toward the handicapped. Often this feeling of severe prejudicial judgment on the part of the nonhandicapped is a misconception. But, whether it is a misconception or an accurate evaluation of the situation, the reality for this severely disabled individual still is that he needs to react as if prejudice were present within his environment. This withdrawal and passivity allows him to recognize the stigmatization which is occurring, and at the same time gives him a safe secure approach to dealing with this stigmatization. Again, as we mentioned above, withdrawal occurs at the beginning of the adjustment process as a mechanism which allows the individual to retreat from the environment during an initial phase which will allow him to gain a new perspective of disability and disabling conditions before he begins to aggressively meet the environment and adjust to the disability. The withdrawal and passivity which Allport is mentioning at this point is not the more healthy withdrawal we mentioned above in the adjustment process. The withdrawal and passivity mentioned at this point is a persistent life style which is developed in order to combat perceived or implied criticism, prejudice, and stigmatization based upon the presence of a disability.

While Allport feels *clowning* is an ego defense mechanism which alleviates the pressure of prejudice by accentuating the particular traits which are most susceptable to prejudice, we have seen clowning used so infrequently that we do not feel this is a true life-style of the disabled. We are not saying this is not evident as a life-style, but we do not feel it is of sufficient prevalence to be singled out as being usual. However, there are examples of this approach to alleviating the internal feelings of prejudice on the part of the disabled. For example, we are aware of a well-known entertainer, a comedian who is active on the nightclub circuit as well as TV. The comedian has a severe hearing loss. His particular and unique brand of comedy is centered around the misperception by a deaf person of words used in a conversation. For example, he converts the word "elocution" into the word "electrocution." He converts the word "diaphragm" to the word "diagram." By making slight changes in the phonemes of the words there are total changes in the meaning of the words and consequently in the meaning of the responses in a dialogue between this individual and a hearing individual and therein lies the humor. There are other examples of this type of clowning. However, again we stress they are so few using clowning we do not feel it is a major life-style of the disabled.

Both of us have had experience in working with blind persons, and we have noticed that in any particular geographical locale the blind form very strong intergroup ties. They have an accurate and active grapevine system in which they exchange information significant to the blind population as a whole. Their ties are so very strong within hours the group can be mobilized for political action, etc. This is an example of a life style characterized by Allport as *strengthening in-group ties*. This example holds true for many of the disability groups. With the cord injured there are very strong groups and very active groups involved in an effort to provide cohesiveness. For example, there are the paraolympics, there are wheelchair basketball conferences, there are groups, clubs and associations which have one underlying theme and that is the association of cord injured individuals. In fact, the Paraplegia Foundation of America is predicated upon the development of cohesiveness in cord injured individuals and for the betterment of the cord injured. This cohesiveness has not been sufficient to the extent or exclusiveness to produce prejudice against this group. Perhaps this is because of the extreme minority status of this group of individuals. We feel that prejudice is demonstrated toward a minority group only when it becomes a substantial minority. And, in the case of disability groups, no one disability group is a viable minority.

While *slyness and cunning* is felt to be a logical life-style according to Allport it is not encountered to any great extent among traditional victims of prejudice. This lack of prevalence is underscored when applied to disabled persons. Rarely does one encounter slyness and cunning as a life-style with disabled persons. One occasionally will see a disabled person who exaggerates the extent of his disability in order to gain a favorable reaction from the nondisabled population. Perhaps the most prevalent example of this type of behavior is with the disabled street beggar who exaggerates his disability in order to excite the urges of generosity in the passersby. Many of us who have worked in rehabilitation for a period of time have seen the disabled street beggar who appears in dire financial straits. Upon offering him a chance for vocational rehabilitation with ultimate vocational adjustment in an occupation of his choosing, we have seen the individual demur and when pushed toward vocational rehabilitation flatly refuse any type of services. We feel this is an example of a disabled individual using slyness and cunning as a life-style to better his financial lot in life.

Identification with the dominant group which is expressed by self-hate is seen quite often in disabled individuals. In this situation the disabled individual attempts to see other disabled individuals through the eyes of nondisabled persons. In doing so he perceives disabled people in a negative light and in turn views himself in this self-depreciating manner. The individual who adopts this life-style generally is a very unhappy person whose adjustment process is rarely, if ever, complete. He is unable to identify with other disabled people and becomes quite rejecting of them as well as of himself. He will try to please the nondisabled in order to be accepted but yet feels that he will not be accepted by them because of his disability. This is a never ending circle, the key to which is his own dissatisfaction with himself and his self-depreciating attitude.

This self-hate which is a symptom of the identification with a dominant group often is paired with the life-style of *aggression against one's own group.* Many times we have seen disabled professionals and paraprofessionals in rehabilitation act quite punitively toward other disabled individuals and specifically other disabled individuals whose disability parallels their own. The level of expectation expressed for a disabled person by a disabled professional or paraprofessional practitioner often is extremely high and almost impossible to meet. And, when the client fails to meet this level of expectation, the punitiveness is accelerated both in counseling sessions and in the quality of services being offered the client. Underlying many of the punitive expressions is the philosophy "I'm disabled, I made it to this level in life, why can't you." This question ignores social level, intellectual level, level of prior training and education, etc. It is a punitive aggression against an individual's own group.

While we feel the life-styles of *prejudice against out-groups, sympathy, militant fighting back* are not particularly prevalent in the disabled, we do feel that *enhanced striving* is quite obvious and is a healthy productive life-style in the disabled. Not only does this enhanced striving result in improving the disabled individual's lot in life he also receives a great deal of positive reinforcement from nondisabled and other disabled in his environment. Compensation or enhanced striving is probably the most socially approved approach to real or perceived disabilities, physical, vocational, social, etc. in our culture. We are part of an aggressive culture. When an individual expresses his frustration at his lot in life by compensation or as Allport puts it "enhanced striving" he will achieve in all spheres of life. This is a very prevalent life-style of disabled people. It is seen in most successful disabled individuals. In fact, this is one of the factors placement counselors use when approaching industry regarding the employment of disabled persons.

The last life-style which we feel is of significance in understanding the personality of disabled people is that of the *self-fulfilling prophecy.* What people think of us we tend to become. This we the authors feel is particularly evident in disabled individuals. Self-fulfilling prophecy begins during the immediate medical crisis after disability or in terms of congenital disabilities, rather than adventitious disabilities, it begins immediately after birth. There may exist many types of subtle influences which set out goals to be reached or standards which preclude an individual achieving certain goals. For example, it has been routinely accepted that paraplegics and quadriplegics could have no viable function in sexual relations. Some of the work being done by Dr. Ted Coles (1971) refutes this thesis. However, many cord injured individuals are still told after cord injury they have no viable sexual functioning therefore they should sublimate the sexual drive through other types of creative activities. Many persons believe this prophecy and fulfill this prophecy. They do not in fact have any sexual functioning. And, in the successful cases they do indeed sublimate their sexual drive in other creative types of activity. We feel the self-fulfilling prophecy exerts many pressures upon the disabled individual at all points in his life not only by family and friends but also by well-meaning medical and paramedical practitioners. When the individual is in a medical facility or rehabilitation center this self-fulfilling prophecy type of activity continues on throughout the rehabilitation process and it is not always a positive pressure. Often it may be a negative pressure which precludes the individual engaging in the enhanced striving we mentioned above.

GENERAL IMPLICATIONS FOR PROFESSIONALS

Almost everyone in our society views handicapping and disabling conditions from an anatomical point of view rather than from a functional point of view. It is imperative that the counselor who is attempting to help the newly cord injured individual view the disability functionally rather than anatomically. The client should gain an appreciation for the abilities he has left rather than classifying himself with a group based solely on an anatomical loss. The counselor should make sure that the information which he gives the client on sexual concerns, adjustment matters, etc. is factual, practical, concise and clear. He should be certain that the cord injured individual's perception of the disability is correct and the cause of the disability is completely understood. This understanding greatly enhances the adjustment of the client to cord injury.

The client should be helped in exploring his feelings regarding the manner in which he is currently being treated by his spouse, other family members, friends, and the treatment team. He should be helped to understand the natural emotional reactions he will have resulting from his newly acquired disability; and he should be aided in understanding that the feelings of family and friends are going to be different for a period of time while they themselves adjust to his disability. He also should be helped to understand that negative feelings which result from his dependent role now that he has become disabled are quite natural. As such he should not repress them but should try to deal with them and look at them very objectively.

The counselor or helping person should not fall into the trap of thinking that degree of disability is correlated with degree of psychological impact. Professional helping persons must realize that each individual's disability will be particular to him.

If the counselor is able to observe that the client is employing the defense mechanisms of denial and withdrawal, he should be sure to make efforts to keep him in complete touch with his environment. Allow his environment to be present for him to call upon as much as he would like without it becoming stifling and demanding in areas where he cannot meet the demands. As the client becomes ego-oriented, the helping person can bring in outside stimulation in the form of news from the world at large, the family, friends, etc., so that he can be reminded that he should function interdependently with his environment rather than independently of his environment.

If aberrant behavior is observed which will hold the client up to ridicule as a result of regression, the counselor should point out the manner in which he is regressing. Help him to understand what he is doing; help him to understand some of the mechanics which are taking place in his adjustment to his cord injury; however, counseling should be done in a manner that will preserve the integrity of the defense mechanism.

The counselor should assist him in his fantasy world. If the counselor is fortunate enough to be called in to become a part of his fantasy life, the counselor should be aware of the fact that he is trying on new roles to see how well he fits in these new roles as such, and he will be asking the counselor to function as a mirror for him to see how he is adjusting to the various new roles in life.

When the defense mechanism of projection is being aired, the client may have difficulty realizing that he is projecting even though it may be patently clear to others. Perhaps the only real role the counselor can play here is one which is highly supportive of him and his abilities; but at the same time, the client should be required to identify the people to whom he is projecting his feelings of inadequacy and inferiority. In other words, the client should be encouraged to identify the "they" to whom he refers so negatively so often.

Lastly, the counselor should remember that the most important aspect of the helping process is that of the personality of the counselor. The counselor must be a warm, empathic, accepting individual who is positive in his regard toward the client and one who is pragmatic in counseling and planning efforts with the client.

REFERENCES

Adler, A.: *The Practice and Theory of Individual Psychology.* New York, Harcourt-Brace, 1927.

Allport, G.: *The Nature of Prejudice.* New York, Addison-Wesley, 1954.

Barker, R., Wright, B. and Gonick, M.: *Adjustment to Physical Handicaps and Illness: A Survey of Social-Psychology of Physique and Disability.* New York, Social Science Research Council, 1947.

Bauman, Mary, and Yoder, Norman N.: *Adjustment to Blindness Reviewed.* Springfield, Thomas, 1966.

Bors, E. and Comarr, A. E.: Neurological disturbances of sexual function with special reference to 529 patients with spinal cord injury. *Urol Survey, 10:*191-222, 1960.

Bors, E.: Sexual functions in patients with spinal cord injury. Proceeding Symposium Royal College of Surgeons of Edinburgh, Scotland, June 8, 1963.

Carroll, Thomas J.: *Blindness.* Boston, Little Brown & Co., 1961.

Cleveland, S. E.: Body image changes associated with personality reorganization. *J. Consult Psychol, 24:*256-261, 1960.

Coles, T.: *Touching.* Sound film available through Multimedia Resource Center, P.O. Box 439, San Francisco, California 94102, 1971.

————: *Just What Can You Do?* Sound Film available through Multimedia Resource Center, P. O. Box 439, San Francisco, California 94102, 1971.

Comarr, A. E.: Marriage and Divorce Among Patients with Spinal Cord Injury, #1. I. J. Indian Medical Profession, Bombay *9:*4353-4359, 1962.

————: Marriage and Divorce Among Patients with Spinal Cord Injury, #2. I. J. Indian Medical Profession, Bombay *9:*4378-4384, 1963.

#3. I. J. Indian Medical Profession, Bombay *9:*4424-4430, 1963.

#4. I. J. Indian Medical Profession, Bombay *9:*4162-4168, 1963.

#5. I. J. Indian Medical Profession, Bombay *9:*4181-4186, 1963.

————: Sexual function among patients with spinal cord injury. *Urol Int,* *25:*134-168, 1970.

English, R. W.: *Assessment of Change in the Personal-Social Self-perceptions of Vocational Rehabilitation Clients.* Unpublished doctoral dissertation, University of Wisconsin, Madison, 1968.

————: The application of personality theory to explain psychological reactions to physical disability. In Cull, J. G. and Hardy, R. E.: *Rehabilitation Techniques in Severe Disability.* Springfield, Thomas, 1974.

Fisher, S. and Cleveland, S. E.: *Body Image and Personality.* New York, Dover Publications, 1968.

Gunther, Meyer S.: Emotional aspects. In Ruge, Daniel (Ed.) : *Spinal Cord Injuries.* Springfield, Thomas, 1969, p. 96.

Hohmann, George: Considerations in management of the psychosexual readjustment in the cord injured male. In Phelps, W. R. (Ed.) : *Proceedings of a Seminar on Serving the Spinal Cord Injured Patient.* West Virginia Rehabilitation Center, Institute, West Virginia, 1972, pp. 105-118.

————: Some effects of spinal cord lesions on experienced emotional feelings, *Psychotherapy, 3* (2) :143-156, 1966.

Luborsky, L., Chandler, M., Auerbach, A. H., Cohen, J. and Bachrach, H.: Factors influencing the outcome of psychotherapy: A review of the quantitative research. *Psychol Bull,* 1971.

McDaniel, J. W.: *Physical Disability and Human Behavior.* New York, Pergamon Press, 1969.

Mitchell, Kevin M., et al.: *Antecedents to Psychotherapeutic Outcome.* Arkansas Rehabilitation Research and Training Center, University of Arkansas NIMH Final Report, MH 12306, March, 1973, p. 11.

Parsons, T.: *The Social System.* Glencoe, Free Press, 1951.

Poor, Charles: Group work with the severely disabled. In Hardy, Richard E. and Cull, John G.: *Group Counseling and Therapy Techniques in Special Settings,* Springfield, Thomas, 1974.

Sarbin, T. R.: Role therapy. In Lindzey, G. *Handbook of Social Psychology.* Cambridge, Addison-Wesley Publishing, 1954, p. 223.

Schilder, P.: *The Image and Appearance of the Human Body.* New York, John Wiley & Sons, 1950.

Talbot, H. S.: A report on sexual functions in paraplegics. *J Urol, 61:*265-270, 1941.

Talbot, H. D.: The sexual function in paraplegics. *J Urol, 73*:91-100, 1955.

Talbot, H. S.: *Psychosocial Aspects of Sexuality in Spinal Cord Injury Patients*. Proceedings of the 17th Spinal Cord Injury Conference, Veterans Administration, Washington, D. C., 1970.

Traux, C. B. and Carkhuff, R. R.: *Toward Effective Counseling in Psychotherapy*. Chicago, Aldine, 1967.

Traux, C. B. and Mitchell, K. M.: Research on certain therapist interpersonal skills in relation to process and outcome. In Bergin, A. E. and Garfield, S. E. (Eds.) : *Handbook of Psychotherapy and Behavior Change: An Empirical Analysis*. New York, Wiley, 1971.

Wapner, S. and Werner, H.: *The Body Perception*. New York, Random House, 1965.

Wright, B.: *Physical Disability: A Psychological Approach*. New York, Harper and Row, 1960.

————: The period of mourning in chronic illness. In Harrow, R. (Ed.) : *Medical and Psychological Team Work in the Care of the Chronically Ill*. Springfield, Thomas, 1955.

Other Suggested Readings

Cull, John G. and Hardy, Richard E.: *Rehabilitation Techniques in Severe Disability: Case Studies*. Springfield, Thomas, 1974.

Hardy, Richard E. and Cull, John G.: *Severe Disabilities: Social and Rehabilitation Approaches*. Springfield, Thomas, 1974.

Kelman, H. R.: Evaluation of rehabilitation for the long-term ill and disabled patient: Some persistent research problems. *J Chronic Dis, 17*:631-639, 1964.

Krause, E. A.: After the rehabilitation center. *Soc Problems, 14* (2) :199-200, 1966.

Litman, Theodor J.: *Biography of the Sociology of Medicine and Medical Care—The First Fifty Years,* Berkeley, Glendessary Press, 1970.

————: Physical rehabilitation: A social psychological approach. In Jaco, E. G. (Ed.) : *Patients, Physicians and Illness*, 2nd ed. New York, Free Press, 1968.

————: Self-concept and physical rehabilitation. In Rose, A. M. (Ed.) : *Human Behavior and Social Process*. Houghton-Mifflin, Boston, 1962.

————: The family and physical rehabilitation. *J Chron Dis, 19*:211-217, 1966.

————: The influence of self-concept and life orientation: Factors in the rehabilitation of the orthopedically disabled. *J Health Hum Behav, 3*:249-257, 1962.

Nagi, Saad Z., et al.: Back disorders and rehabilitation achievement. *J Chron Dis, 18*:181-197, 1965.

Roth, Julius A. and Eddy, Elizabeth M.: *Rehabilitation for the Unwanted*. New York, Atherton, 1967.

Safilios-Rothschild, Constantina: *The Sociology and Social Psychology of Disability and Rehabilitation.* New York, Random House, 1970.

Sussman, Marvin B. (Ed.) : *Sociology and Rehabilitation.* American Sociological Association, Washington, 1965.

Sussman, Marvin B., and Slater, R.: *Chronic Illness Study.* Cleveland, Institute on the Family and Bureaucratic Society: Chronic Disease and the Family, Case Western Reserve University, Cleveland, Ohio.

CHAPTER 6

SPECIAL CONSIDERATIONS IN COUNSELING BLIND AND SEVERELY VISUALLY IMPAIRED PERSONS

Introduction

THIS CHAPTER DEALS with providing counseling and vocational services to blind persons.

Rehabilitation counselors are concerned especially with individuals who have vocational handicaps. These handicaps may result from physical disability, emotional or mental illness, social or cultural deprivation. In each individual case, the counselor must be able to decide what remedy is required in order to move the counselee toward successful personal adjustment in his family, community, and on the job.

Rehabilitation counseling requires the ingredients mentioned earlier for effective counselor-client relationships; however, much of rehabilitation counseling consists of advice-giving and coordination of services to the client. In a sense, "rehabilitation counseling" can be considered a misnomer when the term is applied across the board. A substantial number of clients need considerable advice and information which the counselor has to offer concerning social and rehabilitation services from which they can profit. When the counselee needs advice and information, the rehabilitation counselor must be able to recognize this need and provide what is required. There also will be many instances in which the client and counselor must enter into a number of counseling sessions in depth. The counselor must make the judgment concerning what type of help is needed for the client to solve his particular problems. Rehabilitation counselors need appropriate training that will enable them to decide whether or not they are qualified to do the kind of counseling which is necessary.

Many counselors fall into the trap of wanting to play the role of "junior therapist" and involve high percentages of their clients in in-depth counseling sessions. This is particularly true of the graduates of many rehabilitation counselor training programs. Some workers hide behind "counseling" (as synonomous with quality) in terms of their justifying low numbers of rehabilitated clients. There is much talk of quality services and in-depth counseling which require considerable time. The rehabilitation counselor who is an effective manager of his caseload can "rehabilitate" the number of persons required by his agency administrator and while doing so can provide counseling services as needed to his clients.

Rehabilitation work requires a broad definition of counseling which includes the offering of some, and coordination of other, professional services to clients. Generally, agency administrators —especially those trained in counseling—do not accept the explanation of "the time required and quality services" for a low client rehabilitation rate. Any agency administrator or supervisor knows that some cases require much involved counseling, and that these cases in many instances are the most difficult ones. They are time-consuming, and they can test the fiber of the rehabilitation counselor. Untrained counselors generally cannot handle such cases without help from someone who has had some advanced orientation in counseling. However, counselors who play the role of "junior therapist" in trying to become deeply involved with all of their clients—whether or not this type of service is called for—will be ineffective and probably will not remain long in rehabilitation work.

The rehabilitation counselor will find his coordinating and facilitating role highly rewarding when it is done well and gets needed services. One of the greatest satisfactions that the counselor can have is the assurance that he knows when certain types of services are required and whether these should be more therapeutically oriented or more oriented toward advice, information, and coordination of community resources and professional services.

Rehabilitation counselors should not rank-order their clients in a psychological need hierarchy which places the individual with severe psychological problems at the top of the counselor's list for services. Certainly, these persons should be served immediately upon the counselor's realization that severe psychological problems exist. They should be referred to the appropriate psychologist or psychiatrist if problems are so severe that the counselor cannot handle them alone, or they should be served by rehabilitation counselors who are competent in the type of service required. The point to be made here is that the rehabilitation process is a complicated procedure; the client who may be adjusting normally to a loss and who does not need substantial in-depth therapeutic involvement is as good a case for services as one requiring more therapeutic work. Coordination of services of supportive personnel and professional personnel is a substantial part of the work of the rehabilitation counselor. In many cases, he will have to bring this team together in order that the client can continue to receive effective and necessary rehabilitation services.

The rehabilitation counselor must actively involve himself within the community in order to be fully aware of the many resources which exist that can be of substantial benefit to his clients. Generally, counselors have indicated that so much of their time is taken with counseling and coordination of services that they are unable to put forward enough effort to learn all that the community has to offer. Counselors who utilize community resources effectively are very familiar with the offerings of various agencies and through coordination and cooperation find that their work load is lessened by the support of other social service programs.

The counselor will wish to offer his services to various types of community agencies. For instance, most counselors can give a great deal of useful advice to such programs as the community action and model cities efforts sponsored by the Federal Government. Agencies and organizations such as family service programs and welfare agencies can be of considerable help in getting needed services for the rehabilitation client. The counselor should take a major responsibility in coordinating efforts of agencies and programs that can help in the rehabilitation of clients, and he should volunteer his time and energies to help strengthen other social service programs.

The rehabilitation counselor must keep in mind that he should be moving the client toward end objectives of independence and successful adjustment on the job. Rehabilitation differs from some other social service professions in the regard that a substantial test of the counselor's work is made at the end of the rehabilitation process. That test consists of the appropriateness of the client's behavior in work situations (Hardy, 1972).

REHABILITATION COUNSELING WITH THE BLIND AND SEVERELY VISUALLY IMPAIRED

No special counseling theory need be constructed in order for the rehabilitation counselor to serve blind persons. There is, however, a substantial body of knowledge with which the counselor should be thoroughly familiar. Topics include the etiology of diseases related to blindness, problems in adjustment to visual loss including mobility, social adjustment, occupational advice and job placement. The counselor serving blind persons has a real responsibility to undertake considerable study in order to acquaint himself with what Father Carroll (1961) has called in the title of his book, *Blindness: What It Is, What It Does, and How to Live With It.*

The rehabilitation counselor serving blind persons has as much or more of a coordinating function as does the counselor in a general agency setting. A counselor concerned with the blind will work closely with the educational services specialist, the social worker, the ophthalmologist, the placement specialist, the rehabilitation teacher, and the mobility instructor who help in the team effort of moving the blind individual toward adjustment to his visual problem and later to adjustment on the job.

Rehabilitation counselors serving the blind, just as counselors working with any other rehabilitation clients, must be certain that their clients are without need of further medical or psychological treatment. In this regard, the counselor helping the partially sighted should make certain that no visual aid or professional service can offer additional help to the client. He should be fully aware of the various problems which go hand in hand with a loss of sight. Persons who are experiencing a severe physical inadequacy lose some ability to be independent. They feel socially inadequate and in some cases may have additional problems which at first might not be apparent to the counselor. Advanced age or other physical incapabilities may add to the blind person's adjustment problems.

The client will be very much interested in the prognosis for his future, and the rehabilitation counselor should make sure that valid information is provided. An effective counselor must be ready to help the blind person understand what his opportunities are for education, employment, social activities. He should also talk with those persons who give information to the blind client, especially professional individuals such as ophthalmologists, to make certain that they have useful information concerning blindness and the services of the state rehabilitation agency.

Bauman and Yoder (1966) have suggested that the rehabilitation counselor must offer:

> "a combination of several qualities: (1) his own emotional acceptance of blindness (he must be the first person to whom the client has spoken who did not immediately show great pity and anxiety—a helping new experience for the client); (2) formal or informal instruction in procedures which make it easier to live as a blind person (the home teacher and also some adjustment on prevocational training can help here); (3) realistic planning for the future, including vocational planning if the age and general health of the client make this appropriate. It is true that all of these may be rejected for a time, in which case the counselor must offer (4) understanding, patience, and a gentle persistence which keeps him available until the client and his family are able to reorient themselves to the future instead of clinging to the past."

In counseling with blind persons, the rehabilitation counselor must remember that he is working with individuals who cannot see or whose sight is impaired. The client will differ from fellow blind persons as much as he will differ from sighted persons. Some blind persons are very healthy; others are sickly. Some are well adjusted psychologically; others are poorly adjusted. In many cases, blindness will have caused severe psychological stress which has not been overcome, just as an accident or some other type of traumatic experience may have caused either a sighted or a blind person severe psychological difficulty.

Often, reaction to partial vision causes as much or more frustration and anxiety than reaction to total blindness. One reason for this seems to be that partially sighted persons are unable to function normally and do not want to accept their loss of sight as a reality. They live in a no-man's world between blindness and sight.

The rehabilitation counselor serving blind and severely visually impaired persons must be even more thoughtful than the counselor who is concerned with individuals who are sighted. Often it will be necessary to anticipate problems which may arise for the blind client. For instance, simply getting to and from the counselor's office may become a very troublesome and embarrassing task. The blind client may be traveling over unfamiliar terrain with or without the help of relatives or friends. The counselor, in many cases, may want to visit initially in the home and later during the relationship invite the client to the rehabilitation agency.

The counselor must be very much aware that this blind client is "tuned in" to auditory clues (yes's and unhum's may be helpful), since the usual eye contact and other nonverbal communications are not effective with blind persons. For instance, silence over a considerable period of time often takes place in counseling sessions, but when the counselor is working with a blind client, silence may be interpreted at times as disinterest or rejection.

It is respectful and appropriate for the counselor to look directly into the face and eyes of the client just as if the counselee were fully sighted. Blind persons are often aware that sighted persons are not looking at them and they get the impression, which may be true, that the counselor is not listening.

Counselors should be particularly careful about shuffling papers, tapping a pencil on the desk, or making other sounds that are distracting. They should also be aware that many blind persons, especially the congenitally blind, give the counselor little to go by in terms of facial expression. The counselor who is used to reading emotionality in various facial responses may be at a considerable loss with some persons who have been blind for a number of years and who are not nearly as responsive in this respect as sighted people (Jordan, 1962).

A rehabilitation counselor providing professional services to blind persons must avoid fostering unnecessary dependence. Often counselors, unknowingly as well as knowingly, build their own self-esteem by continually allowing clients to rely on them for personal advice and other services. On the other hand, many rehabilitation counselors are afraid to show sufficient interest in the problems of the client because they are concerned about being forced to give a great deal of time and attention to the client. Neither of these extremes will allow the counselor to be effective.

Summary

It has been said that the most important variable for helping people which the counselor brings to the counseling relationship is "himself." The rehabilitation counselor, whether he is working with blind or sighted clients, must make a substantial effort to maintain genuineness, openness, sincerity, honesty, and respect for the client. While techniques and procedures are important in accomplishing goals in counseling sessions, the real key to successful counseling is whether the counselor genuinely cares for the individual. A rehabilitation counselor provides substantial professional and coordinated services from which the client benefits enormously. Most rehabilitation counselors will have certain quotas to meet and the effective counselor, through proper case load management, will be able to provide quality and quantity services. He will also realize that his coordinative and facilitative function is as important as his counseling function. He must serve clients according to *their needs* and not his own; when this is done, counselees will not claim that his work lacks quality because he will have been much more concerned with them as individuals than with whether or not his services were "professional" in nature.

REFERENCES

American Mutual Insurance Alliance: *Workers Worth Their Hire*. Chicago, 1970.

American Psychiatric Association: *Diagnostic and Statistical Manual of Mental Disorders*. Washington, D. C., American Psychiatric Association, 1965.

Bauman, Mary K. and Yoder, Norman M.: *Adjustment to Blindness—Reviewed*. Springfield, Thomas, 1966.

————: *Placing the Blind and Visually Handicapped in Professional Occupations*. Office of Vocational Rehabilitation, Department of Health, Education and Welfare, Washington, D. C., 1962.

Bridges, C. C.: *Job Placement of the Physically Handicapped*. New York, McGraw-Hill, 1946.

Carroll, Thomas J.: *Blindness: What It Is, What It does, and How to Live With It*. Boston, Little, 1961.

Department of Veterans' Benefits, Veterans' Administration. *They Return to Work*. Washington, D. C., U. S. Government Printing Office, 1963.

English, H. B. and English, A. C.: *A Comprehensive Dictionary of Psychological and Psychoanalytical Terms*. New York, McKay, 1966.

Gustard, J. W.: The definition of counseling. In Berdie, R. F.: *Roles and Relationship in Counseling*. Minneapolis, U. of Minn., 1953.

Hardy, Richard E.: Counseling physically handicapped college students. *New Outlook for Blind, 59*(5):182-183, 1965.

————: Relating psychological data to job analysis information in vocational counseling. *New Outlook for Blind, 63*(7):202-204, 1969.

————: Vocational placement. In Cull, John G. and Hardy, Richard E.: *Vocational Rehabilitation: Profession and Process*. Springfield, Thomas, 1972.

Hardy, Richard E. and Cull, John G.: *Social and Rehabilitation Services for the Blind*. Springfield, Thomas, 1973.

International Society for the Welfare of Cripples: *Selective Placement of the Handicapped*. New York, 1955.

Jeffrey, David L.: Pertinent points on placement. *Clearing House*, Oklahoma State University, 1969.

Jones, J. W.: Problems in defining and classifying blindness. *New Outlook for Blind, 56*(4):115-121, 1962.

Jordan, John E.: Counseling the blind. *Personnel and Guidance Journal, 39* (3):10-214, 1962.

Lofquist, L. H., and Davis, R. V.: *Adjustment to Work—A Psychological View of Man's Problems in Work-Oriented Society*. New York, Appleton, July, 1967.

McGowan, J. F. and Porter, T. L.: *An Introduction to the Vocational Rehabilitation Process*. Washington, D. C., Rehabilitation Services Administration, 1967.

McNamee, H. T. and Jeffrey, R. P.: *Service to the Handicapped 1960*. Phoenix, Arizona State Employment Service, 1960.

Maslow, A. H.: A theory of human motivation. *Psychol Rev, 50:*370-396, 1954.

Morgan, Clayton A.: Personality of counseling. *Blindness*. AAWB Annual, Washington, D. C., American Association of Workers for the Blind, Inc., 1969.

Office of Vocational Rehabilitation: *Training Personnel for the State Vocational Rehabilitation Programs—A Guide for Administrators.* Washington, D. C., U. S. Government Printing Office, 1957.

Sinick, D.: *Placement Training Handbook.* Washington, D. C., Office of Vocational Rehabilitation, 1962.

Stalnaker, W. O., Wright, K. C., and Johnston, L. T.: *Small Business Enterprises in Vocational Rehabilitation.* U. S. Department of Health, Education and Welfare, Vocational Rehabilitation Administration, Rehabilitation Services Series No. 63-47, 1963.

Thomason, B. and Barrett, A.: *The Placement Process in Vocational Rehabilitation Counseling.* U. S. Department of Health, Education and Welfare, Office of Vocational Rehabilitation, GTP Bull. No. 2, Rehabilitation Services Series No. 545, 1960.

Traux, Charles B. and Carkhuff, Robert R.: *Toward Effective Counseling and Psychotherapy: Training and Practice.* Chicago, Aldine, 1967.

U. S. Employment Service: *Dictionary of Occupational Titles.* Washington, D. C., U. S. Government Printing Office, 1965.

————: *Selected Placement for the Handicapped* (Revised ed.), Washington, D. C., U. S. Government Printing Office, 1945.

Weiss, D. J., Davis, R. V., Lofquist, L. H., and England, G. W.: *Minnesota Studies in Vocational Rehabilitation.* University of Minnesota, Industrial Relations Center. (Series published since 1954.)

CHAPTER 7

COUNSELING WITH THE CRITICALLY ILL*

Introduction

IN THIS CHAPTER, material is offered which will be helpful in counseling critically ill persons. The area of renal failure has been chosen as an example of critically ill persons. The principles suggested here can be applied in work with various individuals who are critically ill.

Counseling an end-stage-renal-failure client is most often difficult. The terminal nature of this disease presents victims with devastating psychological conflicts that must be resolved if one is to be rehabilitated. As an example Beard has expressed the paradox that "The fear of dying and the fear of living are an integral part of the whole problem of renal failure and its treatment" (Beard, 1969). The only thing these individuals see in the future is death, or life for an undetermined period, disabled, at the mercy of the disease and the machine (Ebra, 1972).

When the counselor first sees the client, chances are that he is not yet on dialysis. This makes any type of assessment difficult since the level of uremia has a direct cause and effect relationship with organic brain dysfunction which produces lethargy, impaired judgment, drowsiness, and inability to concentrate for extended periods. During terminal stages of uremia, psychological testing for brain damage has to some degree revealed "organicity" (Short and Wilson, 1969). Possibly the only valid information that can be obtained during the initial interview is background information. This is also a good time to contact relatives and to review medical history.

---

* We gratefully acknowledge the substantial contribution of Evan T. Jones in the development of this chapter.

The most important people at this point are the doctors, specialists, and hospital staff since they will be deciding whether or not to treat the individual. If treatment is appropriate they will also prescribe the type of treatment to be used. The counselor should keep in close, direct contact with the hospital staff so that he will be aware of any change in the client's unstable condition. The counselor also should be prepared to consult with hospital staff, since the staff may request his expertise as to the vocational possibilities of a patient.

Depending on the government regulations in the state where the counselor is working, he may be asked to help the patient make some financial arrangements for treatment. This could involve contact with insurance companies, use of rehabilitation funds, contact with charity organizations, and contact with other social service groups.

The patient's initial reaction to the disease and its terminal nature is usually severe. Patients often experience severe depression, anxiety, fear of death, feelings of personal inadequacy and insecurity. It may be difficult to make the patient realize the terminal nature of his disease. Reality orientation and weakening of ego functions are common problems at this point (Kemph, 1966). Ebra has summarized this situation: "Some individuals may necessitate more time and counseling sessions in order to work through these problems and come to the realization that they are, in fact, terminally ill. Until this initial phase of the counseling is successful, the patient cannot be mobilized towards the phase of adaptation and ultimately complete rehabilitation" (Ebra, 1972).

An important aspect of the patient's adjustment centers around how his family, particularly his spouse, view his quandary. It is important that the family include the patient on important decisions. This will help maintain his ego strength and his pre-illness role within the family. As with most disabilities the family should not be oversolicitious or rejecting. The rehabilitation counselor should counsel the patient's family to make them aware of how they can help the psychological adjustment of the patient. The family will also need counseling to facilitate their own adjustment to a new life-style. This will help minimize the great burdens of caring for a terminally ill person and the financial limitations placed on the family.

In order to overcome the rather severe psychological stresses that go along with dialysis, many patients employ a series of defense mechanisms. This procedure allows them to maintain some degree of emotional stability and self-esteem while on dialysis.

The first defense mechanism used is that of denial. Patients often use this defense mechanism when complications arise, seeing them as one-time singular occurrences rather than ongoing problems that develop along with dialysis (Ebra and Toth, 1972). The rehabilitation counselor should alert himself and be aware when a client is using this defense mechanism since he may be covering up serious medical problems. Often this rationale is recognized in potential transplant patients since they often feel that surgery will solve all their problems.

Another mechanism used by dialysis patients is projection. Patients are quick to recognize mutual problems and setbacks in other patients but not in themselves. Often a client will project his fears and anxieties onto other family members. For example, he may report his children find his fistula repulsive when he himself finds it repulsive. Ebra and Toth have summarized: "The patient is not able to attribute certain undesirable emotions or characteristics to himself; instead, he attributes his own negative aspects to others. This mechanism is useful in that it can preserve a healthy self-image and prevent massive ego damage. However, its overuse can distort reality and, therefore, cause a significant amount of problems in reality orientation" (Ebra et al., 1972).

An easily recognized defense mechanism in dialysis patients is that of displacement. A patient may displace his fear of death onto a smaller problem such as care of his shunt. He may become overzealous in keeping his cannulus clean. Another more dangerous form of displacement occurs when the patient displaces feelings of aggression and hostility onto his wife and/or his family. The problems with this are obvious, a patient's wife and family are important in his adjustment and may play an important part in home dialysis. Any family disagreements can upset the delicate relationship of the family and the dialysis patient.

Lastly many patients use reaction formations to protect their egos. Patients who are not feeling well may claim that they never felt better. Hostile feelings toward doctors and hospital staff may result in the patient being exceptionally receptive toward treatment and hospital care.

All of the above defense mechanisms are beneficial and help reduce the tumultuous stress that dialysis patients experience. The rehabilitation counselor should be aware that his client is using these defenses and be prepared to counsel if his client begins distorting reality. Depending on the amount of stress and the use of defenses the rehabilitation counselor may want to arrange for some short-term psychotherapy (Ebra et al., 1972).

Part of the counselor's job is to help the patient through periods when complications arise. The rehabilitation counselor should keep his client informed as to the ramifications of his disease and its complications. One of the most common problems that dialysis patients experience is infection around the cannula. Unless this infection can immediately be cleared up the cannula will have to be removed and a new one placed at some other point on his body. This is always a considerable setback and requires both surgery and a great deal of expense. The client at this time needs reassurance and counseling, the client should be reminded that this is a part of dialysis and that it cannot always be avoided. Lastly, care of the cannula should be reemphasized; the client should keep in mind that this cannula must be treated as a fresh surgical wound.

Another complication the patient should be well aware of is the fact that his body can no longer produce blood at the pre-illness level. The kidneys produce a substance which stimulates a person's bone marrow to produce blood. When the kidneys stop functioning, production of blood is significantly decreased. Blood loss may rise above production and the patient may require a transfusion. Transfusions are fairly dangerous since an already weak anemic dialysis patient is a prime target for hepatitis. Another consideration is that the transfused blood may contain antibodies foreign to the patient. These antibodies may increase a patient's resistance making a successful transplant difficult.

Patients will need counseling about their reduced sexual function. Some will realize limited sexual activity and others may not be able to perform at all. Females generally stop menstruating, although if they do not they face the problems of blood loss mentioned earlier.

A particularly difficult problem for clients is their change in diet. The rehabilitation counselor should understand why a particular diet was selected for his client and give supportive counseling.

Other common complications and problems include osteodystrophy, neuropathy, hemorrhage, blood clots in and around the cannula, hypertensive and cardiovascular complications, chronic anemia, psychologic and behavioral problems. The rehabilitation counselor must be aware of these problems and be ready to answer questions about them. It is during these times of crisis that the rehabilitation counselor can put his expertise to work. Oftentimes it is this strong supportive counseling that can make a meaningful difference in final rehabilitation.

Throughout this period of time the patient will have questions about his disability. Although the patient's doctors will relate much of this information, the rehabilitation counselor must be ready to answer questions about the disability and its future effects. Ebra has found that the rehabilitation counselor is often in a better position to answer questions about the disease than doctors and paramedical staff since patients often withdraw from their doctors and are unable to communicate with them satisfactorily (Ebra, 1972).

As the client's condition (psychological and physical) begins to stabilize, hospital staff will be evaluating him for possible home dialysis. The rehabilitation counselor is often helpful by explaining details of home dialysis and the training that goes with it. The counselor may again be asked to help arrange the financial end of dialysis as it moves into the home. The patient will have to have an appropriate partner to help him administer dialysis at home. This partner, preferably a family member, will need counseling in order to prepare for the eventual homecoming.

About this time the rehabilitation counselor should be making an assessment of the client's rehabilitation potential. The counselor should consider such things as: Will the patient receive dialysis at home or at a neighborhood center? What was his previous job? How much physical activity will a specific vocational objective require? Will he need to be retrained? Does he have any complications? As the counselor answers these questions and lists the client's strengths and weaknesses, he should keep in mind some of the general trends that have been observed in rehabilitation renal failure patients. First, the patients that lead the closest to normal lives are those that have had a successful transplantation. These patients are for the most part physically restored and can enter most jobs or training programs. The only employment problem facing transplant patients is that they are predisposed toward disease and infection since they must take considerable amounts of immunosuppressive drugs to combat rejection. A transplant patient should be placed in a job that would not lower his resistance to the point that he would be dangerously vulnerable to disease and infection.

The patient on dialysis has more serious restrictions placed on his employment. If the client is being dialyzed at the hospital, he would need two or three working days a week away from the job since hospital dialysis is done Monday through Friday during the day. If the patient is receiving dialysis at an ambulatory care facility he will still have to schedule work around dialysis. A client on a home dialysis plan usually has the most available time for employment, he can schedule his treatment around his job since he and his partner can administer home dialysis at any time it fits their schedule. The rehabilitation counselor should remember that often dialysis patients are anemic which makes physically strenuous jobs very difficult for them. Also these patients should avoid exertion or strain of the cannulated limb. Generally dialysis clients do much better at sedentary or intellectual type tasks rather than labor or physical type jobs. The patient receiving dialysis will have to find an understanding employer who will put up with periodic short-term absences from work when the client finds he must be hospitalized for complications.

As stated earlier counseling an end-stage-renal-failure patient is difficult. The rehabilitation counselor needs to know everything about the disability and the client he is counseling. There are many setbacks and frustrations and the rehabilitation process may take a considerably long time. In order to rehabilitate these rather dramatically ill individuals the rehabilitation counselor must develop and utilize truly professional counseling techniques and qualities.

REFERENCES

Beard, Bruce H.: Fear of death and fear of life. *Arch of Gen Psychiatry, 21:373-380,* 1969.

Ebra, George and Toth, John C.: Chronic hemodialysis: Some psychological and rehabilitative considerations. *Rehab Lit, 33:2-10,* 1972.

Ebra, George: Rehabilitation counseling considerations in end-stage renal disease. *J Appl Rehab Counsel, 3*(2), 1972.

Hardy, R. E. and Cull, J. G.: *Social and Rehabilitation Services for the Blind.* Springfield, Thomas, 1972.

Kemph, John P.: Renal failure, artificial kidney and kidney transplant. *Am J Psychiatry, 122:*1270-1274, 1966.

Massachusetts Rehabilitation Commission: *Chronic Hemodialysis and the Vocational Rehabilitation Program.* Third Progress Report: July, 1969.

Medical World News: Hemodialysis for all who need it. April 30, *12:*29-36, 1971.

National Kidney Foundation: *Kidney Transplantation and the Organ Donor Program,* 1971.

Read, M. and Mallison, M.: External arteriovenous shunts. *Am J Nursing, 72*(1), 1972.

Sapperstien, M.: Dialysis. *Am J Nursing, 72*(1), 1972.

Short, M. J. and Wilson, W. D.: Roles of denial in chronic hemodialysis. *Arch Gen Psychiatry, 20:*433-437, 1969.

Smirnow, V. and Colmen, J. G.: *1971 Re-Survey Programs and Services of State Rehabilitation Agencies for Clients with Chronic Kidney Disease.* Virgil Smirnow Associates. Community Health Consultants, Sept., 1971.

University of Alabama in Birmingham: Morgan, Jean M., M.D., Project Director. *Final Report: A comprehensive study of the rehabilitation process in patients in a chronic dialysis program,* March, 1971.

Webster's New World Dictionary: Cleveland, World Publishing, 1966.

CHAPTER 8

COUNSELING WITH PHYSICALLY HANDICAPPED COLLEGE STUDENTS*

I NSTITUTIONS OF HIGHER EDUCATION are accepting hundreds of blind and other handicapped students each year, and for this reason, certain questions such as the following must be asked and answered: How can the physically handicapped student best be served? Should counselors be trained to counsel handicapped college students? Should college counselors who work in counseling center settings be trained to do rehabilitation counseling?

Research has shown that there is no set pattern by which state rehabilitation agencies select those students who are to enter college training. Some agencies, for instance, require intelligence tests, while others put major emphasis on class standing or quality of the high school scholastic record. In addition to these combinations of requirements, the prospective college student who is handicapped is subjected to careful evaluation by a rehabilitation counselor (Brown, 1965). This evaluation often results in what might be termed a personal endorsement by the counselor.

Efforts have been made to study the handicapped student's adjustment to college life. A survey of fifty-three general rehabilitation agencies has recently shown that the main reason for discontinuing college training is student behavior which requires disciplinary action by the institution. Students who are unable to interact in a socially acceptable way with pressures of the college environment often have problems in maturity, self-management, insight, problem solving, lack of information, and dependence. The counselor who is working with the physically handicapped college student has a threefold job: He must help the counselee toward self-management through the development of insight; he must be certain that the counselee has the necessary information

---

* Reprinted with permission of *The New Outlook for the Blind*.

124

for problem solving; and he must attempt to help the counselee develop social maturity through interaction with individuals and groups. Campus student bodies are able to solve many disciplinary problems through an increased degree of participation by students in such activities as student government, planning intellectual cultural activities, and developing plans for solutions of social problems both on and off campus. (Volunteering in the mental health movement is an example of constructive off-campus student involvement.)

The counselor has the opportunity not only to counsel in the strict definition of the word, but also to give information and guide the development of the student through special extracurricular activity. What does the counselor need to know in order to facilitate the physically handicapped student's successful adjustment to the environmental pressures of college life? The college counselor should consider himself a rehabilitation counselor, and the rehabilitation counselor should consider himself a college counselor. Each must take on new responsibilities. Both counselors may find that additional graduate course work and self-directed study will strengthen weak areas. The college counselor should become knowledgeable in such areas as medical information for rehabilitation, special problems in rehabilitating the handicapped, and psychological problems of the handicapped. He should understand the job placement process in rehabilitation, the use of occupational information in relation to physical handicaps, and the influence of architectural barriers on optimum student adjustment. He must become aware of rehabilitation resources in the community and should develop a close working relationship with the rehabilitation agency.

The counselor must acquire information that can be used to help students select the type of college best suited to vocational and personal goals, and to the personality and ability of the particular student. He should be knowledgeable concerning college curricula, student activities, administrative regulations, special facilities for the handicapped, causes of disciplinary problems among college students, remedial services, placement office services, opportunities for educational, vocational and personal counseling at the college counseling center, special health services, and financial aid. He also has responsibility for seeing that a high degree of cooperation exists between the rehabilitation agency and the college.

In addition, he must understand the general philosophy of the institution to which he plans to send clients for college training. Institutions usually adopt one of the following as an admission guideline:

1. Accept only the highly selected and the drop-out rate will be small;
2. Accept all for good public relations, although many will fail;
3. Take a middle road in accepting those who meet standards.

The counselor will find that some institutions not only will accept clients, but additional special services and modified facilities will be provided. Such might include physical therapy, speech correction, hearing diagnosis, reading rooms for blind students, and modified residence halls with wide doors for students in wheelchairs. Other institutions are less rehabilitation-oriented, and some will provide no special services.

Eventually, student personnel administrators hope to extend placement services to all students, including those who drop out as well as those who are graduated. Plans include interinstitutional cooperation which would lead to placement services in all geographical areas where colleges are located. In other words, colleges would provide placement services to college students regardless of whether or not the student attended that particular institution. From these plans the rehabilitation counselor can see that he has an excellent resource in the college placement office.

The area of placement in professional occupations is one in which the rehabilitation counselor joins forces with the college placement officer and the client in the job location and selection. The client should share responsibility for developing employment opportunities and the rehabilitation counselor must be prepared to discuss problems and coordinate efforts when necessary. Of course, before college training begins the rehabilitation counselor has studied professional opportunities for his client in specific areas. He is therefore ready to give vocational information and help the client select vocational goals in professional areas at least two years before a student's graduation.

The counselor will greatly facilitate placement of the handicapped student through an effective program of community public relations. He is responsible for fully informing placement office personnel concerning the vocational rehabilitation process and the problems involved in the placement of handicapped students. The placement officer should understand that the handicapped college student, aided by the rehabilitation counselor, will play an important part in his own job location. The vocational placement of handicapped college graduates in the well-informed community should be no more difficult than the placement of nonhandicapped college graduates.

American colleges and universities are now educating thousands of physically handicapped students each year. The college population explosion has taken place and students including those who are physically handicapped will continue to seek higher education in coming years. The closer the sense of cooperation between institutions of higher education and rehabilitation agencies, the more effective will be the education experience and the rehabilitation process for the student.

SELECTED READINGS

Bauman, Mary K., and Yoder, Norman M.: *Placing the Blind and Visually Handicapped in Professional Occupations.* Harrisburg, Office for the Blind, 1962. (Prepared under a grant from the Office of Vocational Rehabilitation.)

Brown, H. R.: Orienting Blind College Students. *The New Outlook for the blind, 59*(5):180-181, 1965.

Bruebacher, John and Rudy, Willis: *Higher Education in Transition.* New York, Harper and Brothers, 1958.

Byrne, Richard H.: Proposed revision of the Bordin-Pepinsky diagnostic constructs. *J Counseling Psychol, 5* (3) , 1958.

Hardy, R. E. and Cull, J. G.: *Social and Rehabilitation Services for the Blind.* Thomas, Springfield, 1972.

Rusalem, Herbert: *Guiding the Physically Handicapped College Student.* Teachers College, Columbia University, 1962.

Williamson, E. G.: *Student Personnel Services in Colleges and Universities.* New York, McGraw-Hill, 1961.

Wrenn, C. Gilbert: *Student Personnel Work in Colleges.* New York, Ronald Press, 1951.

PART THREE

COUNSELING STRATEGIES WITH THE SOCIALLY DISABLED

Counseling the Culturally Different Disabled
Rehabilitation Counseling in the Correctional Institution
Group Counseling in the Correctional Setting
Working With the Functionally Retarded

CHAPTER 9

COUNSELING THE CULTURALLY DIFFERENT DISABLED

- Impact of Poverty on the Individual
- Special Problems in Adolescence
- Implications for Counselors

PERHAPS ONE OF THE LEAST understood minority groups in our society is that of culturally different individuals who have suffered disability. When we think about how an individual will react to illness or disability we can safely say that each person reacts according to what is characteristic for his own personality. For instance, the person who has in the past shown a strong need for dependence on others, who has shown that he cannot lead an independent life, will usually react in an even more dependent fashion once disability is evident. The person who has been strongly independent and mature in his own adjustment to life in general probably will make an adequate or more than adequate adjustment to disability.

In order to be successful in counseling this group of individuals the counselor needs to understand the outstanding cluster of problems centered around the lack of understanding of the background and motivation of this type of individual. The counselor needs to better understand the general cultural stock pile of the disadvantaged—his family togetherness, his reluctance to relocate, his acceptance of poverty as a way of life, his distrust of others and the various communication barriers which exists between the counselor and the client. Again, to be effective, the counselor should be prepared to try to overcome some of the ignorance, apathy and resistance to the problems of the disadvantaged by the general public and the ultimate employers of this group of people.

Most counseling strategies have been developed for the middle-class clientele. They were not developed for the public welfare recipient type of client. Counseling strategies work very smoothly and efficiently if there is an underlying motivation for success and if the client is able to forego short-range goals for long-range planning.

While values of poor persons seem to differ from those of the middle-class person, it should be remembered that these values do not differ in all respects. Persons living in poverty seem to have a strong orientation in the present and short-term perspectives rather than long-range planning and goals. In addition, there is a definite feeling of fatalism and the belief in chances; impulsiveness and a general inability to delay immediate gratification or make definite plans for the future. Also, there is a thinking process that could be termed much more concrete in character than abstract. There are general feelings of inferiority and an acceptance of authoritarianism. Therefore, when an individual who has lived in a poverty environment during the formative years of his growth and development becomes disabled the reaction is generally substantially different from those who have been reared in a middle-class environment.

The pattern or culture of poverty is at times viewed as a causative factor in poverty and in other times as a result. In other words general feelings and emotions resulting from impoverished conditions either can perpetuate the poverty or these same psychological feelings can be viewed as those consequences of the actual environmental conditions. The important question revolves around whether the environment causes the internal psychological makeup or whether the internal psychological makeup helps create the environmental state in which the individual lives. There are affirmative and negative answers to both questions and there is considerable overlap in any type of explanation which might attempt to give answers.

Poverty is a relative condition since it varies enormously from country to country and region to region. The subculture of poverty, however, in terms of the traits it seems to bring with it transcends regional, racial, social class and national differences. Of course there are definite variations among countries and over periods of time. It is a well-known fact that poverty in the nineteenth century was a much more tolerable state than poverty in the twentieth century.

It is important for counselors working with the disabled disadvantaged to show that they have confidence in these clients' abilities to improve themselves not only from the poverty condition, but also from the point of view of whatever handicap the individual may have. In a recent study by Rosenthal and Jacobson (1968) results indicated that teachers who were led to believe that certain lower-class students could show unusual gains during the year actually brought about these gains in the children (the students for whom they held positive expectations).

IMPACT OF POVERTY ON THE INDIVIDUAL

Poverty very definitely constitutes one of the most persistent and critical problems of modern life. The factors associated with poverty and destitution influence the individual's feelings of self-worth, self-regard and general self-concept. When the self-concept is altered, the individual's behavior is altered. In other words, what a man thinks of himself determines to a great extent how he will behave in any given situation. Self-concept greatly influences the behavior an individual exhibits to others. Pockets of poverty, then, offer their own patterns and their own subcultures, and ways of behavior are determined by persons living within these pockets of poverty. In order for an individual to maintain the level of self-esteem he wishes to hold, he must be accepted by those persons who are important to him. The persons he knows within these pockets of poverty determine his life goals, meanings, and social roles to a considerable degree. The individual identifies himself and gives status to his being according to the value system of those around him, especially those important others who also predetermine his present and future behavioral roles. This fact is important in understanding why many persons who live within these pockets of poverty in both our rural areas and our urban areas do not avail themselves of various programs and opportunities, and in general, the services of the counselor. These individuals have found their present identity, and any threat to their way of life represents a threat to their person. Proposed changes bring about great feelings of anxiety; and while persons in poverty are unhappy about their fate, they do not have the strength to change what they have become. They do not have the immediate motivation to change the life pattern with which they are comfortable and that pattern of behavior through which they have found identity.

Few individuals are strong enough to make an identity change on their own, and changes within these pockets of destitution often must come through a total community development process. Persons can change as a group, once change has begun, easier than they can change as separate individuals. Change, then, within these pockets of destitution must come about within individuals in groups and cannot be achieved just by moving people to new geographic areas or mounting new programs which are aimed at the individual and which put basic and primary responsibility on the individual.

In order for individuals or groups to change they must be somewhat dissatisfied with their present state and their present self-image. People in poverty as well as people in the middle class and higher classes vary in their satisfaction with their self-image, and this is why some are more susceptible to change than others. It is important for the professionals in the rehabilitation field to ask for opinions of persons living in poverty in order that they can evaluate the present conditions of these individuals' lives and see whether or not the individuals wish to change in their communities and in their individual physical environment. Many poverty-stricken individuals have no idea that they can bring about change in their lives and most have given little thought to the possibility of improving living conditions. Counselors must be cognizant of the fact that the most effective way to change people is to treat them in accordance with the status in life which they would like to achieve. If an individual is to change behavioral patterns, he must be treated in a different manner from that to which he is accustomed.

The counselor concerned with the culturally disadvantaged and disabled disadvantaged should keep in mind that the economic system does not provide a sufficient number of employment opportunities in terms of jobs which are actually available to and appropriate for the poor. There is a chronic depression among many poor persons which results from inadequate occupational, educational, social and economic opportunity. This chronic depression is accentuated in our rural areas. This depression leads to a considerable lack of sufficient motivation for adjustment and achievement within the highly competitive society of the United States today. Various facts of life of the hard core jobless are interrelated and multiple. There is a high level of physical and mental deficiency, a low education level and property abounds. There is a general feeling of alienation, a lack of training and employment opportunity and severe racial and cultural problems.

Persons who live in the culture of poverty adapt to the conditions of that culture. The conditions and general culture of poverty perpetuates itself to its effects on children from generation to generation. It is believed that by the time children are six or seven they have taken on attitudes and values of their subculture, and they are not able, psychologically, to cope with the changing conditions and take advantage of various training and job opportunities which may occur later in life. If a break alone is offered to these individuals, it would soon be apparent that they are not favorably disposed toward the generosity. Measures to overcome their basic cultural, social and economic experiences must be included as a part of any social action program or rehabilitative program before positive change can be expected.

Moynihan (1968) has indicated that intensive family and personal rehabilitation must make up a major part of the war on impoverished conditions. He has said that increased opportunity for decent and well-paying jobs are simply not enough. Moynihan maintains that for an unspecified number of American poor deprivation over a long period of time has caused such serious personality difficulties (personality structure problems) that many of these persons are psychologically unable to avail themselves of the various training and job opportunities which might be available to them. When these personality structure problems have a chronic or permanent disability superimposed upon them the reaction to the disability is severe and often devastating.

While under the best of circumstances, the integrity of the family constellation is severely tested when disability occurs. The integrity of the family is definitely threatened when disability occurs in poverty families. One very important characteristic of poverty families is that they are in constant crisis. It seems that no sooner is one crisis worked out than another takes its place. There is always the financial situation; there is always sickness; there is always the situation of the possibility of divorce due to increased stress; there is always crime and a lack of a safe living environment for the weaker members of the family structure; there is always the child in trouble; and there is always the possibility of the loss of employment. There is always the stress of insufficient nutrition; insufficient provision for activities, entertainment, etc. When these deficiencies are superimposed upon a crisis situation in the family such as disability, the psychological reaction to the disability by both family members and the disabled is heightened. These constant crises have the effect of draining all the energy from the family and its members. Such emotionality takes a high toll in terms of the overall ability of the family unit or of an individual within the family.

To a large portion of the newly disabled from the deprived environment, the newly acquired status of disability is merely one more of a long series of misfortunes which he has encountered. While those from more affluent backgrounds are concerned about the future impact of the disability, those from the ghetto areas are more concerned with the here and now aspects of the disability.

When an individual accepts that his disability is of a permanent nature and that it is irrevocable, there will then be a period of what can be called reactive depression, and depending upon the severity of the disability, there may be various suicidal inclinations. This period of extreme depression after severe injury is a normal phase of adjustment. It is at this time that often much harm is done by well-meaning individuals who offer too much hope in terms of what may or may not be accomplished by science in order to aid the individual in the future. This is a period when candid advice and information can be of great value to the individual in planning what he is able to do in reference to his particular circumstance.

Accepting disability is of paramount importance. Persons vary in their reactions to a disability. Some think they are being punished for their own or for their parents' sin. Others may give the disability societal meaning in terms of their never being full members again with equal status. Still others may put sexual meanings on the disability problems. In addition, the economic aspect of the problem is often emphasized.

The meaning of disability to the family and friends of the individual cannot be overly stressed. If a child, for instance, is born disabled the family is not only grief-stricken, but since the child represents the family's position in the community the disabled child is more than a disappointment. Often the families of these children can find little happiness in caring for them. Often they enter upon every expensive endeavor to ameliorate a disability which cannot be corrected. In some cases the father will completely abandon the disabled child and his family saying that the defective child is the mother's responsibility since she gave birth to him. The family often can disintegrate around arguments and disputes which center around a disabled child.

SPECIAL PROBLEMS IN ADOLESCENCE

There are important reasons why traumatic experiences during adolescence can be of particular significance to the individual. Physique plays an especially important part in how we look at ourselves and in adolescence the body is constantly changing. In addition, the adolescent period overlaps both childhood and adulthood, and it is during the period of adolescence that important self-concept changes take place. During this period an individual is making a real effort to get to know himself, his abilities, and his limitations. If traumatic injury causes disability during this period, the adjustment to such disability can be of extreme difficulty.

During adolescence, the young person is particularly concerned about his physique in terms of sexuality. The young person is very interested in learning how others will view him from the point of view of his sexual role. He has constantly heard about marriage and bearing offspring and is evaluating how he will measure up to the criteria established by society. The adolescent who sustains a disability must tolerate the frustration and psychological meaning to him as an individual of this disability plus the overlapping child-adult status which he holds. The fact that he is disabled may cause the overlapping of childhood and adulthood to persist into years beyond that of the usual adolescent period. When the person is denied adulthood status, due to disability which may retard his forward movement, insecurities increase. It should also be noted that the tremendous influence of the adolescent's peer group during this period has a great deal to do with how he evaluates himself in comparison with what he would like to be later as an adult. It is easy for the adolescent during this difficult period to develop contempt for adult authority and to become very cynical even without the added burden of a disabling circumstance.

Slums offer their own patterns, their own subcultures, their ways of behavior are determined by persons living within them. In order for an individual to maintain the level of self-esteem he wishes to hold, he must be accepted by those persons who are important to him within his environment. The persons he knows within the slums or ghetto determine life goals, meanings, and social roles for him to a considerable degree. It is of prime importance for him to be accepted by them and to be accepted by himself at the same time. The individual identifies himself and gives status to his "being" according to the values of those around him, especially to those important "others" who almost predetermine his present and future behavior and goals. This fact is important in understanding why many persons who live within the ghetto and within slums do not avail themselves of various training and placement opportunities and in general, the services of the rehabilitation counselor. These individuals have found their present identity and any threat to their way of life represents a threat to their "person." Proposed changes by the re-habilitation counselor bring about great feelings of anxiety. While persons in poverty are unhappy with their fate, they do not have the strength to change that which they have become comfortable with and that pattern of behavior through which they have found identity. Consequently in the face of the onset of disability, it is much more likely that the individual will seek to achieve a level of adjustment in the environment in which he lives which existed prior to the onset of disability than strike out in a new area and achieve at a higher level even though he may be fully capable intellectually and vocationally to accomplish at a higher level. The problem here is that disability has added an additional stress in the equilibrium he has established between his own personality integration and the demands and stress of the environment. The psychological adjustment to disability among poverty groups is most difficult with individuals in early adolescence up through early adulthood since they are adjusting to a life-style which make unusual and somewhat severe psychological demands upon them thereby reducing the available psychic reserves to adjust to other conditions.

Few individuals are strong enough to make an identity change on their own and changes within areas of the ghetto and slum often must come through a total community development process. Persons can change once change has begun easier than they can change on their own initiative as separate individuals. Change then within slums and ghettos must come about within individuals and groups and cannot be achieved just by moving people to new geographical areas and physical surroundings and providing rehabilitation services in these new surroundings.

In order for disabled individuals to change they must be somewhat dissatisfied with their present state—their present self-image. Disabled people in poverty, as well as people in middle and higher classes vary in their satisfaction with their self-image and this is why some are more susceptible to change than others. This is why some are more receptive to counseling services than others. It is important for social service workers to ask for opinions of the disabled living in poverty in order that they can evaluate the present conditions of these individuals' lives and see whether or not they wish to change in their communities and in their individual physical environments. Many of these people have no idea that they could bring about a change in their lives and have given little thought to the possibilities of improving their living conditions. The concept of counseling in many of these instances is totally alien and incompatible with their life-style. At this point we want to repeat and emphasize the concept that counselors working with the disabled in these areas must be cognizant of the fact that the most effective way to change people is to treat them in accordance with the status in life which they would like to achieve. If an individual is to change behavioral patterns he must be treated or rewarded in a manner different from that to which he is accustomed.

IMPLICATIONS FOR COUNSELORS

Now, based upon this pattern, the counselors within our communities will be challenged in working with this large segment of our population. Old approaches will no longer work. Counselors who do not tool up and modify their basic approaches in evaluating clients and providing counseling services will be left behind during the mid and later seventies when the clamor for welfare reform will reach its peak. Not only must we work with the individual as we have in the past, but we must now work with his family in a more intimate and dramatic fashion. We must work with other community organizations which are organized for meeting some of the clients' needs. Additionally, we must work with the client in different program approaches and different counseling approaches than we have recognized in the past.

In working with the disadvantaged it is clearly indicated that different counseling approaches will need to be developed. Some old counseling strategies may be modified for the particular needs of this segment of our culture but we feel new levels of involvement need to be developed and new counseling strategies need to emerge in order to adequately meet counseling needs of this population. The counselor will need to work more closely with the community to learn how to uncover community resources, to work with family members, to deal with the basic problems of transportation, housing, food supplement, etc. Concepts such as self-actualization, client self-direction, etc. should not be ignored, but emphasis in the counseling strategy must be upon meeting current emergencies. With this approach self-direction and other long-range goals may eventually become a meaningful reality to the client; however, they should not be interjected as early in the process as they have been in the past. This is a quite obvious conclusion when one considers the level of our clients in the past in relationship to Maslow's hierarchy (Maslow, 1954). According to Maslow's hierarchy, most of our clients in the past have fulfilled the specific needs at the most basic two levels and are involved in fulfilling love and esteem needs. This new segment of clients with which we will be dealing is concerned more with physiological needs and safety needs. Therefore, their concerns are much more immediate and much more urgent.

Basic security in coping with the environment and with immediate concerns and problems are paramount values of the disadvantaged. Planning ahead is often a futile exercise and holds little personal value or rewards. For example, the possibility of discontinuance of a basic income supplement through a Social Security pension or welfare is apt to be viewed negatively in light of previous limited job success and long periods of unemployment frustration. Such clients have little assurance that social services, counseling and rehabilitation will make them better off than they are now.

An important problem affecting the counseling outcome is that the client may feel counselors really do not understand him or his needs; furthermore, he may feel that the team members working in the rehabilitation process may try to convey the attitude of understanding, but from the client's viewpoint, these individuals really do not and cannot understand. For example, the client will agree that personal motivation is necessary for people to get ahead in the world; however, the client is apt to disagree seriously if the counselor questions the client's motivation. The need for immediate assistance, medical care, transportation, money and so on are seen as the most important first steps. Many people needing the services of rehabilitation counseling feel they previously have been given unfulfilled promises by the professional personnel in the various fields of social service. There are psychological needs requiring immediate reward or service. Long-term planning and vague expectations and promises fail to motivate most disabled disadvantaged people.

Furthermore, a client has a general pessimism which is hard for the highly goal-oriented, motivated professionals to understand. The client has seen few of his people make it. Those who have escaped from poverty seldom remain in his social group, and hence, are not present to serve as models with whom the client might identify. Thus, the things which the client considers to be important are not apt to be congruent with what the counselor considers to be of importance.

In light of the these considerations, perhaps now it can be understood why a client may drop a training program, which could eventually lead to a two or three dollar an hour job, for an immediate opportunity to accept a job paying $1.50 per hour. Such behavior is understandable even though it appears to us to be a dead-end and self-defeating action.

The client desperately needs to be considered important and may really want to feel that he is being accepted by professionals working with him; yet many clients may have had previous experience with public agencies when they felt that their own personal integrity was questioned and their experience with the agency was a personally degrading one. Thus, they are now apt to view the counselor with suspicion and he must be proven not guilty. Demonstrating and conveying instant acceptance of the client as a worthwhile individual is a first major step towards establishing a working relationship.

The counselor has a prime opportunity to serve in a very basic capacity—that of being the focal point of community action and rehabilitation services. The counselor should serve not only as a focal point but as an energizer of services. There is a common concept that there is a paucity or a lacking of services within our communities organized to meet the needs of this segment of our population. This is not true. Upon investigation, one will find a plethora of services; however, they tend to be somewhat disjointed and directed more toward specific groups of people.

Quite often their approach is less broad than we would desire. Therefore, the counselor should assume the role of being the uniting force between these diverse service agencies for the benefit of these disadvantaged disabled clients. He should develop a very active information and referral program in order to be able to know who is providing services to what groups, where the clientele are located and what their needs are. In order to serve the welfare recipient, we have to find him. If the rehabilitation counselor is not able to locate and identify concentrations of welfare recipient clients, he cannot serve as an effective ingredient in the rehabilitation process.

Therefore, it would behoove the counselor to take time to learn each agency's function and solicit its cooperation. In order for the counselor to achieve the bright promise which lies ahead in fulfilling his role in the rehabilitation of this segment of our population, he should become the guiding force in welding the community together and directing it toward this goal.

Since communicating with the public welfare recipient is a prime obstacle to successful rehabilitation, we feel the counselor should initiate the employment of indigenous workers to communicate with these clients. The indigenous worker who is carefully selected to work with his people can do much more in the way of communicating to these citizens in bringing about the necessary changes that are indicated in order for the client to be employed than can a professional worker in many cases.

Since there is a shortage of available manpower within our professional areas, we need to turn to innovative approaches in staffing patterns. One innovative approach is the use of volunteer workers. We have a large reservoir of untapped manpower within the retired ranks of our communities. We feel the rehabilitation facilities within the country have missed the boat by not mobilizing these people for rehabilitation purposes. We have seen evidence that retired people from all walks of life are interested in volunteering their services to rehabilitation facilities. We have seen demonstrated that these individuals are eager to accept responsibility for the transportation of clients to rehabilitation facilities, to clinics to various other facilities. We have seen clients who are eager to accept responsibility in functioning as remedial educators for clients who are in need of remedial education; we have seen retired individuals who will volunteer to work with clients who are involved in homebound programs. It is our opinion that the counselor should make maximum utilization of voluntary activity.

REFERENCES AND SELECTED READINGS

Cull, J. G. and Hardy, R. E.: *Rehabilitation of the Urban Disadvantaged.* Springfield, Thomas, 1973.

Maslow, A. H.: *Motivation and Personality.* New York, Harper & Row Publishers, 1954.

Moynihan, D. P.: *Maximum Feasible Misunderstanding.* New York, Free Press, 1968.

Rosenthal, R. and Jacobson, L. F.: Teacher expectations for the disadvantaged. *Sci Am, 218*:19-23, 1968.

CHAPTER 10

REHABILITATION COUNSELING IN THE CORRECTIONAL INSTITUTION*

- History of Vocational Rehabilitation's Involvement With the Public Offender
- Counselor's Role in the Correctional Setting
- To Whom Is the Counselor Administratively Responsible?
- The Counselor's Relationship With the Correctional Administration
- The Counselor's Relationship With Prison Staff
- The Rehabilitation Counselor's Relationship With the Public Offender
- Complementary Programs and Their Participation in Public Offender Rehabilitation
- Community Participation in Inmate Rehabilitation
- Eligibility Determination of the Public Offender
- The Counselor's Responsibility in Serving the Inmate Population
- The Three Criteria of Eligibility

General Overview

VOCATIONAL REHABILITATION's collaboration with correctional institutions has become a reality. The rationale for its existence is supported in the Federal Offenders Program publication (Fulton, 1969) outlining the future of correctional rehabilitation. The writers of this research report state that in addition to the humanitarian aspects inherent in the rehabilitation movement, the primary impetus for creating a treatment program for the

---

* We gratefully acknowledge the substantial contribution of Craig R. Colvin in the development of this chapter.

public offender emerged from the complementary needs of vocational rehabilitation and corrections. This research study continues by saying that vocational rehabilitation was eager to develop a new source of clientele and had developed the resourcefulness to serve such a population. If one examines, even superficially, the composition of several correctional facilities, he will see that they have an abundance of clients with insufficient community resources to provide at least minimum treatment services. Therefore, it becomes obvious that these two agencies, vocational rehabilitation and corrections, must join forces in an attempt to provide meaningful services which will increase the probability of the public offender's returning to the community as a respected and trusted citizen.

Even though enthusiastic advances have been made, in the majority of articles pertaining to public offender programs, *rehabilitation* of the inmate within the institution has never quite caught up to the age-old concept of *restraint* and, to some degree, *retribution*. To be effective with this population, professionals must realign philosophies regarding institutionalization. Present-day ideologies existing in our country are undergoing massive and sometimes disruptive changes. Vocational rehabilitation can play a vital role in the assertion of rehabilitation techniques and methodologies enabling the inmate, after a predetermined treatment program, to reenter the community (society) as a productive member.

The inclusion of the following editorial written by a prison inmate serves a dual function of introducing the chapter as well as allowing the counselor to read some of the thoughts going through the mind of one man who is confined behind stark barren walls. After all, to whom will the professional be directing his efforts if it is not the inmate himself? Let's read what rehabilitation means to him.

The Great Rehabilitation Hoax*

"REHABILITATE, according to the *Webster's Seventh New Collegiate Dictionary,* means: la: to restore to a former capacity; to re-

* This editorial appeared in the February 7, 1969, publication of the *Prison Mirror.*

store to good repute by vindicating; 2a: to restore to a state of efficiency, good management, or solvency; b: to restore to a condition of health or useful and constructive activity. Unfortunately, as often is the case, either my dictionary is obsolete or Webster has failed to grasp the colloquial connotation of the word.

"Perhaps I can offer a more up-to-date, workable definition— REHABILITATE: to transform, by some mysterious, miraculous process, convicted felons into model, contributing members of society. This definition seems a little more apropos, and now that we have arrived at a more current definition, let's examine the perpetrators of 'THE GREAT REHABILITATION HOAX.'

"The primary offenders are all those well-meaning judges, social workers, penologists, and pseudo-penologists, criminologists, writers, newspapermen, etc. who persist in misusing and misapplying the term 'rehabilitation.' Rehabilitation has become the standard one-word answer to a myriad of questions concerning prisons, correctional programs, and penal philosophy. It is the answer that leaves the questioner with that 'Oh, I see' feeling, even though he really doesn't 'see' at all. 'Rehabilitation' has become idiomatic aspirin, to be dispensed by the sociologist as a cure-all for the headache of crime and punishment in these United States.

"The aforementioned group of conspirators are not solely responsible for the hoax. They have tens of thousands of 'rap partners' inhabiting the prisons and correctional institutions throughout the land—the wise guys and old cons, the youthful offenders who follow idealistically the example of their 'elders' and say, 'Okay, so rehabilitate me!' It's no secret the vast majority of convicts are waiting for an invisible Merlin to wave a wand, stamp their backsides 'RE-HABILITATED,' and send them off to the free world with the keys to a new Cadillac in their pocket and a 25,000-dollar-a-year income waiting for them, just as soon as they report to their parole officers. Oh yes, to all of 'us'—all the smart guys and would-be big shots—half the rap belongs to us.

"The answer to the problem does not lie in the application of sociological terminology, for mere words cannot correct a problem of this magnitude. It has taken most of us a lifetime to acquire the ignominy of the label 'convict.' Words and good intentions are not enough to cure the illness that afflicts us. You sociologists, you penologists—you cannot rehabilitate us! We must rehabilitate ourselves! OOPS! Pardon me, for I have committed the cardinal sin myself. We must HELP ourselves! I think, though, that you must be aware of this fact already, for some of you aren't trying very hard to rehabilitate us anyway.

"There is no magic formula that you can apply, no elixir you can prescribe to cure our malady. At best you can but offer the facility, the vehicle, the tools with which we may help ourselves. The degree to which you offer your cooperation and the quality of the tools available will, in the long run, determine how successful you have been. The rate of recidivism is the only yardstick you can apply to measure the success or failure of your part of the bargain, and in the end, one can hardly blame a poor harvest on the man who sold him the seed.

"There is one commodity you can furnish—one that has been sorely lacking in the past—EMPATHY! In simpler terms, a genuine under-standing of our problems from our point of view and an unqualified belief in the worth of each one of us as a human being. Try to bear this in mind when we approach you with palms extended, asking for a push to get us started. It has taken the courage of a martyr to bring us to this stage. Don't ask us to defend our motives! Don't make us suspects of devious plots and schemes merely because we want to change! The prime mover for all of us is universal—we want to get out and stay out!

"The biggest task is ours alone. You cannot make it easy for us, but you can make it difficult. You cannot ensure our success, but you can ensure our failure. Give us the tools, give us consideration, and above all, be flexible enough to treat us as individuals, and you will have done your job. Not all of us will win that battle, some of us will fail and return. To be sure, some will attempt to deceive you from the very first, but more will succeed than are succeeding now!

"So far we have uncovered the perpetrators of the hoax, but who are the victims? You are, all of you on the other side of the concrete curtain—you, the taxpayers, that great uninformed electorate, and conglomeration we call 'society.' You have bought the 'Brooklyn Bridge' of rehabilitation. You have allowed your all too infrequent queries into crime and punishment to be satisfied with the classic one-word answer. You have swallowed the hook and are proceeding to choke on the bait. You've been fleeced and it's your own fault.

"Now I've gotten you mad and you want to know why and how you've been taken. It's really quite simple. Your tax dollars have been spent to foster 'rehabilitation programs' carried on in every prison in the land. Dedicated men have worked untold hours with us, the convicts, helping us reshape our lives. Time and effort, ours and theirs, and your money are invested in a process which yields a product, a parolee. When that product is placed on the 'market' you proceed to destroy it! You saddle it with the burden of a label—EX-CONVICT, which seems to be synonymous with EX-HUMAN BEING, and you ride it into the ground. You beat it over the head with a billy club labeled 'Once a thief. . . .' You speak aloud of

Christian charity and every man deserving another chance, then whisper behind your hand, 'They never change.' You stretch a thread-like tightrope across the chasm that separates ignominy from respectability, then ask us to carry an elephant on our shoulders when we attempt to cross. Is it any wonder so many wind up on the rocks below?

"Why bother to 'rehabilitate' us if you are going to allow an attitude to prevail which prevents us from coming all the way back? Our 'debt to society' you always speak of, is a debt we have ostensibly paid when we walk out of the shadows of these walls. But somehow you never get around to marking our account 'paid in full.' Some of us have paid a terrific price to settle that account, perhaps others have not paid enough. But that is a judgment no mortal man can make for certain! So in the end you are like a hunter caught in his own trap. You are your own victim!

"To succeed, to reenter the civilized world of everyday life, we need a tricycle to ride upon. We need the professional guidance and effective administration of dedicated sociologists, psychologists and criminologists; the acceptance of an understanding, unprejudiced society; and the fortitude, the 'guts' to start again ourselves. Take away one of the wheels and the rides get a little shaky—it's easier to ride a tricycle than a bicycle. Take away two of the wheels and it requires the prodigious effort and skill of a unicyclist! To be sure, some of us will find the tricycle too difficult to ride, but don't condemn the rest of that unicycle ride on that account. Give us all the chance to ride the tricycle and rehabilitation will cease to be a hoax and indeed become a reality."

This is the challenge we must accept if there is hope of returning and keeping the public offender within the guidelines established by society.

HISTORY OF VOCATIONAL REHABILITATION'S INVOLVEMENT WITH THE PUBLIC OFFENDER

When considering vocational rehabilitation's participation in public offender programs, one need not go back too many years. To gain a better perspective of this relatively new area called correctional rehabilitation in relation to the total development of vocational rehabilitation, it is imperative to examine briefly some of the legislative movements affecting its growth.

It is important to look at several of the laws and amendments to see how rehabilitation became interested in serving the incarcerated. This public service organization, vocational rehabilitation, has grown on the concepts of helping one's fellowman. The initial program began in 1918 with the original mandate of providing services to World War I veterans that had been wounded. The ultimate objective was, of course, to "place them" back into the labor market. It did not take long to see that this program could be expanded to include the civilian population. Even though we don't have records indicating the provision of services to the public offender population, we are quite sure that a few were accepted for rehabilitation services during these early years.

In 1939, the agency broadened its delivery of services to include a full spectrum of physical disabilities. Prior to this date, the organization had directed its energy toward those individuals with orthopedic handicaps. A small number of inmates were being provided services under the auspices of vocational rehabilitation even though no formal programs had been developed.

Probably the greatest impetus given to public offender rehabilitation was with the passage of Public Law 565 in 1954 when mental retardation and emotional illness were added to the traditional services which vocational rehabilitation could provide. Studies have indicated that approximately 15 percent of the inmates in penitentiaries have diagnosable mental illnesses and that 85 percent have some emotional problem (Tessler, 1966). Additionally, and as importantly, research and demonstration projects were approved to be carried out across the nation in specific areas relative to the rehabilitation of various disability groups. Several of these early demonstration projects dealt with the feasibility of working with the inmate population.

Following the 1954 legislation was the passage of Public Law 333 in 1965. Through the expansion of the definition of disability to include behavior disorders, it was determined the public offender could be considered eligible under this category. Within this piece of legislation, vocational rehabilitation states that the socially handicapped were feasible candidates for services; included in this group was the public offender. Research and demonstration projects from previous years supported the rationale for extending services to this group. The 1969 law redefined the disability category of behavior disorders which definitely made the public offender more accessible to the rehabilitation counselor.

Even though adequate legislation has been written at the federal level, all state rehabilitation agencies have not adopted an open-door policy of accepting the public offender as a client. Some states have only "token" programs in which nothing more than an occasional simple physical restoration case is accepted (and usually the inmate is determined feasible only if he has been awarded parole and a job has been secured for him by someone else).

Other state rehabilitation agencies, on the other hand, have accepted the challenge of working with the public offender. California, Georgia, North and South Carolina, Massachusetts, and Texas, as well as others, have enacted comprehensive programs with the objective of providing a multitude of rehabilitation services for the majority of each state's respective inmate population. Cooperative agreements have been written—utilizing the broad federal guidelines—outlining the authority, types of services, and future direction of participating agencies.

Future developments in correctional rehabilitation will depend upon increased state agency acceptance of the feasibility of working with inmates and the commitment of people to force continued legislative action.

COUNSELOR'S ROLE IN THE CORRECTIONAL SETTING

There is a multitude of variables which must be considered by the rehabilitation counselor prior to his actual contact with clients in a penal institution: The counselor must evaluate his own inadequacies and how they might interfere with the counselor-client relationship; the counselor has to determine to whom he is responsible (the rehabilitation administration or the correctional administration); and the counselor must define his professional relationship with the correctional administration and other members of the prison staff in terms of a treatment approach to inmate rehabilitation. Each of these variables will be expanded to help the neophyte counselor become aware of and adjust to many of the idiosyncrasies prevalent in the correctional setting.

Understanding One's Own Limitations

We all have our "hang-ups," both personal as well as professional. Many of us in corrections and rehabilitation envision idealistic approaches to inmate treatment. Before involving many people in a theoretical or academic exercise, a realistic attitude is necessary. This means that the counselor has to maintain a level of maturity capable of functioning within a professional framework.

The quality of maturity is a necessary component anyone working with public offenders must possess. Without it the naive counselor soon will fall to the manipulative devices of some inmates, will be "snowed" under with inmate requests for counseling sessions, and in a short period will become so overly involved with some inmates that the only recourse is to resign.

If a counselor cannot realistically face those problems confronting him, he surely will have a difficult time in the correctional setting. Every day will be filled with new "crisis" situations that seem to require the counselor's undivided attention. If he is insecure in his personal life, this will soon become evident in the counselor's activities. Decisions must be made with authority; yet, if the decision is wrong or inappropriate the counselor must have the strength to admit such a mistake.

If, as a counselor, one is anticipating a great deal of "success" in rehabilitating the public offender, the fulfilling of expectations will be rather limited. No matter what degree of preparation one might have prior to engaging in correctional rehabilitation, the criteria utilized to evaluate success must be reevaluated. Most authors concerned with this topic first mention the failure syndrome surrounding the inmate; he has been a failure in society; he has been a failure to himself; he has even been a failure in crime; and he has been a failure to those people who have tried to help him. No rehabilitation counselor is going to come along and change things overnight. Rehabilitation should attempt to bring about change. We must design, realistically, a plan for constructive rehabilitation which is relevant to the inmate's own needs rather than the needs imposed upon him by some counselor representing a "bureaucratic organization."

False values, the inability to make decisions, insecurity, a poor attitude toward one's work, and other forms of inappropriate behavior will become magnified many times if one enters the correctional rehabilitation field. After all, these types of behavior and personality problems are manifested by the majority of people the counselor has the responsibility of serving! Therefore, prior to accepting an appointment within a correctional facility, the counselor should critically examine his own behavior and attitudes toward the job. This soul-searching will go a long way if it is approached with conscientiousness. One's assignment in the penal institution can be either a rewarding professional experience or it can become just the opposite.

TO WHOM IS THE COUNSELOR ADMINISTRATIVELY RESPONSIBLE?

Upon entering professional work in correctional rehabilitation, the counselor often asks regarding administrative policy, "To whom am I responsible, the department of correction or vocational rehabilitation?" Administrative responsibility is directed toward vocational rehabilitation, even though line supervision may be coming from the correctional unit.

For some newly employed counselors there is a tendency for them to believe that they are accountable to both corrections and vocational rehabilitation. This is true in some situations and false in others. Administrative responsibility is given usually to the agency which has the counselor on its payroll. Since professionals involved in vocational rehabilitation control the purse strings, they will be directing specific problems concerned with rehabilitation policies and procedures.

Yet, at the same time, there is a fine line separating administrative policies of these two organizations which must be understood. Even though the counselor reports to rehabilitation, he must function under the structure of the correctional administration since you share, in most instances, the facilities. This approach "makes for better neighbors."

Delineation of organizational roles is understood better if the counselor can peruse the formal cooperative agreement established. For those counselors working in situations where no formal agreement has been written, specific agency roles and their respective responsibilities will be more difficult to determine. The counselor should plan a meeting with his immediate vocational rehabilitation supervisor and also a similar meeting with the appropriate institutional supervisor. A get-together of this nature should provide the new employee adequate feedback regarding his responsibility to rehabilitation, corrections, and ultimately, the inmate.

THE COUNSELOR'S RELATIONSHIP WITH THE CORRECTIONAL ADMINISTRATION

There are several predominant factors which must be identified prior to becoming involved in any treatment program for the public offender. The rehabilitation counselor must be aware of and appreciate the dilemma facing the correctional institution's administration. This organization has two primary goals which at times may be antithetical—they are custody and rehabilitation.

While it may be objectionable to the newly employed counselor's ideals, the custodial facet of the institution is of the utmost concern to correction's administration. Actually vocational rehabilitation becomes a disruptive influence in the overall operation of a correctional unit. To a prison administrator, a rehabilitation program often creates more problems than it solves. In a custodial-oriented institution, a routine is established to maintain order and, in turn, security. If a rehabilitation program is interjected into this routinized system, many changes are required; exceptions to prison procedure which previously were rare now occur with increasing frequency. But in this dichotomy of administrative philosophy, the development and support of rehabilitation programs must evolve.

To further define the rehabilitation counselor's relationship with the correctional administration, the counselor has to realize he must function within this militaristically-oriented work environment.

Administrative officials have operated penal institutions for decades under a militarily-oriented regimen. Such a design allows a few people (with the aid of high walls and iron bars) to control a large number of other individuals. As a counselor one must be cognizant of the realities of such a dehumanizing but essential operation.

Sometimes the stark raw attitude of prison officials confuses the counselor's expectations regarding prison rehabilitation. The counselor has been taught that a permissive attitude and a humanitarian approach are mandatory requisites for work with the public offender. Prison officials do consider the welfare of the inmates; but with the primary objective of maintaining security for the welfare of the institution and its employees. The administration has difficulty relaxing their defenses, knowing well that if they do some inmate will escape or at least attempt to do so.

The counselor's understanding and acceptance of the administration's security precautions have priority over everything. His personal and professional endeavors to rehabilitate the public offender cannot violate security policies. With this in mind, it is suggested that any counselor considering employment in this challenging area peruse the administration's policies and procedures manual. If there are questions regarding the various areas of this manual, the counselor should make note and attempt to have them answered by the respective prison officials.

Another factor which must be identified and understood in a prison work setting is that there are prescribed channels of communication through which all facets of institutional information flow. If the counselor is to be considered effective in such an organization, he quickly must assess his role and determine how it will fit into the overall plan of the institution. This counselor is obliged to understand the various channels of command and learn how he might interject appropriate comments and suggestions regarding implementation of rehabilitation techniques without feeling or becoming ostracized.

One must remember that the correctional organization has developed over the years with a very rigid philosophy. Implementation of rehabilitation concepts will not occur without some degree of resistance.

THE COUNSELOR'S RELATIONSHIP WITH PRISON STAFF

Enthusiasm toward one's work as a correctional rehabilitation counselor is an important asset which should not be stymied by others who, seemingly, do not share this jubilation. Continuous effort must be made to convince the prison staff that dedicated teamwork may eventually result in restoring a percentage of public offenders to a level of behavior acceptable by society. Yet blatant assertion of one's role as a vocational rehabilitation counselor will not get one anywhere, especially among members of the correctional institution's staff. Initial involvement with other staff members should be approached with conscientiousness and tactfulness, recalling that for most of the staff, adherence to a correctional regimen has become a way of life.

Previous discussion has pointed out the rigid military-like and dehumanizing attitude by some correctional authorities. Many staff members functioning under this system soon begin unconsciously to imitate and carry out this philosophy in their own work assignments. In relation to the provision of services, the effectiveness of the classification committee members, social workers, psychologists, correctional officers, and even chaplains and physicians should be evaluated.

Idealistically, all of these professional groups should be active in every penal institution where inmates reside; but realistically this is not the case. The involvement of these disciplines range from a mere token effort to provide a few basic services to a sophisticated and integrated team approach utilizing every available resource.

Theoretically, the classification committee in most correctional facilities has three fundamental responsibilities: (a) diagnosis, categorization and orientation to the newly arrived inmate; (b) the development of his treatment program; and (c) the establishment of guidelines regarding inmate custody. Under these directives the committee attempts to formulate an individualized rehabilitation program for each inmate.* To facilitate their decision-making processes, a team of professionals is utilized and

---

* Realistically, the custodial facet takes precedence over everything. With this in mind, it is difficult to envision any program which could be considered effective.

its contributions are defined briefly in the following paragraphs.

After the public offender's arrival at the institution, he enters the first phase of the classification process. Here he is given a preliminary medical and psychological examination in an attempt to detect physical or mental abnormalities which may need immediate attention. If problems or other deficiencies are noted, the inmate usually will receive a more detailed and comprehensive examination.

During his first few days of institutionalization, the inmate is subjected, at the request of the classification committee, to a barrage of aptitude, interest and achievement tests. In part these test results serve as a factor in determining what responsibilities the inmate may have within the unit such as janitorial duties, cooking detail, a maintenance department job or assignment to an educational program. If a gross deficiency pattern is noted from these tests or the psychologicals, further psychiatric services may be warranted.

The reception unit, staffed by social workers, has the responsibility of developing an inmate's social history record. This staff concentrates on the individual's background, pertinent family data, special interests he may have and what role the inmate expects to fulfill within the institution. Due to the ever-increasing admission rates and the pressure to interview a greater number of inmates, the worth of such derived material is questioned since the social workers usually have enough time only to record information which is rather objective in nature. An in-depth analysis of an inmate's past cannot be justified when an interviewer has three or four people waiting outside his office.

Also, it should be pointed out that these staff members soon begin to become calloused in their thinking, often forgetting that they are serving someone who most likely has never encountered anyone willing to listen to his problems. This is a rut the counselor in an institution easily can get into; he soon sees all inmates as the same person, with the same problems, with the same social, educational, and environmental history. If we call ourselves professionals, we must make a concerted effort to see each inmate as an individual who needs our undivided attention.

There are others who usually see the inmate during this orientation phase; the chaplain, the orientation committee, physicians and dentists. The chaplain tries to talk with each man individually to explain the availability of religious programs within the institution. The unit chaplain attempts to relate with the inmate on an individual basis, letting him know that he always has someone to whom he can confide without fear of reprimand.

Most units have at least an informal orientation committee whose primary responsibility is to explain the prison regulations and procedures to the new arrival. The inmate is briefed regarding what is expected of him during his imprisonment and he is told at the outset what consequences will evolve if he violates prison policy.

Medical services similar to those found in the community are provided—a general physical examination along with a blood and urine test, chest x-ray and other diagnostic work-ups are administered. Usually routine dental exams are given to each inmate at the beginning of his incarceration.

After all of the above services have been offered, the respective staff reports are typed and sent to the classification committee so that they may use them to carry out their other responsibilities (development of a treatment program and custody assignment).

Classification committees vary in size from three to seven or more members, with one of them acting as chairman. Each member surveys all diagnostic and related material prior to the committee meeting. Following a discussion of the particular inmate being evaluated, specific recommendations are made regarding his rehabilitation program and his custody assignment. As stated in the introduction to this chapter, here we see again the dilemma confronting correctional authorities: rehabilitation versus custody.

Thus far there has been no indication of vocational rehabilitation's involvement in any of the classification committee's activities. Probably the simplest explanation is that in the majority of correctional institutions vocational rehabilitation has not been given the opportunity to help develop constructive inmate rehabilitation programs. Too many facilities feel that vocational rehabilitation is trying to infringe upon their territory. It is imperative that archaic attitudes associated with prisons be eliminated and replaced by advanced attitudes which effect positive change.

Active participation on the classification committee should become a personal as well as professional goal of all counselors functioning within the correctional setting. One's involvement at this stage of the inmate's contact with the institution will, more than likely, increase the probability of success once an integrated rehabilitation program can be devised for him. In those few penal facilities where vocational rehabilitation has a clearly defined role, the attitude of correctional staff members responsible for modifying inmate behavior has been positive. Rehabilitation counselors have acted as catalysts in causing a renewed awareness—on the part of the prison staff—of the public offender's intended life-style after release rather than relying only on his life-style during imprisonment. The rationale for this is quite obvious: rehabilitation traditionally has been a community-based program, whereas corrections has divorced itself from the community to become an isolate. Therefore, by joining forces with vocational rehabilitation, the classification committee is in a better position to plan a logical and constructive program facilitating inmate development.

The same holds true regarding the counselor's involvement with the physicians. As in the past, vocational rehabilitation counselors have relied heavily on the medical profession in the free community. This should not change to any significant degree within the institution. Where most of the other professional services found in the community are lacking behind prison walls, the provision of medical services is the least affected.

Counselors should avail themselves of this material and, at the same time, undertake a public relations program promoting vocational rehabilitation. Unfortunately all too often physicians working solely within the prison setting have removed themselves from the current mainstream of continued professional development. They also are not particularly interested in learning about or becoming associated with the other helping disciplines. Again, the reasons for this should be obvious: Since most institutions do not have adequate legislative and community support, salaries are relatively low in comparison to those same positions outside the walls. This, in turn, creates a vacuum or void which regretfully is filled by the retiring or misplaced physician. Also, as it has been stated several times in this chapter, prison staff including physicians, some picture all public offenders as "con" men attempting to "get something for nothing." As an example, one should visit a physician's office inside a prison during sick call. Here one will find most of the waiting chairs occupied by inmates who solemnly attest to the fact that they are in acute pain and are, therefore, in need of drugs. It is true that after a short length of time the physician or any other person, for that matter, would tire of such actions.

Yet a hardened and negative attitude is not a solution to the problem. Returning to what was said earlier, rehabilitation can become the agent of attitude change. By becoming interested in the physician's role in the institution, the counselor automatically has the chance to increase the doctor's perceptions of vocational rehabilitation and this agency's objective of helping the inmate adapt to the demands of society. Additionally, the counselor can provide the physician appropriate feedback regarding medical information required by vocational rehabilitation to aid in the determination of eligibility. This approach should initiate the doctor's subscribing to rehabilitation-oriented concepts rather than the antiquated regimen of medical practice solely for maintenance of the inmate while he is institutionalized.

Social workers too can become valuable allies in vocational rehabilitation. Through the coordination of services the duplication of similar programs can be eliminated. Again, as with other disciplines, the combined effort undoubtedly will be greater than the services any one agency could hope to provide the inmate.

There is more to inmate rehabilitation than helping him while he is behind bars. Total rehabilitation must extend out into the community once the man has served his time. What better opportunity would the releasee have through the concentrated efforts of these two (and why not other) organizations who have had successful programs in the community for quite some time? If success with the inmate is what we are looking for, we must discard and bury whatever hostilities, jealousies or negative attitudes that have been fostered through the years. A marriage of all disciplines must come about; yet the dissolution of each organization's professional identity is not necessary nor would it be advisable. Let each agency keep its separate identity, but let each cooperate with one another for the benefit of those people the organizations have said they would serve.

Downtrodden and often neglected, the correctional officer rarely receives the attention he so rightfully deserves. He is probably the most underrated prison staff member, though he is the one in the best position to help inmates with their immediate problems. The correctional officer (he has been designated in the past as guard or "turn key") has responsibility to watch over the inmate twenty-four hours a day, seven days a week, fifty-two weeks a year or until such time release is granted. No one else within the institutional setting has a better chance to influence inmate behavior change. But as evidenced in most prisons, the officer has been relegated an assignment of "watchdog." If an inmate "breaks" or violates any of the outmoded prison rules, he is reported by the officer to a higher level authority who, in turn, continues the transmittal of violation(s) until they have exhausted the chain of command. The point here is that the correctional officer has not been given the responsibility to act on behalf of the inmate as an agent of change; he is there only to carry out the function of surveillance.

The writers feel that if these men were accorded a specific role in the total design of an inmate's rehabilitation program, we would experience a dramatic decrease in recidivism (a public offender's return to prison). Realizing that custody is the primary concern of prison officials there must be an attempt to realign responsibilities so that a delicate balance could be achieved between rehabilitation and custody. Combining both of these facets and having staff control this balance will not be easy, but it is mandatory. If such effort is to occur, it is necessary to involve the correctional officer on the firing line.

THE REHABILITATION COUNSELOR'S RELATIONSHIP
WITH THE PUBLIC OFFENDER

Following the counselor's development of an affiliation with those people held responsible for effecting inmate behavior change within the institution, we finally examine the counselor's involvement with the public offender. This section will be directed toward several factors that influence the counselor-inmate relationship and how the counselor can improve or strengthen his competency in working with this population.

Utilization of Diagnostic Information

In respect to the history of incarceration, correctional personnel only recently have begun accumulating adequate diagnostic material on each inmate's entering the system. These diagnostic reports or work-ups usually include a comprehensive medical examination with appropriate laboratory tests; a rather elaborate psychological test battery composed of Wechsler Adult Intelligence Scale, Minnesota Multiphasic Personality Inventory, Kuder Preference Record, Bender-*Gestalt* Test, Purdue Pegboard, and a host of other personality and achievement tests. A psychiatric examination is necessary in some cases. As stated previously a detailed social history is gathered containing educational, religious and economic information.

A thorough and objective analysis of this existing material should be made prior to the counselor's first interview with the potential client. After a counselor has perused such diagnostic material, he should determine whether or not additional information is required. If such material is deemed necessary, the counselor in conjunction with the correctional unit can activate a program to secure such without breaching security or established prison routines.

Counseling Aspects

Generally, counseling as practiced by vocational rehabilitation counselors does not vary to any significant degree from one rehabilitation setting to another. Nevertheless, there is a definite facade existing between a correctional unit counselor and his inmate client which normally does not exist between a field counselor and his client in the community. An "on-guard" or defensive attitude prevails between counselor and inmate which does not lend itself to the establishment of a favorable counseling relationship. The counselor feels compelled to remain "uptight" so as not to become a pawn of the inmate's manipulative devices.

Continuing along this thought and reiterating a point brought out several times in the preceding sections, it is mandatory that the vocational rehabilitation counselor concern himself with security precautions although his ultimate objective is for the rehabilitation of an individual who will be reentering the free world. Without this awareness the counselor may jeopardize his relationship not only with the institution's administration but also with the inmate as well.

For the correctional rehabilitation counselor to be effective in performing his responsibilities, he must discuss his role with the inmate during their initial interview. The counselor must set somewhat rigid limits on the relationship he establishes with this man, yet convince him that he is there to help him rehabilitate himself. As one readily can imagine, such an arrangement is no simple matter that can be sloughed over nonchalantly; to achieve this precarious balance requires a great deal of insight and perceptiveness on the counselor's part.

Inmate Motivation Versus Manipulation

Motivation as defined by Webster means a "stimulus to action or something that causes a person to act." If there is one recurring characteristic or quality found within the prison population, it is motivation; but we must ask ourselves, "Motivation for what?" There is both an unconscious as well as conscious desire operating within the inmate that can be defined as motivation. One might even call it a driving impulse which suggests a power arising from personal temperament and desire. It sounds as if the vocational rehabilitation counselor has found the "perfect" client! Again, we have to ask ourselves what the inmate is motivated for or towards. Freedom!

Probably freedom occupies his mind more than any other single facet connected with his institutionalization; his main objective is to get out of prison as soon as humanly possible. Even so, each inmate responds differently to the ever-present desires for freedom: There is the inmate who will resort to escape to reach his freedom; another will quietly sit back and wait out his time in idleness; a third type will try to con his way out; and then there is the individual who will work conscientiously toward earning his freedom by productive work and obeying the institution's regulations.

Vocational rehabilitation will find the greatest degree of success with this last man, and yet it will be difficult for the counselor to separate one from another during the initial interviews. As an example, the motivation of one inmate may be directed toward manipulation of the staff. From our side of the fence, we often see this inmate's external behavior as being conducive for positive rehabilitation efforts. Because of the public offender's isolation, he will strive to manipulate or convince some professionals that he is "motivated" toward whatever objective they are wanting him to achieve.

Upon release from the institution, this man usually rejects the likely benefits of rehabilitation programs. As an illustration, in the writers' experience in working with the public offender, we have seen individuals really look forward to their training in such areas as bakery, welding, printing, and offset. As their counselors we felt that adjustment and progression in these training areas were more than satisfactory and that upon release, there would be no difficulty in placing them in the labor market. Prior to their departure from the institution, the counselor would make the usual arrangements regarding work and a place to stay for these men. After one or two weeks on the job, the majority of these people came to see if they could be trained in some other area. When asked why, they answered invariably that the training they received did come from "behind the wall" and it reminded them of an experience they would rather forget; the best way of doing so was to be retrained in another area and go their own way.

Additional Considerations

When the public offender makes a mistake, he often is ridiculed or punished unduly. If this same mistake were made by another client in the community, he probably would not be reprimanded as severely. After all, mistakes are a vital part of the learning process, and we have to examine and, if necessary, continually reexamine the reasons underlying their failure.

We must give the inmate more responsibility for his actions. As is found in most correctional institutions today the inmate is told when to get up, when to wash and shave, when to eat, when to go to the bathroom, when to go to work, when to participate in recreation, and on and on. What happens to this individual when it comes time for him to reenter the community and face the everyday grind? Self-control has been inhibited or even squelched during his institutionalization and after release we expect him, as if by magic, to regain all those intricate components which are identifiable as "normal" behavior patterns exhibited by the majority.

Treatment, rehabilitation, habilitation or any word which expresses a return to normalcy must include responsibility for one's own behavior. This behavioral change process has no predetermined solution which can be applied to all inmates; individual approaches to individual problems are required if we expect to see positive results. Such an approach necessitates greater coordination and teamwork of all disciplines that have dedicated themselves to helping the imprisoned.

COMPLEMENTARY PROGRAMS AND THEIR PARTICIPATION IN PUBLIC OFFENDER REHABILITATION

Thus far we have concerned ourselves primarily with various personnel in the correctional system and the counselor's involvement in public offender rehabilitation. A quick glance at several programs designed specifically to help the individual who has been committed for violating societal laws should provide the reader additional insight into inmate problems and how they might be resolved.

Probation and Parole

A discussion of correctional rehabilitation is meaningless without briefly mentioning two other important agencies and their contributions toward the rehabilitation of the public offender— the probation and parole systems.

Probation as it is known today has changed very little since its inception in the mid-1800's. Those chosen as potential candidates have been screened thoroughly by the probation agency prior to the judge's final sentencing. The probation department's basic responsibility then is to select an individual who has been convicted of a crime and, under a threat of being put into prison, provide him with necessary guidance and supervision in the community. The rationale supporting probation is that if the individual is capable of handling his personal activities, he should be given the opportunity of doing so by remaining in society as a productive member.

Due to vocational rehabilitation's traditional role as a community-based program, it is logical that a cooperative effort should be established whereby both agencies would share in the supervision of the individual on probation. If services are indicated to ensure the probationer's remaining on a job, the counselor and the probation officer should collaborate so that complementary services are provided rather than the duplication of services.

The parole system becomes a factor after an individual has been incarcerated for a length of time. The parole department selects certain inmates which have proven to the establishment that they can function readily in the community. Actual work must be available and awaiting the inmate upon release before he is considered eligible for parole. In fact, the philosophy of work is the crux of both the department of probation and the department of parole; without the availability of work in the form of a specific job, an inmate will not be placed on probation or be paroled from the prison. Immediately one can visualize the implications for vocational rehabilitation involvement in both of these organizations as well as with the department of correction. Through a unified team approach a host of interrelated services can be provided with the ultimate objective of placing the inmate back into the community to function on a socially accepted level.

Work Release

The prison work release program has gained wide recognition, especially in the last decade. This program originally began in Wisconsin in 1913 with the passage of the Huber Act. This act, along with further legislative refinements over the years, capitalizes on or uses as a basis a concept which is one of the most perplexing problems confronting the public offender—unemployment.

Prior to commitment this individual has gotten into trouble usually because he has been out of work. After conviction, the inmate is placed in an isolated environment where idle time or at best limited educational or vocational instruction is provided. Many of the training areas existing within correctional facilities either have become obsolete or are not taught by adequately trained staff. In our highly complex society, job obsolescence becomes a major factor; this means that upon release, the inmate will be entering the labor market unprepared to hold a specific job.

Work release programs, as these are known today, are based on the premise that an inmate must show he can cooperate with and function under authority before he be considered a candidate for the program. Usually it is necessary for him to serve a predetermined prison sentence in order to decide if he can behave accordingly as set forth in the guidelines established by correctional administration.

Through the recommendations of the classification committee, a candidate for work release is transferred to another section of the prison or sometimes outside the unit into a "halfway house" situation. During the day he works on a job *within the community* at this carefully chosen vocation. After work the inmate returns to the work release complex where he spends his nights and weekends. His earnings not only provide some measure of his ability to reintegrate into the free society, especially the world of work, but this money helps pay room and board while at the facility. A part of his earnings are used to help support his family; the remainder of these funds is deposited in a savings account to which he will have access after his release from the institution.

The implications supporting total inmate rehabilitation rather than fragmented rehabilitation are evidenced in the success rates or statistics gathered on the unfortunately small number of work release programs across the country. Of those inmates selected to participate in work release, fewer than 15 percent have failed to complete their sentence without accumulating additional offenses (Colvin, 1972). Most of these infractions were minor in that the work releasee stopped off for a beer on the way back to the unit or the inmate "extended" his allotted time in the community. A smaller percentage forfeited their right to continue on work release after they committed further crimes for which they were reincarcerated.

Some people feel that before work release can be considered a success, it must completely eliminate failure—that is, the inmate will not commit any more crime. The writers believe that such a feat would be next to impossible and that the program is serving its intended purpose beyond the expectations of those who are responsible for its administration. The prediction of inmate success in a work release program is difficult, but as professionals we can eliminate inmate failure by utilizing every available resource at our disposal. Effective screening devices are necessary to select the inmate showing the most potential to reenter the community as a productive member of its work force.

COMMUNITY PARTICIPATION IN INMATE REHABILITATION

In discussing the challenging field of correctional rehabilitation, it is extremely important to be aware of as many different facets as possible so that one may have a better understanding of the total program. The possibility of inmate manipulation and the rigidity of the correctional unit itself has been discussed along with a brief glimpse of several of the helping agencies working for the inmate's rehabilitation; but we have failed to mention the inadequacies existing within our own community relative to inmate needs. Here is the main problem confronting the newly released individual.

From the very outset of the inmate's institutionalization, the correctional process must be directed back toward the community. It is within the community that either further crimes will be committed or a useful life lived. As a society we have formulated laws which he has violated and, in turn, placed him behind bars; and we have determined the sentence which should be imposed upon him. After he has fulfilled his obligation in relation to the law and the amount of time he should remain segregated from society, he is released. Where does he go? Right back out into the community. Instead of accepting him for what he is, we will see him as a "bad guy" or "ex-con" and every other negative connotation that can be depicted. There must be a breakdown in this structure if we ever expect a correctional rehabilitation program to be successful.

Vocational rehabilitation's own field program can alleviate or at least reduce some of the anxiety found within the community. By referring the ex-inmate to a counselor in the field with a complete case history developed by the rehabilitation team within the prison unit, there is a strong likelihood this counselor can become an influential link in the resocialization of the releasee.

To summarize vocational rehabilitation's overall commitment to the total correctional process and, in turn, the reintegration of the public offender back into the community, Table 10-I* has been provided.

As evidenced in Table 10-I, vocational rehabilitation can play a dynamic role in each step of the convicted individual's progress through the correctional process. Most often with the inmate, human dignity is lost. As professionals we must make every effort to restore or build this dignity into the person. A purpose in life

---

* This table adopted from a seminar presented by Mr. Robert Philbeck, State Coordinator for Correctional Rehabilitation, North Carolina Division of Vocational Rehabilitation. It is published with permission of Mr. Philbeck.

TABLE 10-I

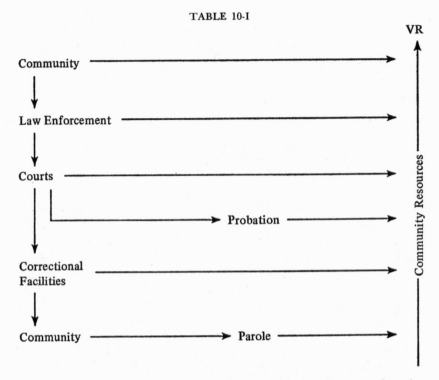

must be found and then appropriate action taken so that he might achieve his goal. Rehabilitation efforts can provide the impetus for the public offender to help himself.

ELIGIBILITY DETERMINATION OF
THE PUBLIC OFFENDER

People knowledgeable of the legal aspects of rehabilitation realize that before any state rehabilitation agency can provide vocational rehabilitation services, three basic criteria of eligibility must be met. Each of the following questions (criteria) must be answered "yes" before the client can be considered for rehabilitation services: (a) Does the individual have a disability? (b) Does the individual possess a handicap to employment? (c) Is there a reasonable expectation that vocational rehabilitation services may help the individual toward engagement in a gainful occupation?

These eligibility requirements were formulated and written

into law in 1920 via the Smith-Fess Act. Therefore, these criteria must be met no matter what target population or individual is being considered for services. The mere fact that a public offender is or has been incarcerated does not automatically signify he is eligible for rehabilitation services; he must have his eligibility established on the basis of an individual evaluation as is the case of *any* applicant for services (Fifth Institute of Rehabilitation Services, 1967).

Since 1965, the law does not state that the client's disability must be a handicap to employment; however, this relationship continues to be implied and has been the *modus operandi* for quite some time. But if rehabilitation is to advance realistically toward its goal of serving people, counselors must consider separately criterion one and criterion two. There is much more in determining eligibility than merely "checking off" whether or not a client meets or fulfills the basic requirements as established by federal law.

THE COUNSELOR'S RESPONSIBILITY IN SERVING THE INMATE POPULATION

We feel that incarceration definitely is a handicap to employment in and of itself. Imprisonment per se is a social stigma and has such an overbearing influence on the man after release that it is next to impossible for him to locate a suitable job. Citizens in the community do not differentiate between types of offenses committed let alone the type of people convicted for these crimes; citizens visualize the majority of inmates as hardened criminals committed to the institution for severely violating societal norms. As rehabilitation workers we must differentiate each inmate and individually evaluate his need for and desire to receive rehabilitation services.

As evidence of vocational rehabilitation's involvement with the correctional institution there can be established a mutual relationship for the ultimate objective of helping inmate-clients. But in order to do so the rehabilitation worker must make a justifiable alignment or assessment of personal and professional ideologies. Therefore, the acquisition of new values or at least a new perspective on old ones must be achieved prior to working with the correctional institution and specifically the inmate population (Colvin, 1972).

The Inmate: A Potential Rehabilitation Client

The inmate population in the United States is composed of a variety of people with different educational and vocational backgrounds as well as having a multitude of disabilities and handicapping conditions.

In 1968, one of the authors had the privilege of working with a psychiatrist at the North Carolina Department of Correction in an attempt to justify vocational rehabilitation's affiliation with the Department of Correction. A study was conducted by sampling one hundred consecutive admissions to the alcoholic ward. The purpose of this study was to examine the feasibility of establishing a cooperative agreement between the two agencies using contemporary correctional rehabilitation philosophy as a focal point.

Upon admission to this program, all men were given an extensive physical and psychiatric examination. Through these examinations it was anticipated that legal and medical authorities, as well as administrators in the social service agencies, might get a realistic appraisal of actual medical and psychological problems existing in a prison population. After a critical analysis of clinical findings the following diagnoses were reported:

1. Five of these one hundred inmates had severe hearing disorders which were not being treated, and these conditions were considered severe enough to warrant immediate treatment.
2. Five inmates had lung diseases in need of medical attention.
3. Ten people had severe problems with hypertension.
4. Twelve of the inmates had psychiatric problems such as paranoia, schizophrenia (including chronic undifferentiated type), acute and chronic brain syndrome, and mental deficiency with and without psychoses.
5. Five more inmates had acute infections which required immediate antibiotic treatment.

6. Another five needed surgery for hernias and hemorrhoids of a rather acute nature.*

7. Eighteen of the inmates needed other surgical and medical treatment for a variety of disorders.

The above represents 60 percent of the initial one hundred inmates sampled. A majority of these cases were assisted so that reasonable control of the disorder was achieved. The remaining 40 percent were by no means in excellent health; almost all inmates suffered from neglect and malnutrition, symptoms of gastritis, in addition to dental and visual problems.

Readers should not assume that the *entire* inmate population of this country is composed of such severe medical and emotional problems but one can extrapolate this data to gather that representative problems do exist in significant numbers to warrant further investigation by rehabilitation personnel. Also it should be realized that the problems described above have been compounded due to the inherent nature of the sample chosen for study (i.e. inmates entering the system diagnostically tagged "alcoholic"). And yet by the same token, of those public offenders arrested and convicted in the United States, many have attributed their getting into trouble to alcohol consumption. This observation leads to the inevitable. This sample does not deviate abnormally, after all, from the total inmate population. Therefore, by using our established criteria of eligibility it can be assumed that the majority of inmates need to be evaluated for possible rehabilitation services.

An item which immediately comes before us when we consider serving the inmate population is their exact location within the

---

* Familiarity with the word "acute" especially in terms of vocational rehabilitation nomenclature deserves further consideration here. These inmates with "acute" conditions had had a variety of medical and psychological disorders for an extended duration and at the time of imprisonment these disorders had increased in severity to the point that immediate medical attention was imperative to ensure reasonable recovery. In rehabilitation terminology the word "acute" means "having a short and relatively severe course" whereas "chronic" means "persisting over a long period of time" (Dorland's, 1965). Therefore, the chronicity of these various diagnoses is obvious and, in turn, would qualify them for rehabilitation consideration.

institution. The following is a description of how potential inmate-clients can be found so that the rehabilitation counselor can initiate contact.

All newly admitted inmates should be considered as automatic referrals and should be given an initial screening by vocational rehabilitation agency personnel. This needs to be done during the admission or quarantine period in order that a representative of the agency can meet with both the inmate and the classification board and participate in the planning of an appropriate program for the inmate (this should come about whether or not vocational rehabilitation has an active role). Of course, this is assuming vocational rehabilitation will have active participation in *all* intake cases, and disregarding the presence of traditional physical or mental disability cases as we have known it in the past. Clients selected for rehabilitation programs should be assigned to an individually tailored program for evaluation, physical and/or psychiatric restoration, education, training, or a combination of these services immediately after completion of the initial classification process.

All inmates currently participating in specific vocational training programs at the time of vocational rehabilitation's initial input should be screened by the correctional unit counselor. Those found to be ineligible will continue their assigned program through completion or until paroled. Subsequently, persons assigned to authorized vocational rehabilitation programs will be eligible clients of the agency. It is intended that a substantial majority of such trainees would fall within the latter category. Eventually as time permits, the backlog of the current population in other areas of the prison should be screened for possible rehabilitation services.

Variables to Consider in Serving the Inmate

The effects of extended unemployment, institutionalization, job obsolescence, and cultural deprivation may be basic considerations in determining the vocational handicap of public offenders for vocational rehabilitation services. Prime consideration also should be given to secondary disabilities since they so often hinder the client as much as primary disabilities in achieving successful vocational adjustment.

The significance of a "substantial handicap to employment" must be considered as well. The medical, psychological, vocational, educational, cultural, social, or environmental factors which may impede an individual's occupational performance affecting gainful employment should be weighed. Such factors as age, establishment of disability, and stability of residence also should be examined. If the client is eligible for rehabilitation services, he should be accepted by the counselor and a plan of services developed. As usual, the action must be based upon adequate diagnostic information and an accurate, realistic interpretation of the information that is secured by the counselor. Each rehabilitation inmate-client must be served on the basis of a sound plan rather than the sometimes unrealistic and whimisical needs of a counselor or his client.

In most bureaucratic organizations paperwork is a fundamental aspect of the job. Even though it is abhorred by staff, adequate records must be kept as is the case with any client being served by vocational rehabilitation. Case records should be complete to the point that if a counselor working with an inmate were to transfer or leave the institution, another counselor could resume activities without interrupting the inmate's plan.

Case records should contain as a minimum the following items to the extent pertinent for each client:

1. Data supporting the determination of eligibility or ineligibility.
2. Data supporting the decision to provide extended evaluation services to determine the rehabilitation potential for those individuals for whom the third condition of eligibility cannot be determined immediately, the extended evaluation plan, and progress reports on the extended evaluation.
3. Data relating to client participation in the cost of services if the agency elects to condition the provision of any services on the financial need of the client.

4. Data relating to the eligibility of the individual for similar benefits by way of pension, compensation, insurance or other benefits.

5. Data supporting the clinical status of the client's disabling condition as stable or slowly progressive in the event that the physical restoration services are provided after the establishment of the three basic conditions of eligibility.

6. Data supporting the decision to provide services to family members.

7. A vocational rehabilitation plan, setting forth the vocational rehabilitation objective of the individual, the services needed for his vocational rehabilitation (including services to family members) as determined through the case study and extended evaluation, if provided, and the way in which such services will be provided.

8. The reason and justification for closing the case, including the employment status of the client, and, if the case is closed as employed, the basis on which the employment was determined to be suitable.

9. Data supporting the provision of follow-up services after case closure to assist the individual to maintain his employment (*Federal Register*, 1969).

As with the traditional client population being served in the free community, the major objective of rehabilitation holds true for the inmate-client population working under the auspices of vocational rehabilitation, i.e. the process is culminated with successful placement and follow-up of the client on his job. The unique characteristic which distinguishes and differentiates the vocational rehabilitation process from all other types of counseling is its insistence upon the realistic and permanent vocational adjustment of the inmate-client as its primary objective. The possible services follow the gamut found in any rehabilitation setting: physical restoration; maintenance; transportation; vocational and related training; the provision of books, training materials, tools, equipment, initial stocks and supplies; job placement; and other goods and services necessary to complete successfully the rehabilitation of the individual.

Often a counselor asks what criteria should he take into consideration regarding the evaluation of potential inmate-clients for rehabilitation services. The following description has been developed by the North Carolina Division of Vocational Rehabilitation and the United States Probation Office. Regarding an *excellent* vocational rehabilitation prognosis, an inmate should have the majority of these characteristics: (a) age not over forty-five; (b) a very positive attitude toward work and self-rehabilitation efforts in his own behalf; (c) education (at least to the eighth grade); (d) disability stabilized or remedial to the point that the applicant is either mobile or potentially mobile to meet the demands of competitive employment, and in good general health; (e) possession of usable job skills or capacity to acquire job skills; (f) absences of social or family problems potentially detrimental to the rehabilitation outlook; (g) not isolated from potential job opportunity by area of residence or the inmate agrees to relocate if necessary.

An inmate with a *good* vocational rehabilitation prognosis should have the following characteristics: (a) not over sixty-five years of age; (b) literate—trainable for selective employment; (c) strongly motivated for work and participation in a rehabilitation program; (d) possessing satisfactory work records; (e) not grossly handicapped by any physical or mental condition; (f) not isolated from potential work or is amenable to relocate.

Inmates with other conditions not described above probably would be considered candidates for vocational rehabilitation services, or at least, they could be considered to have a guarded rehabilitation prognosis.

THE THREE CRITERIA OF ELIGIBILITY FOR VOCATIONAL REHABILITATION

The rehabilitation counselor's initial input toward any client's plan development deals primarily with eligibility determination. Let us return and separately examine each of the three criteria of eligibility. Not only must we look at the essential factors within each criterion, but we must evaluate the combined effects of establishing eligibility toward our ultimate objective of placing the inmate into the community as a productive member of the labor market.

Is There a Disability?

Medical Information

Before an inmate can receive rehabilitation services, the counselor must secure medical information showing the presence of a physical or mental disability. A counselor cannot determine eligibility following agency standards until the general medical report and the specialist's report have been procured and have become a part of the case records. This information should be presented in the form of a report from qualified physicians. Medical reports must contain, as a minimum, the diagnosis, prognosis, limitations, and recommendations of the examining practitoner.

Secondary and, in some cases, other established disabilities should be given utmost attention by the physician *and* the rehabilitation worker. All too often the counselor is concerned solely in finding the primary disability so that he may initiate services. We pose the question, "How can you be effective in prescribing a rehabilitation plan if you do not consider all facets which may influence the inmate's functional capacity?" Unfortunately many rehabilitation specialists provide services based only on the primary disability without considering the effects of other medically or psychiatrically diagnosed problems; this is especially true with counselors working with the inmate population.

A specialist's examination may be necessary whenever it is deemed appropriate by the counselor or his medical consultant in order to make a proper diagnosis. For many types of disabilities, a specialist's report is needed; specifically these reports are on: visual and hearing disabilities, tuberculosis, heart and lung impairments, mental or emotional disorders, amputations resulting from diabetes, gangrene, Buerger's disease, renal failure, and other disabilities not otherwise categorized or described adequately by the general practitioner.

To help the counselor further in his determination of eligibility he should attempt to gather as much information as possible from other medical resources rather than relying solely on the department of correction's medical facilities. As with counselors working outside of the prison system, the counselors within should procure medical information from other state and private agencies, hospitals, or resources the client may have employed in securing various services prior to his incarceration.

Psychiatric Reports

Before an inmate can receive services on the basis of mental illness or an emotional disorder, the counselor must secure an evaluation from a psychiatrist. When the inmate's suspected disability is that of a behavioral disorder or there are indications of mental or emotional disorders, a psychiatric evaluation is mandatory.

Psychiatric reports must include a diagnosis, any foreseeable limitations, as well as recommendations for services. If the counselor cannot obtain this information from the client's preincarceration records, such as from mental hospitals and mental health clinics within the client's area (s) of residence, it becomes necessary for the counselor to authorize and schedule an examination with the correctional psychiatrist. If the institution does not have a psychiatrist assigned to its staff, the counselor must seek the assistance of one located in the community.

In discussing some of the nomenclature prevalent in diagnostic categories, behavioral disorder is a term with many accepted meanings. In recent years it has been used to refer to the full range of psychiatric problems and, to some extent, it has sometimes been used as a synonym for sociopathic personality.

The American Psychiatric Association's (APA) *Diagnostic and Statistical Manual of Mental Disorders* uses the term "disorder" generically to designate a group of related psychiatric syndromes. The personality disorders are related to each other in that they show a relative predominance of unadaptive or maladaptive behavior, rather than subjective anxiety and other mental or emotional symptoms. The APA *Manual* groups broad types of personality disorders together and lists specific diagnoses associated with each. Included within the standard categories as outlined in the *Manual* is the following: "sociopathic personality disturbance." This means that the individual is ill primarily in terms of society and not only in terms of personal discomfort and interpersonal difficulties. This disturbance is very often symptomatic of severe underlying pathology, e.g. neurosis, psychosis, brain injury or disease. These underlying factors, understandably, should be diagnosed when recognized.

Of particular concern to the vocational rehabilitation counselor working within the correctional institution is the behavior disorder terms "antisocial reaction." Within this category chronic antisocial behavior is described (the individual is always in trouble; this individual does not profit from experience and maintains no real loyalty to any person, group, or code). He is frequently callous and shows marked lack of responsibility and judgment. Another trait the counselor should be aware of here is that the inmate-client is skilled at rationalizing his behavior so that it appears warranted and justified.

Dissocial reaction is another diagnosis which the counselor should consider in determining inmate eligibility. These people disregard usual social codes as a result of rearing in an abnormal moral environment. Even so, they may be capable of strong loyalties, and typically show no significant personality deviations other than adherence to the values and code of their own criminal, or other social groups (Nielson, 1968).

Sexual deviation and addiction (alcohol or drugs) are two categories deserving special attention when considering vocational rehabilitation's input. Using the definitions established by APA, one immediately can see the necessity of procuring adequate medical information including a psychiatric examination.

The first classification (sexual deviation) covers a wide range of problems including homosexuality, transvestism, pedophilia, fetishism, and sexual sadism such as rape, sexual assault, or mutilation. The rehabilitation counselor's responsibility is to evaluate the inmate possessing one or a combination of the above problems in terms of his potential adjustment and ultimately his job placement.

In the past, vocational rehabilitation and the other helping disciplines have had only limited contact with the sexual deviant primarily because the governing laws were such that an anticipated release date could not be secured since the inmate was usually not eligible for parole. Within the last decade courts have become more lenient in their sentencing and more rehabilitation-oriented; thence, judges have committed these people under the indeterminate sentence where specific psychiatric, vocational and educational programs are established for the inmate. An individual convicted today for rape has as good a chance to receive the majority of rehabilitation services as do misdemeanants or felons. He is considered for parole and has the same rights as other inmates within the correctional system.

Individuals committed for alcohol and drug addiction related crimes should be given every consideration for rehabilitation services. During the initial phase of commitment they may be segregated due to withdrawal or severe medical problems. The counselor should not divorce himself from the fact that even though the inmate is experiencing some immediate difficulties he may have problems necessitating vocational rehabilitation involvement.

From the above information it is obvious that people with many different kinds of personality problems potentially are eligible for services by reason of behavior or personality disorder. In the general agency program, a wide variety of these disorders may be seen, and the possibility of one of them should be kept in mind when an applicant (with or without an accompanying physical disability) shows a poor employment history. In correctional rehabilitation programs; the most common type of personality disorders will include the inadequate personality, the emotionally unstable personality, the passive-aggressive, and sociopathic disturbance.

Once the prospective inmate-client has received the diagnosis of behavior disorder and the rest of the diagnostic studies (including the general medical examination) has been completed, the other criteria of eligibility may then be applied.

Psychological Reports

Psychological evaluations are required in all cases where eligibility is based on suspected mental retardation. When the inmate's disability is that of behavioral disorder and there are indications of mental retardation, an evaluation by an agency-certified psychologist is mandatory. His evaluation of the inmate usually includes a valid test of intelligence, an assessment of social, functional, and educational progress and achievement. It is best to employ the services of a psychologist willing to give a battery of tests rather than a psychologist relying solely on a single test of intelligence and personality. This way you are increasing the probability of securing test results typical of the inmate's behavior patterns associated with intelligence and personality, rather than focusing in on a suspected atypical intelligence level or behavior pattern which may have arisen from one testing session. Even though many of the inmates with which the counselor will be working in the correctional institution have dropped out of school, psychological information and various test results often are available at the guidance counselor's office. This material may supplement information derived by the correctional psychologist.

Does the Inmate Have an Employment Handicap?

We must remind ourselves constantly of the phrase "substantial handicap to employment." In order to be determined eligible for rehabilitation services, the individual must possess a substantial handicap to employment which impedes an individual's occupational performance by preventing his obtaining, retaining, or preparing for a gainful occupation consistent with his capacities and abilities.

In making the judgment as to employment handicap, the counselor may take into account such factors as the effects of institutionalization or cultural deprivation on employment possibilities. In the determination of rehabilitation potential for many of these prospective clients, a clear dilemma exists. The prognosis is better for the nonsociopathic personality disorders than for those with genuine sociopathic trends. On the other hand, we may not refuse services solely on the basis of the disability. Whether a prospective client appears able to profit from services is always a matter for individual counselor decision, on the basis of a full case study investigation and taking into account the prognosis as seen by the physician, psychiatrist and/or psychologist. Extended evaluation, with the final determination based on the client's response to services, may sometimes be the answer but, as suggested in the Federal guidelines, "The only way we can, in the future, guide our efforts in rehabilitating persons with this disorder is to move ahead, using our good instincts, and provide services to them. We will then assess our results as we gain experience" (*Vocational Rehabilitation Manual*, 1971).

Another aid in helping the counselor determine eligibility is to secure the records regarding scholastic achievement, especially in those instances where vocational training is to be provided to the client-inmate. Additionally, school records as well as a transcript is required when the inmate is being considered for academic training, such as college, business school, and correspondence courses (Colvin, 1973).

Many correctional facilities today have professional staff members who compile a magnitude of social information on each inmate entering the system. This social history is of vital necessity for the vocational rehabilitation counselor's use in determining eligibility (if this report is not automatically sent to the counselor upon the inmate's admission, the counselor should take immediate steps to secure this information). In many instances social work agencies, hospitals, and other institutions have relevant social history information to supplement that which has already been developed. A signed release from the inmate should be made available to the counselor and, in turn, mailed to these other organizations so that they are assured material provided will be used with discretion.

Continuing with the concept developed previously regarding behavioral disorders and using it within the framework of the second criterion, an individual may exhibit abnormal behavior which persists over a period of time and manifests itself in various settings such as in school, on the job, before legal authorities, and even before his family. In some instances, the counselor may have to supplement psychiatric or psychological evaluations with reports from a variety of examiners and observers such as teachers, employers, probation officers, or members of social service agencies. The counselor's entering the inmate's home environment is not at all unreasonable if this enables him to better understand the problem (s) his client alleges. Such incidents of behavior, as family quarrels, arrests, truancy, or other idiosyncrasies or mannerisms do not, in and of themselves, constitute a behavioral disorder, but may be suggestive of this disability's existence.

Factors such as cultural and social deprivation, chronic poverty, public offense, illiteracy and educational deficit, and long-term unemployment do not constitute behavioral disorders by themselves, but may contribute to the formation of behavioral disorders at some later point in time. Therefore, when the counselor is studying psychiatric reports, he should look for material which may help him in deciding whether or not the inmate has an employment handicap.

Other employment handicaps are as follows: a lack of marketable skills, low educational level, community and employer prejudices, and poor or ill-defined attitudes concerning disability, long-term unemployment, unstable work record, belonging to a disadvantaged group, residence in ghetto areas or pockets of poverty, long history of dependency, and poor attitudes toward work, family, and community. As an example, Alexander (1966) has estimated that approximately 90 percent of federal public offenders do not have appropriate or adequate work skills.

Often overlooked in determining inmate eligibility is the expected date of release from the institution. The counselor must make a realistic appraisal of intended services to be provided an inmate in relation to this date. It would seem ridiculous to sponsor someone for vocational training lasting only twelve months if the inmate just entered the prison under a twenty year sentence; and yet if we are dedicated to the philosophy of our profession, we *must* entertain this notion.

With the assistance of the prison's administration, especially the classification committee and the parole board, a counselor should know and have recorded in each inmate's casefolder a tentative release date. As additional information is derived regarding this date more definitive action should take place. The ultimate objective would be to correlate development of the re-habilitation plan with the release date so that upon termination of institutionalization the inmate would be ready to reenter the community and take a job commensurate with his training.

Is There Reasonable Expectation That Vocational Rehabilitation Services Will Help the Individual Attain a Gainful Occupation?

Since vocational rehabilitation's involvement in correctional work, there has been argument regarding the term "rehabilita-tion" of the inmate. If rehabilitation services are successful only to the extent of enabling an incarcerated public offender to be-come employed within the correctional setting, such as in prison industry, the requirements of gainful occupation as defined in the Federal guidelines are not met. Often it is difficult to predict an exact date of release from prison; therefore, flexibility should be exercised in attempting to synchronize the completion of a re-habilitation plan with the projected release date. This plan must provide a continuum of services not only during the man's im-prisonment but also after his release to the free community (Newman, 1970).

Inmates should not be considered rehabilitated until they have either been released from the institution and appropriately placed at a job in the community or they have been placed in a job via a work release program. In order to meet the require-ments of gainful employment, a work release program must in-clude the following elements:

1. Employment in a job outside the prison system.
2. Compensation is within the standards established by federal labor laws.
3. Wages earned are for the benefit of the individual and/or his family. As stated in the federal guidelines, this would not preclude a reasonable portion of wages earned to be used in defraying the inmate's living expenses while incar-cerated or expenses associated with the job.
4. Work is productive and on a predetermined schedule.
5. Services, including placement in the work-release program,

have been carried out in accordance with an approved vocational rehabilitation plan (*Vocational Rehabilitation Manual*, 1971).

However, whether the client is in an instutition or in the free world, the rehabilitation counselor has the responsibility of judging the client's rehabilitation potential. The rehabilitation counselor is better able to predict future behavior of clients from the general community than that of those from prisons. The client has established a much more predictable life-style. This responsibility of judging rehabilitation potential is more difficult at times with a prison population. The client in the prison community has a much less predictable behavior pattern; he also has established a life-style which is interpreted as a failure when judged by society's criterion of adjustment (e.g., the individual is a contributing and productive member of the community).

Probably the rehabilitation counselor's most valuable tool in determining eligibility and specifically the third criterion of eligibility is that of extended evaluation. The provisions for extended evaluation are relatively new since they were added to the rehabilitation process in 1965 with the passage of Public Law 89-333. Briefly defined, the law reads that if the counselor is unsure of the client's rehabilitation potential, the counselor may provide a majority of the rehabilitation services to the client in extended evaluation. This is done in order to determine his rehabilitation potential or to establish the fact there is a reasonable expectation that after rehabilitation services are provided the client will become gainfully employed.

The counselor who is unsure of a client's rehabilitation potential should use the extended evaluation approach rather freely. While the client is in this status the counselor should use consultations with other members of the rehabilitation unit as well as with the wide variety of institution employees who have contact with the inmate-client. These consultations are used to determine such things as the client's attitude toward work; his attitude toward authority figures and direct supervision; his skills as a worker (not technical vocational skills, but skills such as perseverance, initiative, ability to get along with fellow employees, and consistency of effort); his attitude toward himself and his concept of his future; his level of motivation; and his willingness or ability to accept as his goals the goals of another individual or an organization. For it is these attributes and attitudes which determine his potential for rehabilitation.

Conclusion

The extension and provision of limited vocational rehabilitation services to the public offender has been made possible through legislative developments and the determination of a few dedicated people. But before inmate rehabilitation can be considered successful, the counselor must understand his role in relation to the correctional institution and its personnel, his relationship with the public offender himself, and complementary programs outside the institution that provide auxiliary services.

The realization of our rehabilitation efforts can be summarized in the following article by George Fraleigh.*

The Last Night

It wasn't so bad while the lights were on. He could pace up and down, making his legs tired, hoping he'd be able to sleep, but knowing he was only kidding himself. He could walk his legs off up to his knees and there would be no sleep for him on his last night.

The lights went out the way they always do in prison, with something akin to a mild shock to him. One minute there was light, then there were darkness, no click of light switch as a warning, just the sudden transition from light to dark and it still was able to shake him up, even after the nights that had gone by.

He stopped his restless pacing and sat on the edge of the bed. Even in stocking feet he might get a rumble from the guy in the cell below. Prisoners are sensitive to even the faint vibration from barefoot pacing on the floor above them and he didn't want to set the joint off into a bedlam of angry shouting and cursing. Not on his last night in this world. Might as well go out with a few good words behind him instead of shouted invective.

He remained on the bed until the steel edge cutting into the under-

* This article appeared in the May-June 1969 issue of the *Island Lantern*, published by men of the U.S. Penitentiary, McNeil Island, Washington. Acknowledgement is extended to the author and the editor of the *Island Lantern*.

side of his legs stopped the blood and his feet began to feel numb, then prickled with a thousand needle points as he stood up and silently jiggled first one foot, then the other in the air shaking off the numbness the way he was trying to shake off the terror which was hovering silently over his head waiting for the morning to pounce.

He walked to the barred front of the cell and leaned his hot forehead against the cold steel. Funny how it was always cold, winter and summer the bars were always cold. The cement walls, too, they never warmed up. His hands came up and grasped the bars above his head as high as he could reach while his eyes sought to pierce the darkness over the water that surrounded the island prison.

A tug with red and white running lights fore and aft moved into view, the sound of its diesels a faint chug-chug in the distance, and a few minutes later low lying lights followed, seeming to be riding on top of the water. He knew they were the riding lights on a huge log raft which the tug was towing to the mill. He'd looked out the same window in the daylight and watched the tugs as they strained against the current with their log rafts fighting, inch by inch it seemed, to master the powerful pull of the tide sweeping relentlessly in from the ocean.

The tug and its raft disappeared and he turned wearily away and sought the refuge of his bed, covering his burning eyes with his arms, trying to shut out even the blackness of his cell, trying to escape the spectre which haunted the darkness. Tomorrow it would be all over. They'd come for him early, he knew, they always came early so they could get it over with and go on with their daily routine. They'd walk him down the long corridor, one on each side of him, through the door at the end and there it would be, waiting. He wondered if he could go quietly and expressionlessly the way most of the others went. He hoped so. It wouldn't do any good to make a fuss. Tomorrow morning was his last day and he had to go and all the fighting and screaming and dragging his feet wouldn't change a thing.

He wondered how severe the shock would be. Pretty bad, the way he heard it told, but it only lasted an instant, they said. Maybe the pain came later. He'd never talked to anyone about that though, he'd never seen anyone who'd come back. He was starting to sweat now, could feel the runnels of sticky perspiration coursing down his face, trickling off his chest, sliding down his legs. He leaped off the bed in sudden panic, stood on the cold floor, felt the icy cement through the soles of his stockings, fought the trembling that wracked his body like an attack of ague. Then reason took over, he sank back into the bed and stared wide-eyed at the ceiling. He wanted a cigarette but he knew what it would taste like, hot and acrid in his feverish mouth, so he fought down the craving while he tried to recall events which had led up to his last night. Everything was a confused jumble in his mind and he couldn't sort out the pieces. It had all started too long ago and too many things had happened between then and now, and anyway, all that mattered was that in a few hours he'd be walking down that long, long corridor and through that door. They'd take his prison clothes off him and give him new ones, fresh and clean, and they'd walk with him through the last door and down the road, put him on the boat, then, turn around and walk away, and he'd be all alone in the free world, all alone.

REFERENCES

Alexander, M.: The disabled public offender in federal institutions. In Margolin, R. J. et al. (Eds.): *Effective Approaches to the Rehabilitation of the Disabled Public Offender.* Boston, Department of Rehabilitation and Special Education, Northeastern University, 1966.

American Psychiatric Association: *Diagnostic and Statistical Manual of Mental Disorders (DSM-11).* Washington, D. C., 1968.

Colvin, C. R.: The correctional institution and vocational rehabilitation. In Cull, J. G. and Hardy, R. E. (Eds.): *Vocational Rehabilitation: Profession and Process.* Springfield, Thomas, 1972.

————: The role of higher education in corrections. In Cull, J. G. and Hardy, R. E. (Eds.): *Fundamentals of Criminal Behavior and Correctional Systems.* Springfield, Thomas, 1973.

Department of Health, Education and Welfare, Social and Rehabilitation Services: *Federal Register.* Washington, D. C., Vol. 34, Number 200, Part II, October 17, 1969.

Dorland's Illustrated Medical Dictionary, 24th ed. Philadelphia, W. B. Saunders Co., 1965.

Fulton, W. S. (Ed.): *A Future for Correctional Rehabilitation.* Final Report, Federal Offenders Rehabilitation Program, November, 1969. State of Washington, Division of Vocational Rehabilitation, Research and Demonstration Grants, Social and Rehabilitation Services, Department of Health, Education and Welfare.

Newman, E.: General counsel ruling re: Closure of cases of offenders remaining institutionalized. Social and Rehabilitation Services, Department of Health, Education and Welfare. Transmittal Letter to Associate Regional Commissioners, July 16, 1970.

Nielson, W. M.: *Establishing Eligibility on Grounds of "Behavior Disorder,"* Psychological Consultant's Memorandum No. 68-1, North Carolina Division of Vocational Rehabilitation. Raleigh, February 14, 1968.

Fifth Institute of Rehabilitation Services: *Rehabilitation of the Public Offender.* U. S. Department of Health, Education and Welfare, Rehabilitation Services Series Number 68-36, May 22-25, 1967.

Tessler, N.: In Margolin, R. J. et al. (Eds.): *Effective Approaches to the Re-habilitation of the Disabled Public Offender.* May, 1966, Northeastern University, Contract No. VRA 66-35, Vocational Rehabilitation Administration, Department of Health, Education and Welfare.

Vocational Rehabilitation Manual. Washington, D. C., Department of Health, Education and Welfare, Chap. 13, 1967.

Vocational Rehabilitation Manual. Washington, D. C., Department of Health, Education and Welfare, Chap. 16, June, 1971.

CHAPTER 11

GROUP COUNSELING IN THE CORRECTIONAL SETTING

- Further Definition
- What Is Group Counseling and Therapy?
- Differences in Group Counseling and Group Psychotherapy
- Qualifications for Group Counseling Work
- Client Characteristics
- Grouping Inmates
- Goals of Group Counseling
- Group Leadership Methods

COUNSELING HAS BEEN USED as a tool in various therapeutic settings mainly on an individual or one-to-one basis. Recent research has indicated that not only can counseling be done in groups, but there is considerable therapeutic value in the interaction among members of an intimate group. Since professional therapeutic staff persons in prisons are in short supply and group counseling has been shown to be highly effective, it is only natural that the process of group counseling is becoming more widely accepted in the correctional setting.

FURTHER DEFINITION

Delinquent or criminal acts are committed by people at all levels in the society. There is no class of criminals versus noncriminals. There is a group of the "caught" versus the "non-caught."

We can ascertain from the study of arrest records, probation reports, and other statistics related to penal systems that the offender is an individual who has been disadvantaged in education, mental, and physical health. He is likely a member of the lower socioeconomic group who is poorly educated, has been underemployed, is probably unmarried, a product of a broken home, and more than likely has a prior criminal record.

The stereotyping of public offenders just as that of other individuals is a dangerous procedure and this should be carefully noted. Not all offenders fit any composite profile. We must remember that the portrait of the offender just described is taken from those who have been arrested, tried, and sentenced. Many persons, as previously indicated, who are guilty of crime are not included in the portrait. Statistics based on national arrest records indicate that when all offenses are considered together the majority of offenders are over twenty-four years of age, white, and male. The great majority of persons arrested for fraud, embezzlement, gambling, drunkenness, offenses against the family, and vagrancy are over twenty-four years of age. The younger group, those fifteen to seventeen are the ones who commit the most burglaries, larcenies, and auto thefts. Statistics show that males are arrested nearly seven times more frequently than females (I.R.S., 1967).

In terms of the socioeconomic family dimensions of offenders it can be said that often the person is a homeless male, single, divorced, or separated, likely to have had an unstable marriage. He is highly mobile having probably recently changed his residence. He may very well be a member of a minority group and have experience with cultural deprivation. He probably is dependent on public welfare or some other type of financial aid. Intelligence appears to be fairly normally distributed in the offender population. Getting work is a major problem for this group of people and keeping work once it is attained is an additional problem.

In terms of psychological aspects, the offender often is a person who has isolated himself somewhat from others. He tends to be suspicious and to "act out" or have difficulty controlling his impulses. He often is a hypermanic or overactive type of person. He may have difficulty in planning his activities and thinking out various alternative approaches for action. Often there is considerable hostility. In addition, offenders may have problems with alcoholism, sexual deviance, and narcotics addiction. The number who are emotionally disturbed and mentally ill is significant.

Group counseling can probably be of particular value to the offender soon after he is incarcerated. After remaining in the penal system for some time he will become accustomed to the institutional way of life and group counseling or any other type of counseling is hampered. Toward the end of the inmate's stay in prison, group or individual counseling again has a better chance for success since he is planning on getting himself ready for the outside world and is more receptive than when he is in the middle of a long stay in a penal institution.

WHAT IS GROUP COUNSELING AND THERAPY?

According to Moreno, "group psychotherapy" means simply to treat people in groups. A composite definition of group counseling has been presented by Gazda. "Group counseling is a dynamic interpersonal process focusing on conscious thought and behavior and involving the therapy functions of permissiveness, orientation to reality, catharsis, and mutual trust, caring, understanding, acceptance, and support. The therapy functions are creative and nurtured in a small group through the sharing of personal concerns with one's peers and the counselor (s)" (Gazda, 1970).

In group counseling, counselees are basically normal individuals with various concerns which are not debilitating to the extent requiring extensive personality change. The counselors will utilize the group interaction to increase understanding and acceptance of values and goals and to learn and/or unlearn certain attitudes and behaviors (Gazda et al., 1967).

In group counseling the leader of the group attempts to get members involved in various relationships in order that his (the leader's) role can be reduced. The leader functions by reflecting the feelings as he interprets them of others and gives meaning to what is said by all members of the group. The leader serves as a catalyst in helping different members of the group understand fully what is said or felt by other members of the group. He minimizes differences in perceptions by helping explain the thoughts and feelings of others. He reflects the general feelings of the group.

Of course, he must initially establish certain rules covering the behavior of the group in terms of confidentiality, the general requirements of group members, etc. The group leader often varies his role according to the needs of the group. He may function as facilitator, resource person, or client. Above all, he constantly demonstrates his feeling of warmth and genuine positive regard and respect for the honestly given perceptions and reactions of each member. He provides a role model which group members may use during the group session.

DIFFERENCES IN GROUP COUNSELING
AND GROUP PSYCHOTHERAPY

Group psychotherapy is at a more advanced stage in its development than is group counseling. Group counseling usually is oriented in the Adlerian client-centered or eclectic approach. Stefflre (1965) in his *Theories of Counseling* has said that "indeed, most theorists in the field would agree that counseling is a learning process, although there they may have sharp differences as to what facilitates learning and how learning occurs." According to Gazda (1970), group counseling and group psychotherapy lie on a continuum with an overlapping of goals and professional competencies, but the subtle distinctions are evident in expressions such as "basically normal counselees" focusing on conscious thought and behavior and concerns which are not debilitating to the extent requiring extensive personality change. Counseling is usually described as supportive, situational, and educational in terms of conscious awareness and of a short-term nature. Psychotherapy has been characterized as reconstructive, in depth and analytical, with an emphasis on the unconscious, the neurotic, and severe emotional problems. Psychotherapy is thought of as being of a long-term nature. Truax reported that group cohesiveness was one of three group conditions significantly related to interpersonal exploration. It is extremely important for a cooperative group spirit to exist and there must be empathy among all the clients. Truax (1963) has also stated that the group is perhaps more potent in its effects on interpersonal exploration than is the therapist.

QUALIFICATIONS FOR GROUP COUNSELING WORK

First of all, the group counselor must have a genuine and sympathetic interest in other human beings in order to be effective. He must be a stable individual of considerable insight and maturity. He must have considerable knowledge of psychology and interhuman processes.

Along with these characteristics go appropriate attitudes which allow the group leader to work with inmates of minority groups, ability to handle hostility when inmates direct it at him or other group members. A very important characteristic is knowing when one is in "over his head" in group work and when to request help from individuals more sensitive or competent.

The group leader's role is quite difficult. It requires considerable study, practical types of experience, and a high degree of personal development.

The inmate must be willing to trust the group leader. The leader must be recognized by them as one who will not betray them and he must be able to accept members of the group no matter what their status in life is or their level of adjustment.

The novice in group work, whether he plans to be a lay leader or later a professional group worker, must recognize that there is a substantial body of knowledge to be mastered. He must also recognize the need for supervision by persons trained in group work and he will wish to participate as a group member under the leadership of a highly trained person before deciding he is ready to take on the leadership of the group.

Group work with inmates can be very rewarding. At times it will be difficult to see whether or not progress is being made, and in some cases, inmates will notice growth behavior in others before the group leader becomes aware of this phenomenon. As inmates become better adjusted, they will become more friendly toward other inmates and staff persons. They will be more interested in their previous friends and family. They will react more effectively interpersonally among their peers. Some inmates will take on leadership responsibilities within the group. Group leaders should not become overly concerned in attempting to measure change or progress in his group. This measurement will be particularly difficult in the early days of the group meetings when it is probably most necessary for the group leader to see that he is accomplishing some goals. The leader should expect no rapid changes in behavior. He should just continue his group meetings in an atmosphere of acceptance refraining at all times from authoritarianism.

CLIENT CHARACTERISTICS

The client must be open and genuine if he is to profit fully. He must honestly and genuinely seek to improve his adjustment by understanding his behavior and the reaction of other persons toward him. Truax (1963) reported that as the genuineness of group members in the psychotherapy relationship increases, so does the amount of depth of intrapersonal exploration, the development of insight, and the rate of personal references.

One of the problems which exists in working with clients in penal institutions centers around the fact that they are involuntarily in residence. These persons must understand the therapeutic effects of group counseling to wish to open themselves from the point of view of reviewing personal inadequacies in order to improve their adjustment. If they are permitted to participate for a long enough period to experience basic therapeutic effects, they often will feel much less defensive. The counselor must allow persons who wish to leave the group and not participate to do so.

Counseling in therapy groups does not have highly defined group goals as they may be wished for in vocational advising or counseling. The emphasis is on effective, honest communication. Group counseling is much more goal-oriented than is group therapy. In school settings and similar group settings, goals can be somewhat specific. The counselor will always have to remember that no matter how well individuals accept general goals of the group, the client's goals are always his own.

GROUPING INMATES

Often it will be necessary for the counselor to try trial placements in groups since it is difficult to know how given individuals will react once in a specific group. After several group meetings, the permanency of groups can be established by shifting persons from one group to another. The counselor may want to start with twice as many members in a group as he wants and then divide the group according to the members who seem to fit together in a way which will be most conducive to achieving maximum therapeutic usefulness in the group.

In conducting groups within penal settings, the counselor or therapist will often find that participants are hostile and involuntary. Corsini (1951) has shown that clients can become much more accepting of the group through the technique of the counselor's demonstration of understanding and his reflection of the reason for their hostile feelings.

The research on homogeneous versus heterogeneous groupings has given us little to use in terms of knowing which is most effective. When persons are in homogeneous groups in terms of personality structure, each group member often tends to reinforce another's pattern of behavior. Heterogeneous groups seem to give more learning material to the group as a whole and for this reason heterogeneous groups may be more effective. Certainly groups cannot consist of all aggressive, dominating or shy persons or all persons with psychopathic personalities if groups are to be effective and people are to learn from one another.

The counselor will wish to hold the diagnostic screening interview with each prospective counselee. This will be necessary so that persons can be screened in and out of the grouping experience and so that individuals who are about to join the group will understand how the group operates. They can then make a decision concerning whether they wish to become a member of the group or not. Once the group has begun, it is the responsibility of the leader to explain such matters as confidentiality, attendance, and the right of the leader to remove the person from a group and set certain structures concerning meals, use of bathroom facilities, etc.

GOALS OF GROUP COUNSELING

The group leader must remember that if group counseling is to be effective, it must be a growth experience for the inmate. The inmate must move toward developing from the point of view of maturing of attitudes toward himself and toward others. He must ask himself the question, "What will life consist of in future days?" The answer is often only his to give.

Group counseling should provide an inmate the opportunity to learn about his own individual personality and how it serves him in his relationships with others. He should be helped to understand any unrealistic, fantasy, or day-dreaming behavior that reflect his general adjustment. He must understand the price that he must pay for various types of behavior. Group counseling should offer inmates an opportunity to evaluate and study their own feelings and beliefs and those of others in a constructive group setting. In groups, inmates should be allowed to "spill out" their hostilities and painful experiences with impunity in order that their anxiety may be reduced. One of the substantial advantages of group counseling and therapy is that persons realize their problems are not unique. Other inmates have had the same problematic situation. Group counseling should help the inmate in his adjustment within the institution and improve his ability to adjust once he is outside the institution. Generally, it should improve relationships between staff and inmates within the prison by helping inmates to maintain self-control and develop attitudes of acceptance toward other inmates and prison personnel.

The purpose of group counseling and therapy in prison is not the prevention of escapes or elimination of various in-house troubles; but its main purpose is that of treatment—getting the inmates ready to return to society.

GROUP LEADERSHIP METHODS

1. Upon the initial meeting of the group, join them as a member. Take no immediate leadership role.
2. Introduce yourself once the group has started by giving your name and any other information you wish to give about yourself.
3. Ask the inmates to introduce themselves and say something briefly about themselves.
4. If you are asked the purpose of the group, you may wish to

say that it is simply to help everyone become better adjusted, not only to prison life, but to life on the outside once they are released.

5. The leader must convince the members of the confidentiality of the various sessions. They should be told that whatever is said within the group is not reported to anyone's parole officer, supervisor, etc. Notes should not be taken by the group leader. Generally, it is also best to avoid transcriptions such as tape recording. If the leader must use tape recordings, the purpose of these should be for the group to use in playback sessions in order that they may continue discussions about the group and what has occurred. This procedure should be fully explained.

The group leader should be very cautious, especially at the beginning of group sessions, about getting into highly personal matters related to any crime and/or victims of a crime. He might use as a guideline how he would feel if he were an inmate member of the group and was being questioned about his previous behavior. He must control his eagerness to have all inmates participate at an early period. The group leader will have to learn to relax and bring very little or no pressure on persons in the preliminary sessions of the group.

The leader and group members must remember that in the beginning the group is simply a number of individuals getting together with no specific purposes. It is, in fact, a small meeting of inmates. As the leader begins to move the group and the group members become interested in one another, the group takes on special therapeutic qualities. Some members of the group will be indifferent and skeptical; others will be just attentive; and some will be very active. The group leader keeps the group on a constructive plane; and, while the situation is highly unstructured, he keeps the group from wasting time with "chit-chat" which is meaningless.

The group leader will have to be willing to modify the continuity of the exchanges in groups according to the atmosphere of the prison. For instance, when unpleasant custodial incidents happen in prison, it may be necessary for the group to spend several days discussing various reactions to these events. At this time, the group leader will be recognized even more as an authority figure and a member of the oppressor group, and suspicions and hostilities among group members may be rampant.

He should get across to inmates that the success of the group will be in accordance with what they are able to give to it. In other words, the inmate should understand that unless he is able to talk about how he feels without undue shame during group sessions, he may not get highly helpful feedback from the other group members. The inmate must be frank and be able to look at himself and open himself to others; he must face his problems and explain them as he sees them to others as honestly and genuinely as he can. The inmate must understand that one of the basic goals of group counseling or therapy concerns the handling of impulsive behavior—that which leads to criminal acts. The inmate must learn to handle anxiety feelings, inferiority feelings, and various types of hate and hostility feelings and he must understand that his previous behavior has been extremely costly. He must try to understand why he is in the group, whether he is just trying to get out of prison earlier or whether he wants to be more effectively adjusted once he is outside.

Conclusion

In the prison setting, the emphasis is most often on incarceration rather than treatment; in fact, the atmosphere may not be supportive of treatment concepts. There is often considerable hostility among the inmates and other employees within the prison. These factors influence the attitudes of inmates throughout therapy periods and not only in the beginning sessions. This is why it is particularly important for inmates to understand the purposes and nature of the group work. It is also important for the leader to promise little in terms of results.

Problems often can arise when new inmates enter groups that are on-going; and, in fact, when there is a substantial turnover, the demise of the group can come about. The turnover also can be used effectively in that, in a sense, "new blood" is put into the group as inmates experience on a deeply personal level various new individuals who may wish to sit and listen in their first few sessions and later join in after seeing what advantages have come to older group members through participation. Group leaders should not expect new members of the group to join in too rapidly to the in-depth experience which should be taking place.

The group leader may want to continue his groups indefinitely by allowing persons to drop out and enter, or he may want to bring certain groups to a close according to the feeling of the group members after several sessions. There is no set standard for the number of times the group will meet. In terms of time, two or three hours may be used, or the leader may wish to continue his sessions for six or seven hours. This should be, in effect, decided by members of the group. When groups are of the long-term nature, the leader will gradually learn about individuals in the group. He does not have to spend a great deal of time at the outset in studying case materials; he may learn about the individuals more effectively through interacting with them in the group. The group leader may want to use films or various other materials such as readings, or he may want to simply proceed with interaction among group members.

Role playing can be particularly important and effective with inmates playing the role of the victim, or the victim's relative, or the police. There is always a certain awkwardness in beginning role playing. It often carries with it tremendous anxiety feelings for those who are involved. It is certainly work, however, this amount of unpleasant feeling for all in terms of its end-results.

Role playing can become what has been called "psychodrama" a more complicated and in-depth type of experience which can bring on deeply emotional episodes. The group leader must be particularly effective when this type of in-depth involvement is taking place. The counselor should stay away from this technique unless he has had sufficient training to handle the feelings which may ensue.

As the group continues, some inmates will request individual counseling. This is a good sign that the inmate has real faith in the group leader and the individual counseling should be provided.

Some basic assumptions in counseling are as follows:

1. The client has enough freedom to make his own decisions.
2. The counseling session is a special kind of learning situation.
3. Behavior is learned and, therefore, can be changed.
4. The counselor not only recognizes individual differences in his client, but sincerely respects these differences.
5. The total welfare of the client is the counselor's primary consideration in the counseling process.
6. The counselor is sincere in his desire to help his client.
7. The needs of the counselor are fulfilled mostly outside the counseling session and, therefore, are not expressed in the counseling process at the client's expense.
8. The client is willing to assume some of the responsibility for bringing about changes in himself which will result in the kind of person he wants to become.

REFERENCES

Crosini, R.: The theory of change resulting from group therapy. *Group Psychother, 3,* 1951.

Cull, J. G. and Hardy, R. E.: *Fundamentals of Criminal Behavior and Correctional Systems.* Springfield, Thomas, 1973.

Fenton, Norman: *An Introduction to Group Counseling in Correctional Service.* Washington, D. C., The American Correctional Association, 1959.

Gazda, George M.: *Basic Approaches to Group Psychotherapy and Group Counseling.* Springfield, Thomas, 1970.

Gazda, George M., Duncan, J. A., and Meadows, M. E.: Counseling and group procedures—Report of a survey. *Counselor Education and Supervision, 6:*305, 1967.

Institute on Rehabilitation Services: *Rehabilitation of the Public Offender, A Training Guide.* Washington, D. C., U. S. Department of Health, Education and Welfare, Rehabilitation Services Administration, 1967.

Stefflre, Buford: *Theories of Counseling,* New York, McGraw-Hill, 1965.

Truax, C. B.: Effective ingredients in psychotherapy: An approach to unraveling the patient-therapist interaction. *J Counsel Psychol, 10,* 1963.

CHAPTER 12

WORKING WITH THE
FUNCTIONALLY RETARDED

- Confusion in Definition
- Collecting the Data
- Activities of Daily Working
- An Abbreviated Case Study for Demonstration Purposes

CONFUSION IN DEFINITION

FUNCTIONAL RETARDATION is a disability which is causing great confusion in rehabilitation, education, and other social service agencies. Many counselors and rehabilitation agencies do not recognize functional retardation as a disability. Some agencies designate the condition as a disability which may impose handicapping conditions, but the concept of the condition is hazy. Some professionals view functional retardation as mental retardation. The end result is that few of the unemployed who are handicapped as a result of functional retardation are being provided rehabilitation services. In the opinion of the authors, functional retardation is in existence when an individual is functioning at the retarded range academically and emotionally but not psychometrically. That is, he is at least two or more years behind his age level in academic achievement. He is somewhat immature and tends to prefer a younger group of persons than his chronological age group or if he identifies with the chronological age group, these individuals tend to be functional retardates themselves. In other words, he is academically retarded, emotionally retarded, and socially retarded; although psychometrically he may be average or above average in intelligence. Therefore, by definition he

203

is not mentally retarded but is functioning as if he were retarded.

It is easy to understand this apparent paradox when one considers the environment in which individual intelligence tests are administered. The psychologist establishes a warm accepting, non-threatening environment in which the client is encouraged to perform at his highest capacity. However, when the individual leaves the testing environment and is forced to interact in the everyday world the functionally retarded is unable to maintain his demonstrated level of adjustment.

COLLECTING THE DATA

In order to make the decision concerning whether or not an individual is functionally retarded, one of the first problems concerns sources of information. How can we establish an information system which can be used to clarify the confusion which exists in the area of making persons eligible for rehabilitation services who are functioning as retardates but scoring in the borderline or higher ranges of normal intelligence on intelligence tests? Information generally comes from several sources: the physician, the educator, the psychologist, and the social worker. These sources and others must be utilized fully if we are to complete a useful composite picture of value which will give us a clear definition of retardation. The counselor needs to have a broader understanding of environmental causes of decreased intellectual functioning in order to help the person overcome as many inhibiting factors as possible.

In dealing with the psychological, social, and educational aspects of retardation, the counselor must remember that persons who are called "normal" or "retarded" in intelligence are relegated to two mutually exclusive groups. We have been too rapid in our efforts to draw a distinct line of differentiation between these two groups, and intelligence tests alone are just not rigorous enough to bear the responsibility of designating individuals as being eligible or ineligible for rehabilitation services on the basis of a specific score.

The rehabilitation counselor needs to have a broad understanding of any condition which impedes the progress of the individual. This concept is particularly important in work with border-line retarded persons because now they are erroneously classified as ineligible (nonretarded) for services in many cases when in fact they are *functioning* on a retarded level. In addition, if the individual is classed as retarded and therefore eligible for rehabilitation services, he must be restored to his fullest potential through the vocational rehabilitation program. The point being stressed here is the importance of using a broad gauged approach to understanding and interpreting physical, social, educational, and psychological conditions which affect the functional level of the client. The counselor should evaluate medical reports carefully. Pathology, treatment, and prevention approaches should be outlined in the medical report. The combination of medical, psychological, and social data should help the counselor in developing a schema for definition purposes.

Correct and early identification of functional retardation is extremely important in that deprivation in youth adversely affects the ability to achieve in later life. The ideal time to identify, diagnose, and serve the functionally retarded individual is in late adolescence in order that the youngster can develop good adjustment habits. If rehabilitation counselors wait until early adulthood or later to provide rehabilitation services to the individual, the client by that time will have developed a chronic personality pattern which is almost impossible to change. Additionally, the client will be almost devoid of information about jobs and the world of work. For this reason, it is difficult to overemphasize knowing clients well, especially adolescent "functionally retarded" clients. When persons having learning handicaps, a thorough understanding of their background becomes most important. Complete case recording is essential in order to determine the eligibility of a functionally retarded individual. To neglect the full development of information in this complex area of eligibility determination for rehabilitation services is often equivalent to denying the client's eligibility for services.

ACTIVITIES OF DAILY WORKING

Doyle and Seidenfeld (1965) have offered excellent suggestions on the general subject of defining retardation behavioristically as opposed to the traditional psychometric definition. The concepts they discuss have been called Activities of Daily Working (ADW). Activities of Daily Working include:

1. Can the individual adapt to and accept the impact of interpersonal relationships with the people on the job?
2. Can he successfully get to and from work on a regularly available form of transportation?
3. Can he understand and perform all regular activities of the job on which he is placed, and does he have sufficient flexibility to perform and emotionally tolerate at least two other related jobs to which he may be displaced?
4. Can he understand the importance of carrying out time and attendance obligations of the job?
5. Does he possess sufficient initiative to maintain job performance at acceptable levels with no more supervision than the employer or the supervisor believes feasible?
6. Does he possess sufficient emotional stability to remain on the job until his work merits advancement or until a supervisor can correct annoyances?
7. Does he possess sufficient basic educational skills to manage himself without undue dependence on others to interpret or explain what is expected of him?
8. Does he possess sufficient self-control and social judgment to prevent others from taking advantage of his mental limitations?
9. Does he manage all of his ordinary financial activities without help from others?

The work evaluator's report is of real use in developing a case for or against eligibility for rehabilitation services in that it answers many of the above questions. An individual who is capable of functioning at the average level on a psychometric test, but who is not able to function in these activities of daily working is definitely a functionally retarded individual in that he is behavioristically a retarded person but he is psychometrically a nonretarded individual.

AN ABBREVIATED CASE STUDY FOR
DEMONSTRATION PURPOSES

Billy is sixteen years old and is in the tenth grade. He has failed one year in school and has a history of educational problems. Specifically he has had no severe difficulty with authority figures or persons in the school including his significant peers. His attendance is irregular, but he is not a seriously disruptive force in the classroom. He has not demonstrated a chronic maladaptive behavior pattern which would allow his being diagnosed by vocational rehabilitation as having a behavior disorder.

Psychological tests have been administered and test results are as follows:

WECHSLER ADULT INTELLIGENCE SCALE

> Full scale IQ 91
> Verbal scale IQ 90
> Performance scale IQ 94

Verbal Scale Subtests:		Performance Scale Subtests:	
Information	7	Picture completion	10
Computation	8	Picture arrangement	9
Arithmetic	6	Block design	8
Similarities	8	Object assembly	8
Vocabulary	7	Digit symbol	9
Digit span	8		

No significant score scatter was observed (normal responses). Intelligence is low normal.

BENDER-GESTALT: On the test essentially normal reproductions were achieved. There was no evidence of disturbance or organicity.

WIDE RANGE ACHIEVEMENT TEST:

Reading grade placement, 7.8—25th percentile
Spelling grade placement, 7.9—27th percentile
Arithmetic grade placement, 7.7—25th percentile

Billy is not mentally retarded according to psychological test scores; and as a result, is ineligible for rehabilitation according to most state agency requirements under retardation. Is he functionally retarded? Through this simple case description and the Activities of Daily Working Scale, we can readily answer that he has difficulty adapting to and accepting the impact of interpersonal relationships in that he is unable to get along well with his fellow students and teachers. He is borderline in attendance in school and probably would be borderline in attendance on the job. We feel that he would have difficulty in performing emotionally in two types of jobs other than the one in which he has been involved—the job of being a student in school. He has no vocational training and there is no way to assume that he would make a positive adjustment on the job without evaluation and prevocational training. In addition, he seems to be poorly adjusted in the school so we might assume that his work adjustment also would be poor. He must not understand the importance of attendance obligations on the job since he is missing substantial time from school.

How many work evaluators and other professional persons would predict that he has the emotional stability to remain on the job until his work would permit advancement or until a supervisor could correct any annoyances which may be making difficulty for him? He certainly does not seem to have sufficient educational skills to manage himself without undue dependence on others. His self-control is in question in terms of adjustment problems in school. The question concerning financial activities is difficult to answer and maybe cannot be answered from the data we have.

According to the Activities of Daily Working Scale, this person is functionally retarded. Since work is one of the main concerns in rehabilitation, it would seem that we are indicating that this person is definitely not educationally, socially, or vocationally adjusted at this time in his development; and yet he is ineligible for vocational rehabilitation services according to an intelligence test score. However, the point that we would like to stress is that even though he is not mentally retarded, he is functioning as if he were retarded and should be considered seriously for vocational rehabilitation services under the diagnosis of functional retardation.

Summary

In developing and using various types of information in evaluation of retarded persons, counselors and others often do not give enough thought to readily available data which often provide more information than do psychological tests results. The mystique surrounding psychological tests has helped move them further down the continuum of "assumed" effectiveness than their achieved level of successful prediction. Rehabilitation personnel have put far more emphasis on psychological test results than has been recommended by the test developers.

It should be remembered that although IQ scores are most useful, the measures must not be used as the only indices for educational or vocational diagnosis or predictions. In addition to intellectual capacity, information should be obtained on the client's effectiveness in interpersonal relationships, his feelings about himself, his frustration tolerance, and his motivational level. After the collection of necessary data has been completed, the Activities of Daily Working Scale should be used by the counselor when deciding eligibility for rehabilitation services in cases of suspected functional retardation.

REFERENCES

Doyle, P. J. and Seidenfeld, M. A.: Mental retardation. In Myers, J. S. (Ed.): *An Orientation of Chronic Disease and Disability*, New York, Macmillan Company, 1965.

Suggested Readings

American Medical Association: *Mental Retardation, Handbook for the Primary Physician*. Chicago, AMA, 1964.

Baumeister, Alfred A.: *Mental Retardation: Appraisal, Education and Rehabilitation*. Chicago, Aldine Publishing Co., 1967.

Gilmore, Alden S. and Rich, Thomas A.: *Mental Retardation, A Programmed Manual for Volunteer Workers*. Springfield, Thomas, 1967.

Hardy, R. E. and Cull, J. G.: *Mental Retardation and Physical Disability, A Book of Readings*. Springfield, Thomas, 1974.

————: *Modification of Behavior of the Mentally Retarded: Applied Principles.* Springfield, Thomas, 1974.

Karner, Leo: *History of the Care and Study of the Mentally Retarded.* Springfield, Thomas, 1964.

Rothstein, Jerome H.: *Mental Retardation, Readings and Resources.* New York, Holt, Rinehart & Winston, 1961.

PART FOUR

SPECIAL COUNSELING PROBLEM AREAS

The Work of the Family Counselor
Group Family Counseling
Counseling With Non-College Bound Youth
Working With Runaway Youth
Counseling With the Older American
The Use of Peer Pressure in Group Work
Case Study Descriptions of Rehabilitation Counseling Services in
    Drug Abuse and Dependency
Language of the Drug Abuser

CHAPTER 13

THE WORK OF THE FAMILY COUNSELOR

- Rapid Social Change
- What Is Marital and Family Counseling?
- Individual Role Change
- Responsibilities of the Counselor

F EW COUNSELORS who are concerned in the broad areas of social services including psychiatry, rehabilitation, education, the ministry, social work, and/or psychology can do their work without becoming involved at times with their clients' marital problems. The entire field of marital counseling could be described as a very recent addition to the social service helping field and for this reason there is considerable ambiguity concerning its dimensions and who is qualified to practice.

The marital counselor faces many difficult problems with his clients. He will not give them direct advice concerning what they should do to solve various problems, but he will work with them on a one-to-one basis, in husband-wife sessions and/or in group helping situations in order to explore various approaches to problem solving. The counselor must have considerable information for ready use. This information concerns family stability, feelings, budgets, attitudes, sexual beliefs, marital roles and others.

RAPID SOCIAL CHANGE

Our society is experiencing so much change at such a fast pace that adjustment to change itself is becoming a social problem. This rapid social change which includes, of course, attitudes of all of us concerning moral values, ethics and family behavior is changing life in America and throughout much of the world. In-

213

stitutions such as the church, the family, governmental structures of service, the university and other educational systems are changing so rapidly that many persons are losing their anchor points for emotional stability. People look around them and find little or no certainty in their jobs, their family life, or the traditional and religious beliefs formerly held sacrosanct. All of us are deeply influenced by the effects of the mass media such as television. These media depict to us what the outside world seems to be doing. In many cases persons outside of our world seem to be involved in much more exciting activities. Many people live vicariously and some people wish to change their life patterns and family structure in order to relieve boredom and go "where the action is." This immature approach to achieving one's personal goals seldom brings happiness.

With an increased amount of leisure time and a deemphasis on full work days and work weeks, many persons are finding difficulty in managing their personal lives. The changing social environment in which we live has forced the marital counselor into a role of increased importance as a social service professional. His responsibilities affect individuals, their families, work, leisure enjoyment and hopes for personal stability.

WHAT IS MARITAL AND FAMILY COUNSELING?

Marital counseling can be considered as a relationship between two or more persons which is conducive to good mental health. Inherent in an effective counseling relationship is the absence of threat. The counselor must remove threat if the client is to grow and be able to solve his problems in an uninhibited manner. Counseling as a relationship is also typified by the types of feelings many of us have for our closest friends. True close friendships are characterized by honest caring, genuine interest and a high level of concern about helping in a time of need. Real friendships often require one person to put aside his own selfish needs in order to listen long enough with enough empathy so that a friend's problem may begin to work itself out in a natural and constructive manner.

Family counseling services vary according to the needs of the client—not the counselor. Often when a counselee comes to the counselor for help he at first will outline a concern which is not the real problem. The counselor must have considerable flexibility and insight in order to know what is required in each individual situation and the appropriate responses for given situations.

The counselor in a marital session always has the goal of bringing about change in the marital relationship. Marital counseling may be effective in helping clients decide whether or not they can "live" with their situation as it is, in changing that situation without separation, in separating for a period of time, or divorcing. All these alternatives are realistic possibilities for end results in successful family counseling.

Any solution short of total reconciliation is generally considered by our society as indicative of personal failure. This very fact inhibits many people in their exploration of possibilities other than total reconciliation. Many persons fall in line with society's enforced rules and regulations which have particularly forced many persons in the past to remain in unhappy and maladjusted marital situations. The aspect of going for help to a marital counselor for personal adjustment or to a lawyer in order to discuss legal aspects of separation and divorce is also indicative of personal shortcoming in terms of the attitudes of many persons in the society in general. Relatives, peer persons and groups put enormous pressure on the individuals concerned to go back together at all "costs." This "getting back together" in effect saves the family from what some people think of as "disgrace" and makes both family and friends feel more comfortable. Every counselor must take into consideration and impart to his clients the knowledge that while many friends and relatives wish to help, their first thoughts concern what they would like to see as an end result of the consideration rather than what is necessarily best for the partners in difficulty.

Due to strong societal conformity pressure and the problems which individuals have after threatened or actual separation or divorce, they particularly need counseling. Counseling may be concerned with actual problems or anticipated problems of the separation or divorce and the reaction of the individual to the threatened or terminated marriage; or there may be a combination of both of these problem areas.

INDIVIDUAL ROLE CHANGE

Societal change is now fast-paced and affects roles which individuals have in marital situations as they experience various aspects of their lives, develop new interests and maturity. A common myth holds that the well-adjusted person in our society is one who experiences many worldly things but does not change. All people change and generally change is for the best in terms of an individual's increased maturity. It is important for husband and wife to discuss the redefining of roles which often come about as each grows, matures, and changes in interests. If such discussions are held on a frank basis many questions concerning changes in sexual behavior, business activities, attitudes concerning the importance of work, family entertaining, housekeeping, etc., can be understood more fully.

Role confusion concerning the wife and mother is now profound. Many women no longer are satisfied in devoting their entire lives to family life. Many feel insecure as they see the marriages of their peers "breaking up" with increased regularity. More and more women wish to be self-supporting and self-sufficient and do not wish to relegate themselves to what has been called "housewifery." This fact also can readily threaten the male who has carried the image of himself as the total bread earner and in many cases the master of his domain. The husband often can misconceive the working role of the wife as one of competition and one which can be a threat to his marriage due to the many new contexts his wife will experience in her work. Her work and his reaction to it can affect greatly whether or not additional children are added to the family unit.

We cannot overstress the importance of periodically discussing and defining roles during the years of marriage. People are, for instance, now living longer. At one time when the last child left home it was near to the time for both husband and wife to die. Today parents experience a new adjustment period in that life continues for many more years after the children have left home. There has been no societal definition of roles for middle-aged and older couples. We are seeing now an increase in the number of persons being divorced once the "nest is empty."

RESPONSIBILITIES OF THE COUNSELOR

The counselor must be certain that confidentiality of the marital counseling relationship is maintained and the client must understand this feeling. This includes the counselor's being involved in possible court testimony, at a later date. The counselor must let it be known to his clients and others that he cannot have an effective counseling relationship if either client feels that he is not completely free in discussing various feelings and experiences. Clients must have a clear sense of security.

Counselors come from all segments of society and represent various ages, races, sexes, and religions. Each of them has experienced a variety of conflicts and problems of the same types which trouble their clients. The difference between the client and the counselor (helper and helpee) is that the client is experiencing difficulty and for the most part, counselors feel that their own handicaps and problems are under control. The counselor must guard against automatic feelings of superiority and should see himself as an individual who also has difficulties and who simply wishes to help another individual work his way through problems.

The counselor must be able to recognize when he should refer clients to other counselors or sources of help. There may be problems of counter-transference which interfere with the counseling relationship. Race, age, sex, and religion, almost invariably affect the counseling outcomes. For instance, counselors who are older may be out of touch with some of the problems of the younger generation, or male counselors may not fully understand the emerging role of the female in today's society.

Counselors who have strong religious beliefs may be unable to offer unbiased information and those with racial biases and prejudices may experience difficulties of an obvious nature.

Counselors must be certain that they have received adequate training and supervision. Academic requirements in terms of five or six years of college and at least two degrees should have been completed. Supervision in counseling practice as a part of academic and later training is also most important. Each counselor should continue professional growth by active involvement in appropriate professional organizations (according to his interests and trainings). Examples are the American Psychological Association and the American Association of Marriage and Family Counselors. Ethical codes of conduct of these organizations should be strictly followed.

Again, the counselor must guard against the temptation to play "God." Counselors generally who use directive and authoritation approaches are exposed over and over to rationalizations of their own dictatorial motives.

As indicated earlier the personality of the counselor is the decisive factor in the success or failure of therapeutic activities. Counselors constantly must evaluate their own behavior and attitudes toward their work in general and their clients in particular. The counselor must remember that he is working toward the development of the client's ability to make future satisfactory decisions and to achieve a mature dependability.

REFERENCES

Cull, J. G. and Hardy, R. E.: *Deciding on Divorce: Personal and Family Considerations.* Springfield, Thomas, 1974.

Griffin, Gerald: *The Silent Misery: Why Marriages Fail.* Springfield, Thomas, 1975.

Gustad, J. W.: The definition of counseling. In Berdie, R. F.: *Roles and Relationships in Counseling.* Minneapolis, University of Minnesota Press, 1953.

Hardy, R. E. and Cull, J. G.: *Achieving Creative Divorce: Social and Psychological Approaches.* Springfield, Thomas, 1974.

Hardy, R. E. and Cull, J. G.: *Therapeutic Needs of the Family.* Springfield, Thomas, 1974.

CHAPTER 14

GROUP FAMILY COUNSELING

--- --- --- --- --- --- --- --- --- ---

- Marital Roles in Group Settings
- Marital Counseling in Groups
- Modeling Behavior
- Problems Which May Surface During Group Marital
  Counseling
- Ground Rules for Group Marital Sessions
- Time Periods and Types of Sessions

--- --- --- --- --- --- --- --- --- ---

MARITAL ROLES IN GROUP SETTINGS

DURING THE INITIAL PHASES of marital counseling it often is difficult to discriminate between actual behavior (role played) and behavior which is related by a marriage partner. This period of counseling is difficult. The marriage counselor is interacting on a one-to-one basis or is occasionally seeing both marriage partners together. As a result of the defensiveness and the ego-protective nature of the individual, quite often there is a great degree of uncertainty as to the reality of the roles which are being reported; and when it is evident that there is a reality base for some of the reports of an antagonistic spouse, the question remains concerning the impact of this role, the substance of the role and its prevalence. When a marriage starts deteriorating, it is quite natural for each partner to try to justify his position and to displace blame and responsibility for the deterioration of the marriage through recriminations and the imputing of negative roles on the other partner.

Group work is an ideal approach to be used in separating these diverse roles which are so basic in the marital interaction. As the therapist observes the individuals and their role within the group, he can make a direct connection between the role an individual adopts in the group setting and the role he tends to play most often in the marital setting. In individual counseling the client may appear somewhat passive, withdrawn, taciturn and relate his reaction to others and his reaction to events in a philosophical manner. However, in group interactions, it is quite possible for him to change drastically and become the aggressor rather than the passive receptor in a relationship.

The Aggressive Individual

As an aggressor he may work in many ways to exert his will. He may be oblivious or unconcerned about the feelings of others. He will override their concerns by deflating them, attempting to relegate them to a lower status, either expressing disapproval or ignoring their feelings, their value system, or the acts in which they engage and which are counter to his basic goals. He will appear to be highly goal-oriented regardless of the cost in achieving that goal, and he will work toward the goal regardless of the hurt feelings, the inner damage to his interpersonal relationships. He works toward the goal which he perceives as the one bringing him most recognition. Under this set of circumstances, this individual will be most manipulative in that he will show the highest degree of Machiavellianism. He will be somewhat jealous of individuals who gain more recognition than he does and he will be sympathetic toward the individuals whom he outshines most readily.

The Acceptance Seeker

Related to this individual who has a high degree of need to accomplish the goals he perceives as important and who accomplishes them through aggressive-type behavior is the individual whose concern is not the accomplishment of the goals but whose goal is to receive acceptance by the group or one who feels the need for recognition within the group. This is an individual who is quite insecure and tends to need almost continual positive reinforcement as to his self-adequacy and his value to the group or to the marriage partner. This type of individual demonstrates his needs in the group in many ways. Generally, he will not be as oriented toward the goal which is perceived by the group as the group goal as will be the aggressive-type individual. But he will work toward the goal if he feels it will bring a great deal of recognition. Much of his overt behavior upon examination will be seen to be self-serving and self-gratifying behavior rather than goal-oriented behavior. It has been our experience in group work with marriage partners that this type of individual has many more needs than the aggressive-type individual. If the individual who is seeking the recognition to the exclusion of everything else has a spouse who attempts to meet these needs, quite often the needs are so great, the spouse loses the impact she once had to fulfill his needs; therefore, he looks elsewhere for the recognition which is so essential to his personality integration. He responds to her as being unconcerned about him, as not really understanding his motivations, and gives the impression that the spouse is somewhat self-centered and uncooperative in the marriage pact. In the group situation, the individual demonstrates his need for recognition by behavior and mannerisms both verbal and nonverbal which call attention to himself. He will quite often boast; he will feel the need to relate personal experiences; he will relate his accomplishments and achievements; perhaps he may relate them in a thinly veiled manner under the guise of using them as an example to make a point in some other area; however, he feels compelled to bring forth his accomplishments, his values, his attributes to the group and to hold them out for group approval. His most painful moments in the group will be when he perceives he has been devalued by other members in the group and placed in an inferior position or when he feels he is demonstrating behavior which is characterized by the group as inadequacy.

The Sympathy Seeker

On a continuum down from the aggressive-type individual on to the individual who is seeking recognition from the group, the next type of personality may be characterized as the sympathy seeker. This individual attempts to elicit responses of sympathy from the group thereby obviating any pressures for him to achieve either within the group or without the group. As he depreciates himself and relegates himself to a lower inferior position, he gets the sympathy of the group and at the same time is absolved of responsibility within the group. This provides him a haven of irresponsibility. He is able to go his own way; he can follow the group or he can elect to remain aloof from the group all with the approval of the group as a result of his being in a position to receive sympathy from the group. As the group becomes more demanding and insistent on his contributing, he will reinforce his protestations of inferiority or illness, of devaluation or of a generalized inadequacy. He will attempt to reinforce the group's feelings of sympathy for him in order to free himself from entanglements of the group. If he is unsuccessful in his attempts to get sympathy from the group, he will attempt to split the group into smaller units and will see statements of sympathy from the smaller subgroups. The value of the group interaction is too denote how an individual who is a sympathy seeker in the group setting but in the marriage relationship and when seen on an individual counseling basis may come through as a relatively independent sort of person who expresses feelings of adequacy and concern for the marriage relationship. The group setting will highlight the change when his behavior is observed and the pressures of the group are exerted.

The Confessor

The next type of behavior which is brought out in a group is the confessing behavior. This is behavior that is characterized by rather superficial confessing. As the individual sees that the demands are getting greater to reveal himself and as he sees that his responsibility will have to be fulfilled if he is to maintain membership in the group, quite often he starts confessing in a very superficial manner to the group. Generally, these confessions are characterized by large quantity with a very low quality. He feels that the more he confesses, the more he absolves himself of responsibility for honest group interaction. He confesses to his feelings which are somewhat insignificant in a very sober, concerned fashion. He professes to have immediate insight as a result of the group sessions. When an individual starts to criticize him, this confessing-type individual immediately stifles the criticism or stifles the comments by agreeing with the critic and going even further in confessing these feelings or attributes and feelings and attributes related to these on and on *ad nauseam*.

In a marriage, this is a very effective defense. It's quite frustrating when the marriage partner tries to communicate and he is thwarted through this self-confessing type behavior. Communication is effectively blocked when one marriage partner takes the ball and runs by this superficial type of confessing behavior. When this type of behavior is exhibited, it is quite difficult to get to the core of the problem in individual counseling since the confessor is verbalizing a great deal of concern, flexibility and willingness to cooperate when in fact his behavior is aimed more at stifling communication and blocking effective understandings within the marriage relationship.

The Externalizer

Another type of behavior which is exhibited in groups can be characterized by the term "externalization." The externalizer is an individual who becomes uncomfortable in the interaction and the "give and take" which is occurring in the group or which occurs in close interpersonal relationships; therefore, in order to escape from the impact of these interpersonal relationships, he tends to focus on problems that are external to the group or external to the relationship. As the group starts to focus on the individual or as the group gets too close to the individual, he starts externalizing in order to shift the brunt of an attack or the brunt of an inquisition from him on to some external object. Quite often this can be a very effective maneuver; however, again, it is one which is highly frustrating to an individual who is seriously trying to resolve conflicts. An effective externalizer is able to communicate his values, his impressions, his attitudes and beliefs very effectively without referring to himself. He does this through injecting or projecting his attitudes into the attitudes of groups external to the interaction he is currently engaged in. Consequently, he is able to communicate a point of view which he holds without allowing others to adequately communicate their points of view.

The Isolate

The next type of behavior which is observed in the group setting and has a direct referent back to marital interactions is the isolate. This is the individual who decides to insulate himself from the interaction of the group. He very definitely elects not to interact with the group and decides to disallow the group from interacting with him. He quite often will make a very studied effort to inform the group of his nonchalence, of his decision to be noninvolved. He does this quite often by engaging in strategems which are distracting to the group but which give no indication of his interest or willingness to contribute to the group. He may attract the attention of one or two other members of the group and start to play with them. He may become very animated in doodling. He may develop little games which he plays with himself such as folding paper, making airplanes, drawing pictures of the room. When confronted, his general response is, "I'm paying attention," "I'm listening," "I'm participating," "I just engage in these little activities to heighten my sensitivity to what's going on." This individual generally will not allow himself to be drawn into the interaction within the group. He will stay outside the mainstream of activity and will attempt to communicate his intentions to stay outside the mainstream of activity through nonverbal behavior. His verbal behavior will be one of conciliation and concern.

The Dominator

The next type of behavior on the continuum from highly goal-oriented to highly negativistic will be the individual who tries to dominate one or more individuals in the group or tries to dominate the entire group. His drives toward domination are an effort to convince others of his authority and of his superiority. His interests are not as goal-oriented as the aggressive-type individual who sacrifices others' feelings and his own interpersonal relationship with others in an effort to accomplish a group goal; however, the dominating-type individual is concerned with exerting influence over others not for the goal which can be achieved but just for the sake of dominance. If there is a highly aggressive individual in the group and a dominating individual in the group, the more maladaptive type of behavior will be exhibited by the dominating individual for he will find the need to express his adequacy by wooing group members away from the goal-oriented aggressive-type individual whose drives are to move the group toward a goal. The dominator will achieve his purpose if he subverts the actions or intents of the aggressive individual. The dominating individual is concerned with achieving a status of respect. He may do this through many types of behavior such as being punitive and using the threat of punitive behavior to tower a weaker member. He may use flattery to woo a member. He may use the power of suggestion and persuasion or he may just attempt to verbally and socially overpower the other individuals to force them into submission. In a marriage relationship, this type individual most often has to have a wife who is somewhat passive and one who does not have a high level of need for individuality and expressions of self-adequacy through the approval of her spouse.

The Antagonist

The next and last type of behavior to be discussed is the antagonist. This is the individual who strives for self-adequacy and recognition through the negativistic behavior and values he adopts. He is somewhat arbitrary and capricious in his value judgments. The underlying constant of his judgments is the contrariness of his position. He seems to be at odds with the mainstream of opinion, values, or actions within the group interaction. His negativism can be quite harsh and sharp. He apparently is unconcerned about the feelings of others in the group. The most important thing to him is to exhibit his individuality by disagreeing with the group consensus. He is stubbornly resistant to coercion or persuasion. He will go so far as to disrupt the flow of the work of the group by attempting to change directions, change the topic of concern, alter the goal which the group is working toward, or try to redefine the ground rules which were established in the group. This antagonist takes a negative view of life and is antagonistic to almost all of the members in the group. He is argumentative and can be quite bombastic when thwarted.

In marital counseling, it is essential to see the clients in an individual one-to-one situation. It is equally important to see spouses together; however, we feel that it is of utmost importance for effective marriage counseling to supplement individual counseling with group techniques, for it is through group techniques that much of the behavior which can remain enigmatic in individual counseling is delineated and exemplified by pressures and interactions of the group. Much of the behavior which has constituted irritant factors of the marriage pact are elicited in the group situation. This type of behavior is on the surface in the group. It can be observed by the therapist and in individual sessions which follow can be related to the individual and interpreted for him to review and evaluate and react to. Without the benefit of the group, marital counseling is much slower and a much longer process. Many times, marriage will continue to deteriorate at a faster rate than the therapist is able to diagnose and treat the causes of the deterioration.

MARITAL COUNSELING IN GROUPS

There is an exercise in group behavior which requires working toward the solution of a problem concerned with being marooned on the moon. The problem requires individuals to react by rank ordering a number of various types of equipment which they would choose to have with them if they were so marooned. The exercise which has been checked by space experts at the National Space and Aeronautics Administration is first completed by individuals and later by a group of six to eight persons working together. The usual result of the exercise is that group behavior is demonstrated over and over again to be more effective in getting at correct solutions to problems than is individual effort alone. In some few cases the individual's decision may be more effective than that of the group, but in most cases the group decision is more nearly correct than the individual one.

The purpose of the exercise is to demonstrate the effectiveness of group interaction in problem solving. Just as the exercise does demonstrate the effectiveness of increased interaction among individuals in problem solving so does group marital counseling achieve much more in many cases than does the basic interaction between the client and therapist. While much can be accomplished by individual sessions with the client, it is our feeling that supplemental group sessions can bring about enormous strides in understanding and adjustment.

Selection of Group Participants

In group marital counseling one generally has a decision to make concerning whether he wants to have in his group only husbands, only wives or mix the group. He also needs to make a decision whether husbands and wives will be in the same group. When husband and wife are in the same group, other members of the group can help them explore in considerable detail their problem areas. When husbands or wives are in groups made up of exclusively all males or all females, the group leader will experience some difficulty in keeping the session from turning into a kind of complaint session about the opposite sex. When husbands and wives are in groups separately from one another, group members have been shown to be very eager to help the individual to explore his marital situation and understand it more fully. The best combination seems to be one in which both husband and wife are in the same group or husband or wife are in mixed groups of males and females. Heterogeneity has a great affect upon the effectiveness in group interaction and problem solving. Diversity brings with it a certain breadth of experience and increases the strength of the group to solve both individual problems and group problems. There is no reason why persons from all walks of life cannot be mixed in a heterogeneous marital group counseling situation. This same opinion would extend to persons of various ages and socioeconomic backgrounds.

Relationships Necessary for Effective Group Interaction

Some of the necessary ingredients for effective group problem exploration include acceptance of others, awareness, self acceptance of individuals in the group, and problem centering approaches to behavior. When these conditions exist a high "trust" level has been achieved. People are free to be themselves when a level of trust has been established in the group. When the trust level has not been established or is low, group members tend to be manipulative, to hold back information about themselves, and to be defensive. When individuals within the group trust one another defensiveness is reduced, information flow is multiplied, and the strategies of manipulation are dissipated.

The group leader must create in members a feeling of freedom. They can be most valuable as group members to others in groups and to themselves when they are free and able to be themselves.

MODELING BEHAVIOR

It is the responsibility of the group leader to model the types of behavior which he would like to see exhibited by the various members of the group. The group facilitator or leader should not be overbearing and should not be dominating as a leader but should move the group toward understanding of problems through various behaviors which he not only demonstrates but models. The group leader should be an individual who is friendly, warm, and accepting. He should be a person who works with others and does not practice techniques upon them. The word "with" suggests that the procedure taking place is a relationship and not a technique-oriented process. The atmosphere within the group should be productive of or conducive to good mental and social-psychological health. The goal of all group work is that of the obtainment of good mental health.

Every member of the group should be accorded enough consideration and respect by the group so he is assured of at least a modicum of self-esteem. The individual must be willing and able to accept himself within a group setting. He must feel that he has the respect of others and that he is a person of worth. The group environment should facilitate the development and maintenance of self-esteem.

Members of the group should show considerable acceptance of others and their attitudes regardless of whether or not group members agree with the attitudes or ideas which are being expressed. In other words, group members do not have to agree with the ideas in order to accept them as legitimate personal feelings of the individual expressing them. At times the needs of individuals in the group for self-esteem may interfere with their accepting and respecting others. It has been shown many times that we may want to feel superior to others and we do this by bolstering ourselves. When this is the case, often the person involved does not have enough respect for himself, therefore, he cannot respect others. Listening to another is the simplest and one of the most basic ways through which we can show respect for him.

Group members need to show understanding of others' feelings and the group leader should demonstrate that he understands how others feel and wishes to get to know them better. If the group leader uses psychological terminology glibly, he may "turn off" the group. He should not attempt to demonstrate understanding through such use of professional jargon, but he should demonstrate that he has what has been called accurate empathy in reference to the individual. He can put himself in the other's place and understand feelings as the other person experiences them.

All members of the group must demonstrate some degree of confidence in the other persons in the group. There must be recognition of the rights and privileges and freedoms to action of others. The group must be characterized by sincerity, integrity, openness, and honesty if it is to achieve its goals. These characteristics help eliminate the threat and help to create an environment in which the individual can develop to his fullest potential by exploring all aspects of his particular marital problem. The group leader should give his attention, respect, understanding, and interest to those within the group who are attempting to work toward a solution of their problems and help others in doing likewise.

Artificiality must be avoided on the part of the group leader at all costs. There is no real alternative to genuineness in the group counseling process.

The group leader must demonstrate the types of behavior which participants in the group need to exhibit if problem solving is to take place. There must be a certain amount of risk-taking, in other words, individuals in the group must go beyond what is known to be factual in order to explore their behavior. Persons must be willing to do more than to play it safe. If, for instance, within a session an individual becomes angry or anxious, these behaviors can make him appear foolish, but these may be necessary behaviors and necessary risks to take in order for him to achieve success in problem solving. There must be substantial support for others as members attempt to reach goals that are important. Persons can say in various ways that they may not be sure what an individual is aiming toward or proposing, they support the efforts being made to get something moving or to make others understand a particular problem.

There should be a demonstration that persons are free and able to be open about their feelings and thoughts, and there should be a problem centering or focusing on problems faced by a group rather than on control or method. Problem-centering is based upon the assumption that the group can accomplish much more when individuals in groups learn how to solve problems rather than by the leader having to employ certain technique patterns in order to achieve goals. Group members should clearly recognize the feelings of others and how one's feelings are inter-influencing the behavior of others.

Another characteristic which is most important in achieving the level of problem solving ability necessary for success is that of the individual feeling that he can accept his own emotions without denying them or giving rationalizations or apologies. Such acceptance can be evidenced by such statements "I am disgusted or bored with myself because I feel ineffective."

PROBLEMS WHICH MAY SURFACE
DURING GROUP MARITAL COUNSELING

There is no beginning or end to the types of human situations which may come to light during marital counseling. Group marital counseling just as individual counseling and other group counseling covers the whole realm of human life and experience.

Of course, there are sex problems which include frigidity, sterility, impotence and others. There are the problems of children, there are the problems of incongruencies in expectations, of differences in opinion concerning careers, there is the problem of extramarital affairs, of changing life-style in a rapidly moving society, of parents and in-laws and their influence in the marriage. There are identification problems, problems of personal values, the different meanings of love and substitutes for it which are meaningful to some people and not meaningful to others, the expression and management of feelings, the handling of various financial crises and many others.

The counselor concerned with group marital counseling must be a mature individual who is able to facilitate human learning through the demonstration of the behaviors described earlier. He must know group interactions well and thoroughly understand human behavior.

GROUND RULES FOR GROUP MARITAL SESSIONS

Human interaction includes two major properties: (1) content and (2) process. Content has to do with the subject matter with which the group is concerned. Process has to do with the actual procedure of what is happening between and to group members while the group is working. The group leader must be sensitive to the group process in order to help the group in diagnosing special problems so that these can be dealt with soon and effectively.

One of the important concepts in group interaction is that everyone who is in the group belongs there because he simply is there. This concept is one of the most important ones in effecting successful group behavior. If an individual gets angry with another person, this behavior does not change his belonging in the group. If a person reads himself out of a group, it does not change his belonging in it. If he gives up on himself, the group does not give up on him.

Each person determines what is true for him by what is in him. Whatever he feels makes sense in himself and whatever way he wishes to live inside himself is determined by that which is in him as an individual. Most people live mostly inside themselves. No one knows more about how a person really is than the person himself. The group leader should remember that he should force no one to be more honest than he wants to be just at the moment he is speaking. We should listen for the person who is inside the individual who is living and feeling. This person may not be totally exposed to us at any given time although he may wish to be exposed.

The group leader is always responsible for protecting the belongingness of every member to the group and also his right to be heard. He is also responsible for the confidential aspect of the group disclosures, which means that no one will repeat anything which has been said outside of the group unless it concerns only himself.

Everyone should participate in the group. One indication of involvement is verbal participating. The group leader should look for differences in terms of who are the high and low participators. What are the shifts in participation? How are the persons who are not participating being treated by the others? What subgroups are there? Who keeps the group moving? Which of the groups are high in terms of influence? Are there autocrats and peacemakers? Are there members getting attention by their apparent lack of involvement in the group? Who attempts to include everyone in group discussion decision making? In other words, what are the styles of influence? Is the group drifting from topic to topic? Is this a defensive type of behavior? Do they attempt to become overly organized at the expense of losing effectiveness in problem solving? Are there persons outside of the group?

Is the group avoiding certain topics and setting certain norms for behavior? Is religion or sex avoided, for instance as a topic? Are the group members being overly nice to each other? Are they agreeing too soon, in short are they avoiding facing individual and group problems?

One of the helpful techniques which can be used in group marital counseling is that of spontaneous role playing. This can be done by husband and wife actually sitting in the center of the group and playing out a particular problematic situation. The group members can then react to various aspects of the role playing and make suggestions in order that the individuals may develop fuller understanding of the problem area. It may also be useful to have a surrogate wife or husband role play with an actual husband and wife.

Role reversal is another technique in which individuals reverse their roles and then role play actual situations. This technique can be most interesting in that the husband plays the wife's part and wife plays the husband's part. It is sometimes easy to bring about understanding through the use of this technique. Persons can relive past events or project future occurrences through role playing.

Another technique which is useful is that of repeating the client's key words or statements. This is particularly useful in terms of what has been called free association. In other words, that process of using clues or cues to help the client give meaningful information about himself and his problems.

The group leader should keep in mind that persons who live many psychosomatic complaints may be disguising personal problems and conflicts. He should also remember that the individual group member who offers any complaints about his spouse may be covering his own personal anxieties and inadequacies.

TIME PERIODS AND TYPES OF SESSIONS

The purpose of this chapter has been to describe group marital counseling. Generally, sessions may last for three to four hours and may be ongoing meeting eight to ten or more times. This varies from the individual counseling sessions which usually last from fifty to sixty minutes.

Much of the material given in this chapter concerns the facilitating of groups rather than the actual leading of them as a group therapist. It is felt by the authors that selected encounter group concepts can be of substantial benefit in various types of marital counseling.

Of course, it may be that group members will wish to engage in a type of marathon encounter in which they may continue their group activities for twenty to twenty-four hours. These sessions can later be followed by shorter two to three-hour group sessions for those who are interested. Group leaders should not become discouraged if some of their group members do not choose to return to later group meetings. People vary enormously in their abilities to withstand various types of stress and many people feel a good deal of insecurity and stress during group counseling work even though substantial efforts have been made to establish an atmosphere of warmth and trust. Some people are able to gain a great deal in a short period of time and for these persons individual counseling may be more in accordance with their needs than group experiences.

The group counselor, leader or facilitator—whichever name is chosen—must keep in mind that the purpose of the group session is whatever goal the group decides upon. At times a group session may provide real service in terms of being informational in nature. One of the basic problems related to problems in marriage is the preparation for simply living with another person. At times the counselor will find it necessary to assume the role of information-giver and tutor in individual sessions, and in group sessions members may find it necessary to be informational in order to achieve basic goals which have been established. Group members can greatly help individuals in the group by exploring the needs of each person. In many cases needs are not being met due to the fact that these needs are not understood by the spouse and often the person himself.

SUGGESTED READINGS

Hardy, R. E. and Cull, J. G.: *Therapeutic Needs of the Family,* Springfield, Thomas, 1974.
————: *Achieving Creative Divorce: Social and Psychological Approaches.* Springfield, Thomas, 1974.

CHAPTER 15

COUNSELING WITH NON-COLLEGE BOUND YOUTH

To be even fairly adequately prepared to counsel with non-college bound adolescents in today's complex society, the counselor must have a working knowledge of the various career-development, learning, personality, and counseling theories. He must have a broad knowledge of the economic structure of our society and of the forces at work bringing about very rapidly an increasingly complex and changing world. He must take into account the psychological, sociological, and philosophical basis of career planning and formulate a framework from which he can best assist the young person to plan a satisfying and productive life. The counselor must, first of all, realize that he is counseling with the *whole* person, not just one aspect of his development; therefore, evaluation, assessment, and planning must take into account every area of the individual's life.

The importance of work in the individual's life can hardly be overemphasized; probably no other factor has such a profound impact on his total existence. What a person does identifies him. His occupation labels him at a certain level of education, skill, responsibility, and prestige, and it determines to a large extent where he will live and how much money he will earn, it determines his leisure time activities, his friendships, and often whether he will continue to grow as an individual. Work is one of the most important sources of life satisfaction, and without it most people are unlikely to have a high level of total life satisfaction.

In this country our orientation to work and to career development has been influenced by what has been called the "Protestant ethic," which attaches religious significance to work, and the early frontier attitude toward work, which dictated that each member of the community must contribute his share toward the survival of the group; and by the value orientation that Marshall Lowe terms "theism," which postulates that man's loyalty is to his God and the problems men face are such that they have a solution in religious faith. Man is attempting to mature, to achieve satisfaction and to be fulfilled. At present, automation and other technological changes are causing increasing numbers of workers to do assembly-line types of work which are not in themselves satisfying. As Herzberg (1959) summarizes the situation: "In the last hundred years there has been a growing realization of a sickness in our society and that one source of this sickness is the relationship of people to their work."

Vocational counseling is much more than helping the individual match skills and job opportunities at a specific time in his life. Career planning is a long-range, developmental process, almost a life-time matter. The individual needs some understanding of this pattern of career movement to have the knowledge and skill he needs to make realistic decisions at each stage. Perhaps the most important step is the formulation of goals, a guideline to help him avoid useless foundering that gets him nowhere. What satisfactions is he seeking, what is important to him in the long run, and what types of work or work settings will provide those satisfactions?

Maslow's (1954) hierarchy of basic needs can help the counselor evaluate the young person's present status of need satisfaction and to plan for the future. These needs, in the usual order of prepotency, are: Need for (1) physiological satisfactions, (2) safety, (3) belongingness and love, (4) importance, respect, self-esteem, independence, (5) information, (6) understanding, (7) beauty, and (8) self-actualization. In our society there is no single situation which is potentially so capable of giving satisfaction at all levels of these basic needs as is the occupation, and it is the responsibility of the counselor to help the counselee plan for gratification of as many needs as possible through his work.

After the counselee has studied his needs and values, the counselor should help him develop some sort of understanding of career patterns, how one enters the world of work, and the kinds of movement within the job structure. The work world can be thought of as consisting of three dimensions: (1) field, (2) level, and (3) enterprise. By field we mean the nature of the work being done (such as engineering), level is on some scale from high to low, and enterprise is the source of employment or industry. The point at which the individual enters (entry occupation) is determined by many factors, including his skills, general education, and specialized training. The moves he makes during his career may be verticle (progressing higher within the same field and enterprise) or horizontal (remaining in the same field and level but changing enterprise—doing the same work elsewhere). The individual must have the ability to make decisions as to whether certain moves would be a loss or gain (of perceived value) to him in the long run.

The counselor, as stated previously, will want to know something about the many different theories of occupational choice. Anne Roe (1956) employs Maslow's hierarchal classification of needs and expresses seven basic hypotheses, the four most relevant being these: (1) The intensity of these (primarily) unconscious needs, as well as their organization, is the major determinant of the degree of motivation as expressed in accomplishment, (2) needs satisfied routinely as they appear do not develop into unconscious motivators, (3) higher-order needs for which even minimum satisfaction is rarely achieved will become in effect extinguished lower order needs if rarely satisfied will prevent the appearance of higher order needs, and will become dominant and restricting motivators, and (4) needs, the satisfaction of which are delayed but eventually accomplished, will become unconscious motivators, depending largely upon the degree of satisfaction felt.

Ginzberg's (1951) general theory is: (1) Occupational choice is a process which takes place over a six- to ten-year period; (2) each decision during adolescence is related to prior experience, and has influence on the next decision; the process of decision-making is basically irreversible; (3) occupational choice is a result of combining subjective elements with the opportunities and limitations of reality, choice inevitably has the quality of compromise.

Brill (1949) suggests that (1) normal individuals need no advice in the selection of a vocation; they are able to sense the best activity to follow; (2) there is always some psychic determinant which lays the foundation for a later vocation; (3) a sensible person neither needs nor wants advice in choosing a mate or vocation, and fools will fail in spite of the best guidance.

Caplow (1954) concluded that (1) error and accident play a larger part in occupational choice than we like to admit; (2) occupational choices are made when we are still remote from the world of work. Often choice is dependent on the impersonal pressure of the school curriculum which is remote from the realities of the working situation; (3) typically realistic choices require the abandonment of old aspirations in favor of more limited objectives; (4) it is not until late in the average person's career that he is able to compare his expectations with his aspirations and arrive at a permanent sense of frustration, a glow of complacency, or an irregular fluctuation between the two according to Caplow.

Hoppock (1967) hypothesizes that (1) occupations are chosen to meet our needs, which may be intellectually perceived or only vaguely felt; (2) occupational choice begins when we first become aware that an occupation can help meet our needs; (3) information about ourselves and occupations facilitates successful choice; (4) job satisfaction depends on the extent the job we hold meets the needs we feel it should meet; (5) satisfaction can result from a job which meets our needs today or promises to do so in the future; (6) occupational choice is always subject to change if we feel that a change would better meet our needs.

John L. Holland (1966) describes his theory as a heuristic theory of personality types and environmental data in that its pervasive character suggests ideas for research. Six personality types were used: realistic, intellectual, social, conventional, enterprising, and artistic. Holland believes that the choice of an occupation is an expression of personality, that members of a vocation have similar personalities and similar histories of personal development, that they create characteristic interpersonal environments, and that vocational satisfaction, stability, and achievement depend upon the congruency between one's personality and the environment in which he works.

Super (1957) describes five basic stages of career development: the growth stage, the exploration stage, the establishment stage, the maintenance stage, and the decline stage. Counselors are primarily concerned with the two stages, exploration and establishment. Typical kinds of movement within these two periods are floundering (uncoordinated, useless moves that accomplish nothing); trial movements which result in progressive narrowing of the area of activity and lead to progress; and stagnation, remaining on a given job or in an occupation longer than is good for the individual—dead end jobs which lead nowhere. Finally comes establishment, which is vocational behavior representing stability in an occupation.

The rapidly changing society (automation, space exploration, advances in the sciences, struggles for civil and human rights, increased technology, increasing specialization, manpower shortages, and the changing nature of jobs) increases the complexity of choice, decision-making, and planning confronting the individual. Research shows that the average member of the labor force has been in five or six different types of work for which training was required. It is probable that most people will have two to three careers in the sense of different fields and enterprises. The individual needs increased competency and responsibility for making wise decisions in the light of realistic information relevant to the choices with which he is faced along the way. This seems to be a very strong argument in favor of a broad, liberal education that develops the whole person, his ability to understand and relate to others, his understanding of the environmental forces with which he must cope, and especially his ability to think logically and to use sound judgment. This type of education would seem to be preferable to the narrow, restricted "vocational" course which develops skills in specific types of work, but if both types of education could be given concurrently, so much the better. This type of educational counseling would seem to be especially important for those students who do not expect to further their education in college.

Sound vocational counseling should most certainly take into account the sociological and economic aspects affecting career choice and development. The typical person receives life satisfactions from three sources; family, work, and community, and from combinations of these, and if one of the three is low in the satisfaction it brings, the individual is either unhappy or seeks to get substitute satisfactions from other areas. Sound counseling attempts to help the individual consider all these courses of satisfaction as separate entities and as they relate to each other. The individual must develop sound attitudes relating to social interaction. He must be assisted to become a participating member of the community, to find a meaningful and significant place in society. To do this, he must have an understanding of the needs of the group, what is expected of him, and how he can obtain satisfaction by contributing to society. In other words, he must internalize acceptable values relating to society as a whole. Wise counseling will help the individual obtain a feeling of worth and achieve appropriate job placement in the larger community.

Another very important factor to be considered is geographic mobility, the migration of our youth to urban centers is an example of this. Counselors interested in realistic preparation of students for life and the community in which they are going to live should prepare them not only for a vocation which is meaningful in terms of large, urban labor markets, but for a life in the urban community in which he will live if this is the case.

Another sociological phenomenon of no small import is the social stratification in the local community, which tends, through preconceived notions about the worth of certain individuals and their capabilities (including the family socioeconomic level), to reinforce and strengthen the community social structure. To escape the confines of this "track" system of education and socialization, the individual needs help in understanding his own potential for achievement and the avenues open to him. Certain occupations provide opportunity for improving one's social and economic status. Teaching is a good example of an occupation which is very heavily used by upwardly mobile people.

Many economic factors should be understood and taken into consideration. Included are such important details as the opportunity for employment within certain fields (supply and demand), the economic trends in the various occupations during times of prosperity and recession, competition for the jobs, opportunity for service to society, training required for entry, and the various aspects of the job situation itself. Herzberg (1959) has used the terms "content" and "context" to describe the various factors of the job that serve as satisfiers. Content factors include the nature of the job itself, the responsibility given the worker, and status, and achievement. Context includes working conditions, salary, colleagues, equipment, and supervision. The competent counselor can furnish occupational information which can help the individual study appropriate occupations in the light of his fitness for the work and the work's potential for providing him satisfaction.

In helping the individual appraise his potential for happiness and success in certain occupational fields the counselor may use many processes and procedures. He should have a thorough understanding of how individuals differ, physically, psychologically, in social inheritance, and in education, and how these differences affect occupational choice and development. Personality and learning theory should be a very great part of the counselor's educational background.

Twelve theories* are mentioned as suggestions for further reading: (1) the factor theories, (2) stimulus-response theories, (3) Freud's psychoanalysis, (4) Jung's analytic theory, (5) Lewin's

---

* For a detailed treatment of these theories of personality see: Hall, C. & Lindzey, G.: *Theories of Personality, Primary Sources & Research.* 1965. 8:95. Wiley.

field theory, (6) Allport's psychology of the individual, (7) Murray's need-press theory, (8) self-theory, (9) Sheldon's constitutional psychology, and (10) Murphy's biosocial theory.

The counselor should also have a working knowledge of the various theories of counseling, including the directive, client-centered, and eclectic approaches. While studying the contributions of such stalwarts as Williamson, Rogers, and Thorne, the mature counselor, realizing that our current theory is unsystematized and at times equivocal, will select and rationalize from all the theories those that he can organize into a workable framework for his own counseling. It would seem that it is only when counselors remain open-minded and receptive to new ideas and as they struggle creatively and honestly toward a more highly developed theory that they will offer any worthwhile contributions to the field. As Holland states, while admitting that his theory has gone well beyond empirical data, he agrees with Darwin's words: "Without speculation, there is no good and original observation."

The counselor must bear in mind at all times the nature of individual differences—in intellectual ability, aptitudes, personality, interests, motivation, and perhaps as important as any, his potential for commitment to the job, as Samler (1964) describes it. The counselor has at his command various tools for assessing certain of these differences. High on his list of competencies should be his ability to use psychological instruments—to choose expertly those that will serve his purposes best, to administer and interpret them correctly, correlating the results with other pertinent information into meaningful pattern to assist the individual to understand himself better and to plan more realistically on the basis of this understanding.

Another function of the counselor is to provide a timely, up-to-date occupational information service which will provide the student opportunity to study and correlate information with his own needs and also stimulate him to critically appraise ideas, conditions, and trends in order to derive personal meaning and implications for the present and future. The counselor must be skilled in imparting information to the student in a meaningful, helpful way.

The competent counselor will be confronted from time to time with need for helping the individual cope with crippling barriers to his effective functioning as an individual. Needless to say, the counselor should be highly trained in counseling techniques and procedures, as well as in the basic understandings of the individual as discussed earlier. No doubt, for the true counselor, the goal of his work will be somewhat similar to that synthesized by Byrne (1963):

> The counselor's goal, firmly based on the human worth of the individual, regardless of education, intelligence, color, or background, is to use his technical skills (a) to help each counselee attain and maintain an awareness of self so that he can be responsible for himself, (b) to help each counselee confront threats to his being, and thus to open further the way for the counselee to increase his concern for others' wellbeing, (c) to help each counselee bring into full operation his unique potential in compatibility with his own life-style and within the ethical limits of society.

Included in counseling is helping the individual form and implement a realistic self-concept. Super (1957) sees vocational development as the implementation of the self-concept. When a youth is confronted with the problem of what he is going to be when he "grows up," he is forced to voice "I" projections which tend to become imbedded in his self-structure. In situations in which there is confirmation and approval in the reactions of others to his decisions, his self-picture in this area of experience becomes stabilized and capable of considerable resistance to outside forces. He may become threatened emotionally when his self-picture is questioned. His vocational decision becomes highly ego-involved, an integral part of his self-concept. The goal of vocational counseling, then, would be finding a vocation which is consistent with one's self-concept. This means that the individual must view his work, if it is to meet certain basic psychological needs, in terms of his self-concept; i.e., is his occupational role compatible with his self-concept and consistent with other aspects of his life?

C. H. Patterson (1962) has called for broadened view of vocational counselors and said that:

1. It would create an atmosphere of acceptance and understanding, in which the client is not under pressure or threat, since threat is inhibiting to self-analysis.
2. It would allow the client to express his self-concept in terms of his needs, his conflicts and anxieties, and his hopes, desires, and expectations as they relate to aptitudes, abilities, interests, and concepts of work and occupations.
3. It would provide the client with information about himself through tests and inventories for self-appraisal.
4. It would assist the client to explore vocational opportunities through use of occupational information.
5. It would help the client to relate information about himself and about occupations in terms of his self-concept, and to develop plans or programs, set goals, and increase his understanding of himself in relation to the world of work.

In summary, the counselor's responsibility includes the study of the world of work, the stages an individual goes through, the kinds of movements made and the significance of the career patterns of the individual, whether it is floundering or trial or establishment, or stagnation, and finally, the psychological meaning of work in terms of the total life satisfaction. It includes a knowledge of the economic and sociological aspects of the individual's adjustment in the world of work. His responsibility encompasses a concern for the individual and a desire to continue to upgrade his skills and competencies in helping the individual to seek out and to understand and accept his true nature; to be aware of his aptitudes, interests, and personal characteristics; to have a realistic view of the world of work; and, above all, to face the meaning of life and to formulate a goal and purpose for his lifework.

Maslow's Hierarchy of Needs

Maslow has propounded a theory of human motivation which assumes that needs are arranged along a hierarchy of priority or potency. Needs having the greatest potency and priority must be satisfied before those next in priority emerge and press for satisfaction. Triggered by the satisfaction of more basic needs, those from the next level of the pyramid surface and organize behavior.

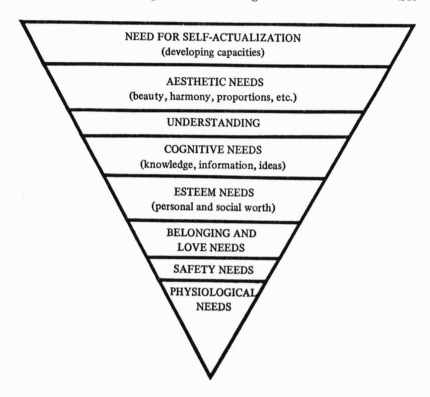

This need structure is represented by the pyramid shown above. Needs emerge in an order from the most to the least potent.

REFERENCES

Brill, A. A.: *Basic Principles of Psychoanalysis.* Garden City, Doubleday and Company, 1949.

Byrne, R. A.: *The School Counselor.* Boston, Houghton Mifflin, 1963.

Caplow, T.: *The Sociology of Work.* Minneapolis, University of Minnesota Press, 1954.

Ginzberg, E., Ginzberg, S. W., Axelrad, S. and Herma, J. L.: *Occupational Choice: An Approach to a General Theory.* New York, Columbia University Press, 1951.

Hardy, R. E. and Cull, J. G.: *Climbing Ghetto Walls: Disadvantagement, Delinquency and Rehabilitation.* Springfield, Thomas, 1973.

Herzberg, S. et al.: *The Motivation to Work.* New York, John Wiley & Sons, 1959.

Holland, John L.: *Psychology of Vocational Choice*. Walthorn, Blaisbell, 1966.

Hoppock, Robert: *Occupational Information*. New York, Mc-Graw-Hill, 1967.

Maslow, A. H.: *Motivation and Personality*. New York, Harper Brothers, 1954.

Patterson, C. H.: *Counseling and Guidance in Schools: A First Course*. New York, Harper & Row, 1962.

Roe, Anne: *The Psychology of Occupations*. New York, Wiley, 1956.

Samler, Joseph: Occupational exploration in counseling: A proposed reorientation. In Borrow, Henry: *Man In a World at Work*. Boston, Houghton-Mifflin, 1964.

Super, Donald E.: *The Psychology of Careers*. New York, Harper & Row, 1957.

CHAPTER 16

WORKING WITH RUNAWAY YOUTH

- Rejection and Resentment
- The Self-Concept
- Relationship Between Runaway Behavior and
  Developmental Tasks

Introduction

THE RECENT DISCOVERY of the sadistic slayings and secret graves of twenty-seven boys in Houston, Texas, has helped in focusing much needed attention of parents, professional helping persons, policemen and others on problems of the teenager who leaves home in what has been called "runaway." The number of young runaways has been estimated to total anywhere from six hundred thousand to one million a year (*Parade Magazine,* 1973).

Anthropologists tell us that the most persistent institution in the history of mankind has been the family unit which has been traced as a phenomenon back to the dawn of man. The family has seemed almost impervious to external pressures which threaten it or external pressures which impinge upon the individuals within it; however, we are now seeing increased evidence within our culture that the family is no longer immune to pressure and change. In fact we are now seeing many types of pressures which are weakening its solidarity. Family disharmony seems on the increase as divorce rates soar, not only in our country and culture but across the world. Perhaps the most persistent attacks on the family unit have centered around questions relating to the effectiveness and purpose of the family. The family now serves a weakened role in inculcating the social and moral values of our society. Other institutions have assumed responsibility for this role and an increased emphasis in molding the opinions and attitudes of young persons has been taken on by their peers. The attacks on the viability and practicality of family units commenced with lower classed families; however, the questions of the efficacy of a family unit have spread to the middle and upper classes so that now it is a generalized concern among sociologists, anthropologists, psychologists and marital counselors.

More and more social scientists are confronted with clients whose basic problem is that of a deteriorating family unit. The spectacle of the deteriorating family is depressing. Figures now show that approximately 50 percent of delinquents come from broken homes (Ambrosia, 1971). The fact that families are increasingly being broken by desertion and divorce is of immediate concern and even among those family units which remain intact, there are exhibited many problems of a social and emotional nature. Alcoholism, other drug addiction, crime and suicide are now rampant.

The family frequently has been cited as the villain of many social evils but with regard to delinquency and runaway behavior there has been substantial agreement that the family is to blame. The difficult and puzzling stage of adolescence brings about many profound problems. As Mead has aptly stated, "Parents have been rearing unknown children for an unknown world since about 1946" (Mead, 1972).

REJECTION AND RESENTMENT

The rejection of either or both parents by the child is certainly an important factor in demonstrated aggressive behavior on the child's part. Many children feel rejected and react with overt aggression toward parents and the family units. Rejected children generally show a marked tendency toward an increased resistance and quarreling in relationship with adults. They also show considerable sibling rivalry.

Many family members who are confronted with a child's hostile, progressive or delinquent behavior react very negatively. In addition to the problems of financial or social misfortunes, the family as a unit is generally ill prepared to deal with these situations. Often there are real communication problems because there are definite differences in values, especially between the outside peer culture and the individual's family.

There are some early signs which can indicate possibilities for runaway behavior. Some of these include resentment of authority figures in the home and school, resentment of overprotection, open conflicts, resentment of discipline, loss of interest in school subjects, impulsivity associated with permissiveness, heavy influence of juvenile peer group, antisocial attitudes, general frustration for involvement with drugs and compensatory behavior.

THE SELF-CONCEPT

It is important for parents and others to understand concepts related to self-esteem. Often persons who are prone toward runaway behavior show inadequate self-confidence and see themselves in negative ways. An individual who maintains a negative self-concept often continues to behave in accordance with this concept by way of expressing hostility. Counseling sessions with a social worker, rehabilitation counselor, psychologist or other helping profession person can be a real help if this helping individual is keenly tuned into the subculture of youth and current mores and patterns of behavior. Professional service workers and parents must be willing to look into the conditions that produce attitudes leading to runaway behavior. These include the environment of the home and the interrelationships between the individual runaway and his parents and peer associates. Every effort should be made to get children inclined toward this behavior to become involved in meaningful activities, if not possible within their home, at least within their community areas. Projects in which students can find meaning through helping others are often of sufficient and substantial value in modifying negative self-concepts and poor attitudes toward the community, home and society in general. If at all possible, families should attempt to have joint projects of mutual interest. These can help in maintaining and improving relationships among family members. Projects should be selected by the family team and not forced upon younger family members by parents or older relatives or siblings.

Another helpful resource is that of grandparents or other relatives who are at least one generation removed from the youth. Since they are less closely associated, there is less ego involvement. Children often can go to such persons and find considerable positive regard and acceptance. In some cases grandparents may be able to be very helpful in that they constantly reinforce positive self-appreciation and more on the part of the young person.

The parent also may wish to consider allowing the young person to get a job in order to become more self-sufficient. This can improve concept of self and cut down on amounts of time which are often used negatively. It should be remembered that most young people get quite bored with themselves, their friends and family units. This is partially due to the large amount of time which many of them use unproductively.

RELATIONSHIP BETWEEN RUNAWAY BEHAVIOR AND DEVELOPMENTAL TASKS

Much behavior of individuals can be explained and better understood through the concept of developmental tasks. Havighurst (1957) has outlined the developmental tasks according to age groups of life. He breaks the life span of individuals into six areas. Infancy and early childhood, middle childhood, adolescence, early adulthood, middle age, and later maturity. Runaway behavior is generally confined to the period of adolescence which runs roughly from age twelve years to eighteen years. According to Havighurst (1957) there are ten specific tasks within this age frame of adolescence. These are:

1. Achieving new and more mature relations with age mates of both sexes.
2. Achieving a masculine or feminine social role.
3. Accepting one's physique and using the body effectively.
4. Achieving emotional independence of parents and other adults.
5. Achieving assurance of economic independence.
6. Selecting and preparing for an occupation.
7. Preparing for marriage and family life.
8. Developing intellectual skills and concepts necessary for civic competence.
9. Desiring and achieving socially responsible behavior.

10. Acquiring a set of values and an ethical system as a guide to behavior.

Many of the causes of runaway behavior among contemporary youth can be tied directly to individual failure at one or more of these developmental tasks of adolescence. Failure to achieve new and more mature relations with age mates leads to a severe social frustration. The individual who fails in this task soon sees that he is out of step with age mates. Successful members of the peer group who are achieving this maturity in their relations with other members of the peer group adjust well and feel more comfortable in social situations. However, the individual who fails in this task feels isolated, alone and has no sense of belonging to the peer group. This is a key factor in precipitating runaway behavior.

Related to the developmental task of achieving new and more mature relations with age mates of both sexes is the task of achieving a masculine or feminine social role. It is at this point that the youngster must assert his identity in the social role and must have a clearly defined self-concept of masculinity or femininity. Again, if he is unable to achieve this level of identity he will be out of step with the peer group and again will feel isolated and rejected. The third developmental task again is related to the first two but is even more specific in its requirement of adjustment. The third task of accepting one's physique and using the body effectively is a very difficult one for adolescents since this is a period of gangliness and lack of muscular control. Therefore, the individual is clumsy, unfamiliar with his body, unfamiliar with its potential and feels strange with himself and with others. Until he can become adjusted to himself he cannot become adjusted to his peer group.

Perhaps the key developmental task which relates to runaway behavior is the need to achieve emotional independence of parents and other adults. If the individual is not able to achieve a masculine or feminine role and declare himself an adequate, separate, competent individual and sever the emotional ties which have bound him to the parents and have rendered him a child, he will experience extreme frustration. He will feel thwarted in many areas and will feel the only solution to this thwarting and isolation is to escape from the environment. This often results in runaway behavior.

Runaway behavior can result when the individual feels the requirements of maturity and those of "the establishment" impinging on him to the extent he feels socially suffocated. In this situation the individual is striving to retain his immature status and is rejecting the demands for maturity. The few developmental tasks outlined above help create the drive for runaway behavior in this instance. For example, when the youth who is reluctant to relinquish his maturity is forced to consider achieving economic independence, selecting and preparing for an occupation, preparing for marriage and family life and developing skills and concepts necessary for civic competence, he will feel that again if he escapes from the environment which is impinging on him, he will be able to delay relinquishing the immature role with which he feels so comfortable. So failure on these developmental tasks will also provide a clue to predicting runaway behavior. The individual who exhibits runaway behavior totally rejects developmental tasks of achieving socially responsible behavior. In fact, runaway behavior generally is characterized by socially irresponsible behavior. It is an attempt to reject participation as a responsible adult in the life of the community and in the life of the family. However, by rejecting this role, the individual is unable to adequately meet the last developmental task, that of acquiring a set of values and an ethical system as a guide to behavior. It is only when an individual is able to function in a socially mature and responsible manner can he get adequate feedback which assists him in developing his own personalized set of values and ethical system which will guide his behavior in a socially responsible manner.

Summary

In summary, runaway behavior is characterized by a panic situation of the young person. He feels he must escape from the environment in which he is functioning for several reasons. All runaways reflect a crisis situation within the family or within the community. There are impinging pressures which are unacceptable and demands are being made which he cannot meet. Therefore, if he runs, he escapes from the reality system which is so unpleasant. There is very little foresight or insightful decision making prior to runaway behavior. If runaway behavior characteristics can be identified by family members or guidance counselors, school teachers, ministers, or other members of the community prior to the run, counseling can be very effective. Pressures in the environment which are so unacceptable can be relieved, demands can be eased and the youth can grow and mature socially and psychologically from the learning experience. However, if the environment becomes so difficult the individual elects runaway behavior, this becomes a habit pattern which may be reinforced throughout life resulting in an aversion on the part of the individual to "face up" to any adversity.

REFERENCES

Ambrosia, Lillian: *Runaways*. Boston, Beacon Press, 1971.

Havighurst, R. J.: *Developmental Tasks,* 2nd Ed., New York, Longmans, Green & Co., 1957.

Mead, Margaret: A conversation with Margaret Mead: On the anthropological age. In *Readings in Psychology Today*. Ted. Bell, Mar, California, CRM Books, 1972.

Parade Magazine, October 7, 1973.

CHAPTER 17

COUNSELING WITH THE OLDER AMERICAN

- Definition of the Older American
- Emotional Aspects of Aging
- Psychological Aspects of Aging
- Employment Needs of the Aging Person
- Social Needs of the Aging Person

DEFINITION OF THE OLDER AMERICAN

THE PURPOSE OF THIS CHAPTER is to outline some of the concerns to be considered in counseling with older Americans. It will cover some of the emotional, psychological, employment, and social needs of these individuals. Before looking at these specific areas, should identify this segment of our population. In counseling and rehabilitation psychology, we tend to be quite exact in our functional descriptions or definitions of a disability group. For example, in mental illness there are numerous specific diagnostic categories which describe the psychological function of the individual; in cardiac involvement there is the functional heart classification; almost all state education and rehabilitation agencies use a rather specific range of IQ to define mental retardation, and IQ is a quantified approach to describing intellectual function; however, the term "older Americans" is filled with ambiguity. We use many other terms which are just as inadequate—the aged, the aging, senior citizens, geriatrics, golden-agers and many others. Not only are the names for this segment of our population indefinite and inadequate, but also the definitions are just as confusing. Almost all the definitions use age rather than function as the criterion. As many will recognize this is foreign to professionals involved in vocational rehabilitation since we pride ourselves on taking the humanistic or functional approach to individuals.

Most professional counselors in rehabilitation psychology prefer the term industrial gerontology or the industrial geriatric. According to Norman Sprague (1970), industrial gerontology is the study of the employment and retirement problems of middle-aged and older workers. It is the science of aging and work.

Industrial gerontology begins where age per se becomes a handicap to employment. Age discrimination in employment may start as early as thirty-five or forty in some industries and occupations, and it begins to take on major dimensions at age forty-five. Federal and state legislation impose age discrimination in employment policies generally around the ages of forty to sixty-five. However, as in other disability areas of vocational rehabilitation, this condition (age) becomes a factor of concern only when it constitutes a handicap to employment.

Industrial gerontology is concerned with aptitude testing, job counseling, vocational training, and placement. It is concerned with job adjustment, job assignment and reassignment, retention on the job, redesign of the work requirements, vocational motivation, and mobility.

The similarity between the concerns of industrial gerontology and rehabilitation psychology and the degree of overlapping in these two areas are impressive. So programs in industrial gerontology are highly significant to the individuals charged with responsibilities for program planning and development in rehabilitation as well as the professional practitioner in the field.

Before discussing the specific needs of this segment of our population as outlined above, the authors would like to state a basic position which we feel most of us all accept but often forget. The similarities between any section of our population and the population as a whole are much greater than the dissimilarities. The industrial geriatric or "older American" is more like than unlike the clients on our existing case loads. Pragmatic changes which are needed to adapt our services to this population will be minor and tend to be changes in emphasis rather than changes in direction.

EMOTIONAL ASPECTS OF AGING

A very interesting trend has occurred in our culture which has resulted in creating emotional needs for the "older American" age is no longer related to conformity behavior (Cull, 1970). Traditionally we have revered our elders. In our culture we can see this reverence in the admonishments of the Old Testament. In the Indo Iranian and Hindu cultures we can turn to the *Rig Vedas, The Upanashads,* and the *Bhagavad-Gita* for the same admonishments. Since the beginning of time, cultures and societies have turned to their elders for judgments, decisions, values, and mores. The elders have determined the future of the tribe, culture, or society. This has been true universally until the past generation. The current generation of elders have been socially, economically, and vocationally emasculated. They have become a lost generation. They grew up expecting, and with every reason to expect, to mature into a role of influence in our culture. This is a very enviable role and one generally anticipated with a degree of eagerness—becoming an elder had meaning, purpose, rewards, and status.

However, after the revolution in technology we now turn to younger, more aggressive, more highly trained individuals to make decisions. The demands for speed and innovation are two factors which have robbed older people of what they viewed as a birthright. Everything which smacks of seniority is under fire—even the committee hierarchy of Congress.

The result is this lost generation of elders have become confused, disoriented, relegated to an inferior role with a great amount of condescending expressions of concern. Rather than arriving at a state which would bring status and reverence and one filled with meaning and purpose, they have been pushed to early retirement, then isolated and forgotten. No wonder many are concerned, bitter, and resentful.

The most important need this group of individuals has is to feel useful. While much can be said for our new sophisticated decision-making theories, there is a great manpower pool of years of experience going to waste. This pool of manpower should be mobilized by our rehabilitation facilities for the benefit of both parties. While production and income supplementation will solve some of the problems of the aging, the workshop facility can solve many others. In workshop operations, it has been found that if older workers are placed with younger retardates, the production of both groups increases and the discipline problems with the retarded youngsters are reduced. This arrangement also seems to be an effective motivating factor for the older worker. Life is becoming more meaningful for him—he is more useful.

PSYCHOLOGICAL ASPECTS OF AGING

When we think of the psychological aspects of aging, we almost automatically think of reduced intellectual ability. Almost all research studies between Galton's in 1883 up to Lorge's in 1947 have indicated there is a decline in intelligence with age. The decline was supposed to be progressive beginning after a peak of age eighteen to twenty-five. However, more recent studies indicate this is not the case. It appears as if there is a plateau established at approximately age twenty-four to twenty-five. This plateau is stable until about age seventy. The objections to decline in intellectual abilities center around (a) the speeded nature of the tests and the decline of the individual's reaction time as opposed to intelligence, (b) the scores being dependent upon acquired and stored knowledge and older subjects being more remote from the time of schooling and having less schooling, and (c) the tests being constructed so they are more appropriate to younger subjects than older subjects. There is little if any reliable evidence that the older individual undergoes significant intellectual decline.

Testing deficits may be explained by lack of motivation, lowered reaction time, lack of familiarity with the testing orientation, as well as the considerations above.

A second factor to consider under psychological aspects of aging is that of the pathological mental conditions among the aged. This factor is probably the largest precluding factor in vocational rehabilitation's accepting and serving the aging population. There are statistics which support the position that age invariably brings on mental aberrations. During the last third of a century the admission rate of geriatrics in our state hospitals has zoomed.

There are many articles now appearing in the literature which indicate that state hospital geriatric wards are serving more as human warehouses and foster homes than bona fide treatment facilities. The high rate of admissions is partially explained by social and cultural factors rather than emotional factors. Due to the removal of much of the stigma attached to mental illness, many adults have older relatives committed on the slightest pretexts since this is a convenient solution to a social problem.

We are not trying to explain away the problems of the aging. Some are very serious and need the attention and concern of all of us; however, the problem is not of the magnitude we in vocational rehabilitation suppose. In the past we have felt the problems were insurmountable so we ignored them. The life expectancy for this attitude is indeed very short. It is incumbent on us to understand the problems of these people and mobilize our efforts to solve them.

In the psychological aspects of aging, one explanation of the increased incidence of a type of mental illness lies in the role which they are required to accept. The current life-style in our culture leads toward older citizens feeling much less secure, unhappy, nonproductive; they generally live in a home situation in which they have at best an ill-defined role; there is a feeling of dependence rather than independence which leads to self-respect. Their future is narrowing, constricting, and bleak with a diminishing health status (physical and emotional).

The last factor we will discuss is on psychological aspects of aging related to rehabilitation psychology is the psychological set of the older individual. All of us view ourselves as workers. If we become unemployed, we still tend to view ourselves as workers and as such are capable of work. The longer we are unemployed the more narrowed and rigid our view of our capabilities of working become. While employed, our psychological set relative to our capabilities for work is highly flexible. We feel we can do our job and many variations of our job in many different locations. The longer we are out of work the more rigid our psychological set of ourselves as workers becomes, until finally we become convinced we are no longer workers. This is very obvious among the coal miners of Appalachia. They can function only as coal miners in their local area. Since there are no jobs, they are unemployable. They no longer view themselves as workers.

This phenomenon is particularly appropriate with the aging. The longer they have been unemployed and the more they felt pushed out of their last job, the less they will characterize themselves as "a worker" or productive individual. Since the older individual has a rather strong need to be considered a useful person, but is unable to do so, his psychological adjustment to aging will be quite difficult.

EMPLOYMENT NEEDS OF THE AGING PERSON

Employment fulfills many functions and needs for all of us. As individuals we are what we do. In our culture we are identified by what we do for a living. Our economic status, self-concept, social status, friends, and community activities are to a great extent determined by our jobs. All of these factors which have direct bearing upon personality integration deteriorate in unemployment.

In the face of economic inflation, more and more concern is being expressed relative to retirement programs which provide fixed incomes. The inflationary spiral which we have had in this country for the last decade has seriously jeopardized or destroyed the stability of fixed-income retirement plans.

Therefore, the employment needs of the aging are two faceted —first, employment supplies many social and psychological needs which are essential to the individual and secondly, and more mundanely, employment needs of the aging include the provision for basic subsistence.

The productive older worker is interested, in many cases, in supplementing his fixed retirement income; therefore, his employment needs are uniquely adapted to part-time work or work involving a piece rate structure. His interests and vocational and production capabilities can be developed to the point of performing a diversity of subcontract work; and, if properly planned programs are instituted, a group of older Americans could attract national industrial contract work on a long-term basis.

Work also can meet the social and psychological aspects of employment needs of older workers who have solved the problems of basic subsistence. For most bright, alert, aggressive retired persons, retirement, unless impeccably planned, soon begins to pall. The avocational pursuits which held so much attraction on the "pre" side of retirement soon become stultifying and deadly on the "past" side of retirement. Fishing, bridge, hiking and so forth soon fail to fill the void left by the demands and rewards of employment. Consequently, many retirees are looking for an opportunity to utilize the talents, abilities and proficiencies they have developed and perfected over many years of employment.

We are amazed that businesses have failed to adapt the SCORE concept (Service Corps of Retired Executives) on the local level. We feel these people represent a vast untapped reservoir of manpower in our communities. In some limited situations businesses have solicited volunteers composed of retired teachers to teach remedial subjects, but we have in our communities retired workers who were supervisors, foremen, managers, and executives concerned with purchasing, marketing, production, accounting, plant layout, and efficiency, and contract procurement —the same concerns we in workshop administration have. We believe a business administration can be highly self-serving and still meet some of the employment needs of retired workers by developing a program to utilize these people's talents in the operation, development, and administration of the industry.

They can be used on a continuing volunteer basis in areas such as staff development, production supervision, quality control, or on a consultative basis for marketing, contract procurement, etc. We feel this approach will gain the business not only improved efficiency in operations and administration but a wider base and greater degree of community support for its programs.

SOCIAL NEEDS OF THE AGING PERSON

It is difficult to separate the social needs of the aging from the other needs discussed above. Almost all of the needs outlined above have direct social implications.

The social needs of the aging, as well as other needs, are the same as for all populations. They need satisfying relationships with their peer groups, security in interpersonal relations (they need to know who they are and have a sense of identity), recognition for achievement and acceptance.

Generally, the aging process is also an isolating process. As people grow old and retire from work, their environment shrinks drastically until, in many instances, the individual withdraws into isolation. In this situation he becomes highly ego-oriented, selfish, and preoccupied with himself and his bodily functions to the point of becoming hypochondriacal. If the social needs of the individual continually fail to be fulfilled, this psychological and physiological deterioration will continue. Once established, this pattern of isolationism is extremely difficult to break since chronic behavior in the aged is relatively easy to establish and the drive for change and new experiences is subdued in them. Individuals in this social isolation system are so obvious or noticeable, regretfully they form the stereotype we have of the older persons. This is an unfair stereotype; but as all stereotypes, it is a highly persistent image highly impervious to change.

Most of the suggestions made above regarding meeting the various needs of the aging will also meet the social needs of the aging.

There are some specific programs of which the counselor should be aware in working with the older American. These programs are designed specifically to overcome the isolationism forces of aging. The tools we have to combat this dreadful isolation for older people exists at least in part in every community (DHEW, 1973). Some of these services specifically include transportation especially adapted to the physical needs of older people, adapted to their timetables, to the routes that will take them where they need and wish to go at a cost they can afford in spite of lowered incomes; senior centers which reach out with real services as well as recreation to bring people into the action center of the community's life; nutrition programs which provide meals for older people and social settings so they may gain friendship, social contacts, education and activity as well as improvement in health through proper nutrition; opportunities in paid employment and in volunteer activities to serve others, provide chances to be needed, the most necessary of human requirements; and home services to make independent living more possible. Older people are not all isolated for the same reasons and they do not all need the same services. Often one service in itself is useless without a companion service. Many excellent health or recreation programs for example are not fully used by older persons because they lack transportation to reach them. Sometimes an older person not only needs transportation to a welfare department office or a health clinic but also needs someone to accompany him and stay with him to see that he gets the service he is entitled to, and to see that he understands what is being done. A counselor should realize that counseling services for this type of client in isolation from other services is wasted effort. Rarely can the service to counseling exclusively be used to solve the multiplicity of problems facing the older American.

Senior centers are places where older persons can come together for a variety of activities and programs. These range from just sitting and talking or playing cards to professionally directed hobby and group activities. Some centers provide counseling services to help individuals make better use of personal and community resources. Some assume responsibility for encouraging other community agencies to provide more help to senior citizens. A few centers serve as central umbrella agencies for all activities and services relating to older people. They serve also as recruiting spots for volunteers offering opportunities to older people to serve others less active. Some people believe that in time the senior center may hold a place in the older person's life equivalent to the central role now played by the school in the lives of children.

Poor nutrition can be caused in part by isolation and loneliness which make it seem hardly worthwhile to prepare the food—only to eat alone. Good nutrition however, provided in a group setting can offer a partial solution to loneliness. Throughout much of life, eating is a social occasion, a time for family gatherings and meetings with friends, birthday parties, holiday picnics—all are associated with pleasant times and food. When the social element is removed entirely, many people abandon regular mealtimes and turn to sporadic snacks to satisfy their hunger. The benefit of eating in a social setting is so important for the mental as well as the physical well-being of older people regardless of income that many organizations are providing group meals in a variety of settings.

Many older people who live alone fear that they may have a fall or be taken suddenly ill and be unable to call for help. Telephone reassurance provides a daily telephone contact for an older person who might otherwise have no outside contact for long periods of time. Persons receiving telephone reassurance are called at a predetermined time each day. If the person does not answer, help is immediately sent to his home. Usually in the event of no answer a neighbor, relative or nearby police or fire station is asked to make a personal check. Such details are worked out when a person begins receiving this service.

Friendly visiting has been called organized neighborliness because in this kind of program volunteers visit isolated homebound older persons on a regular schedule once or more often a week. They do such things as play chess and cards, write letters, provide an arm to lean on during a shopping trip or just sit and chat. The essential element is to provide continuing companionship for an elderly person who has no relative or friend able to do so. This kind of visiting relieves loneliness of older people in a very real way. Older people themselves say such things as, "She has made my life over" . . . "It makes me feel like I am still somebody worth talking to" . . . "It gives me a chance to speak of things which are in my heart" . . . "Her visit is something to look forward to." Professional staff workers have observed that clients look better and take more interest in things outside themselves after receiving friendly visiting services. Frequently there is improvement in actual physical condition or at least less absorption in illness.

Living in their own homes is a great desire of many older people. Home services can help make this possible. Some older persons with chronic conditions need regular continuing help preparing meals, keeping the house tidy and personal grooming. For others help is needed only temporarily while they recover from an illness or while the person who usually gives care is unable to do so. Many older persons may be quite able to handle normal household tasks but need help with heavier chores such as washing walls, moving furniture, cleaning gutters, and taking down storm windows. Accidents which permanently disable people often occur because homes lack minor necessary repair. These in-home services which are available for older people include such things as homemaker service, home health aids, and other similar programs.

Now, what can the counselor do in working with the older American? First, the counselor or psychologist need not modify his approach for the older client. As with other clients counseling should be a sequentially developed or graduated program providing positive concrete feedback relative to progress and should require not only tasks for the older American but should include a program of graduated decision-making responsibility. Most of us in counseling fail to recognize the need for work adjustment for the older worker of average intelligence with a work history. We feel he can just go back to work if he desires. In our approach to the practice of rehabilitation psychology, adjustment training is for the client with just the opposite qualities—youth, mental problems and no work history—but the purpose for the work adjustment training is the same in both instances, that is the establishment of an appropriate psychological set. With the young retardate we are trying to establish the self-concept of a worker. With the older worker we are attempting to reestablish this concept.

There are many indications that the majority of the patients on wards in psychiatric institutions is not in need of psychotherapy as much as they need a redefinition of their role in society. A counseling strategy in working with the older American should be one which reverses the isolationism process of aging and one which is designed to add meaning to the lives of each individual older client as well as activities. A counseling program should also take into consideration the need for remotivation of the older American, the gaining of positive feedback of his capability and adequacy and the introduction of the individual to programs which will facilitate the client's psychological adjustment to aging. There are many activities which need mature individuals. These may be activities which are remunerative for the older American or they may be voluntary activities. There is a severe need in our country today for volunteers to help with the less fortunate and the less self-sufficient (Hardy and Cull, 1973; Cull and Hardy, 1974).

REFERENCES

Cull, J. G.: Age as a factor in achieving conformity behavior. *Ind Gerontol,* 5:28-35, Spring, 1970.

Cull, J. G. and Hardy, R. E.: *Volunteerism: An Emerging Profession.* Springfield, Thomas, 1974.

Galton, F.: *Hereditary Genius.* New York, 1891.

Hardy, R. E. and Cull, J. G.: *Applied Volunteerism in Community Development.* Springfield, Thomas, 1973.

Let's End Isolation, U. S. Department of Health, Education and Welfare, Washington, D. C., DHEW Pub. #(SRS)73-20129, 1973.

Lorge, I.: Intellectual changes during maturity and old age. *Rev Educ Res,* 17, 1947.

Sprague, N.: Industrial gerontology: A definition and a statement of purpose. *Ind Gerontol,* 1970.

Vedder, Clyde B.: *Gerontology, A Book of Readings.* Springfield, Thomas, 1963.

Vedder, Clyde B. and Lefkowitz, Annette S.: *Problems of the Aged.* Springfield, Thomas, 1965.

CHAPTER 18

THE USE OF PEER PRESSURE IN GROUP WORK: A PROGRAM DESCRIPTION

- Application Criteria
- Background of the Program Participants
- Service Delivery System
- Staffing and Training
- Impact and Results

APPROXIMATELY FOUR YEARS AGO, the SEED was founded in Fort Lauderdale, Florida. The basic design of the program is the general treatment model developed by Alcoholics Anonymous; however, there are several modalities which are peculiar to the SEED. The description which follows is basically an outline of the goals and methods of the program; however, certain intangible which are difficult to describe exist in the program.

The SEED was developed because of a desperate need for help which existed for young people in the Fort Lauderdale area as a result of the heightened incidence of drug abuse. It was felt that new approaches to the problem were needed; therefore, the SEED concept evolved. The SEED program's concept was based on the premise that man can change his behavior and can live and cope in his environment. The young people who seek help from the SEED program learn that they can no longer *cop out* with drugs; but that they have daily problems and must learn to live with them. At the SEED, they obtain a sense of belonging to something meaningful along with the knowledge that they can find purpose in their lives with the extra ingredient—a sense of dedication toward helping themselves and helping others to help themselves. The primary function of the SEED program is to provide rehabilitative services for the young person who has become a drug experimenter, user, abuser or addict.

APPLICATION CRITERIA

The SEED is made available to anyone needing help. The addict who must have some sort of maintenance—such as methadone—to assist him in achieving detoxification will not be accepted by the SEED until such time as he is able to tolerate a truly *cold turkey* program of abstinence. Since its main program is not detoxification, the aim is to work with the experimenter, user, abuser or addict who has used drugs less than ten years. Because of the age range—nine years to early twenties—parental consent of the majority of applicants is needed.

Anyone seeking help from the SEED and is in need of detoxification treatment is referred to the appropriate facilities. Those applicants who are in need of medical attention are referred to appropriate hospitals and/or their private physicians. These young people then come back to the SEED program once they are considered to be in sound medical health. Other than these selected criteria, the SEED makes no distinction concerning participation in the program.

Physical discomfort of *withdrawal* is at a minimum among participants. Even those young people who have used heroin for two or more years and have $200-a-day habits (this is equivalent to $60 to $65 in New York) take only approximately three days to pass through the withdrawal symptoms.

BACKGROUND OF THE PROGRAM PARTICIPANTS

A unique factor of the SEED program is that it reaches into the schools. In this community, estimates show that between 70 and 85 percent of the children are experimenting with, using, or abusing drugs. The SEED has been successful in reaching young people through referrals made by principals, teachers and counselors of the various schools in Broward County. The apparent change in students using drugs such as the decline of grades, failures, and dropouts, along with attitude change has added to the frustration and dilemma of educators. Due to the referrals made by educators to the SEED program, the majority of the young people destined to become delinquents and burdens on society have been able to continue in school education and to aid teachers in understanding the drug problems of the young. The young abuser is of considerable help in helping other drug abusers, since he understands not only the values but also the language of the drug culture (Hardy and Cull, 1972).

Many young people, no matter how well they progress, have environmental backgrounds which are quite impossible for them in terms of adjustment. If there is no reinforcement from the family, the young person will meet constantly with disappointment and discouragement. For those young people in this particular situation, the SEED has been able to assist with the cooperation of either the courts and/or various agencies (vocational rehabilitation, family services, etc.) in obtaining foster homes and has been successful in continuing to work with them in their new environments.

SERVICE DELIVERY SYSTEM

The first phase of the SEED's program consists, in most cases, of a two-week program of intensive group discussions, but is expandable when needed. During this two-week period, the group discussion sessions average approximately twelve hours per day. In these sessions, the participant is aided in gaining insight into what he is and what he has done to his life by taking drugs; but more importantly, he learns what his life can be for him and the impact he can have on others if he is *straight*. These two weeks represent the equivalent in time of the participant's going to a psychologist and/or psychiatrist for a period of three years on a one-hour once-a-week basis. The fourteen-day intensive group sessions provide a radical and comprehensive change which facilitates the learning process of the participant. The SEED is operated on a continuous seven-day week basis. The participant in this fourteen-day program is at the SEED from 10 AM to 10 PM during which time he is involved constantly in rap sessions under the supervision of staff. These rap sessions are carefully guided, and the intensity is maintained at a controlled, effective level. When necessary for certain individual needs, rap sessions also are held on a one-to-one basis with a staff member.

Upon successful completion of this first phase, an additional three-month period ensues which requires the participant to attend four group sessions a week. This phase of the program offers practical application of his learning processes. He learns to function and cope in his environment while returning to the group involvement. The criteria of success of this program are based not only on the fact that the young person is drug free, but also on his attitude change toward life; that is, there is a love of self and others, community and country, and a sense of dedication to help his fellow man.

Due to the age of participants, they can adjust well to change. The amount of attitude change in the individual seems to indicate that the three-month period is quite effective. In some instances, individuals require either an extension of the two-week period or an extension of the three-month program. Periodic follow-up is done to see how the participants are doing.

If the participants learn well and grasp the meaning of honesty, love, respect, discipline and affection, there is no need for them to go back to drugs. For the young people who are found to have deep-rooted psychological, or serious physical problems, the SEED makes referrals to medical doctors, psychologists, and/or other community programs. This is true particularly during the individual's participation in the two-week intensive program.

Up until this introduction to the SEED, the *druggie's* most reliable behavior characteristic has been the lie that he speaks and lives in order to mislead his parents and his teachers. This same lie directed to a staff member at the SEED is guaranteed to trigger a *choicely worded* verbal barrage not soon to be forgotten in that some staff members are former "druggies."

The lie must be replaced with something of at least equal strength. This is where the SEED staff asserts its true value and individuality. Just after the above-described verbal barrage, the staff member will close the one-on-one session by saying to the thoroughly deflated recreant, "I love you." No one who has heard this shopworn phrase as it is spoken at the SEED can fail to be deeply moved by the sincerity and purpose behind its use. The reinforcing effect of true concern (love) is quite awesome.

The success of the SEED program also depends largely on

family participation. The families are encouraged to attend two meetings a week to participate with the young people. Through this participation, the parents can get an overall picture of what the SEED is about and can see the gradual improvement of not only their own children but also those of other parents. They also can acquaint themselves with these other parents.

The group participation of parents and children, particularly those parents who are deeply involved with the program, has produced remarkable results in that the family unit is brought close together and gains a better understanding of the dynamics of its problem. Also, with the family, it has been observed that a greater level of love and compassion evolves within the family.

Fundamental to the continuing success of the SEED's program —especially during the period immediately following the two-week initial phase—is a highly effective information network which is composed of ex-druggies, teachers, police and concerned friends. If an apparently rehabilitated participant is seen even talking with a drug user, the director knows about it in a matter of minutes.

STAFFING AND TRAINING

The SEED has been able to train group leaders and help them develop talents of leadership. It also has been successful in encouraging these group leaders to continue more intensively in all endeavors to help combat the drug problem in the Fort Lauderdale area.

The SEED is strictly a paraprofessional organization, with its group leaders and staff coming from the program. Because of its uniqueness, the quality of staffing can be maintained only on this basis. The director is responsible for the overall operation of the program and for seeing that the outline and guidelines which have been developed are followed and the objectives fulfilled. He is also responsible for seeing that the other personnel maintain a high level of proficiency in meeting their obligations and fulfilling job requirements. Additionally, he is a liaison officer with other agencies in the community to effect cooperation and coordinate efforts that benefit the community maximally without duplicating existing services.

There are four senior group leaders whose responsibility it is to maintain group supervision when groups are in session. They assist in training new group leaders and junior group leaders. The junior group leaders are individuals who have gained some insight into the workings of the SEED program, but as yet have not developed the maturity or had experience which would prepare them to take a major responsibility for the conduct of either the initial intensive group sessions or the latter therapeutic group sessions. As they gain responsibility, they move on to being senior group leaders and assume a role of deeper responsibility. The staff of the SEED program, twenty-five paid and fifteen volunteers, can effectively handle the approximately three hundred active participants in the program.

IMPACT AND RESULTS

The SEED has had a demonstrable impact in the Fort Lauderdale area. Its program has reached into the courts, the jails, the minority ghetto areas, and the schools of Broward County. The Broward County Personnel Association officially has adopted the SEED as its 1971 drug project and is assisting in obtaining employment for the successful young people while in, as well as when leaving, the SEED program. The district supervisor of the Florida Parole and Probation Office and his staff have been playing a vital role in the rehabilitation of these people during and after their participation in the SEED program. The SEED also uses resources such as Broward General Hospital, Henderson Clinic, Family Service, Community Services, Vocational Rehabilitation, and adult education on an emergency and referral basis. The SEED recently became a member of the Cooperative Area Manpower Planning System (CAMPS) which is sponsored by the local city governments of Fort Lauderdale and Broward County. CAMPS is attempting to create a force of local agencies to effectively coordinate and cooperate in employment-developing opportunities. One role of the SEED is that of rehabilitating young people to enable them to become employable and constructive members of society and their community; therefore, involvement with these other social action agencies is essential.

It is interesting that the professionals that visit the SEED to observe the program seem to elevate different factors to prominence. One man might be struck by the obvious affection which permeates relationships between staff and participants; another by the sense of discipline displayed; and a third by the basic honesty of the program.

We feel the most effective factor influencing the youthful drug abuser at the SEED is peer pressure. The youthful ex-drugee is a potent influence in exerting conformity behavior. Cull (1971) has shown that peer pressure is influential even among schizophrenics who have rejected interaction with the social world in a manner somewhat similar to the members of the drug culture. Social roles are changing rapidly. No longer do the elders in our culture exert the impact on behavior and judgments as they did in the past (Cull, 1970); consequently, the SEED has turned to the group which can exert sufficient social pressure to change behavior—the youthful "ex-drugees."

The drug dependence problem is one of the most pressing in the country, and Broward County is no exception. This is evidenced primarily by arrests, particularly of the youth between ages thirteen and twenty. The SEED's records substantiate this age span and document the fact that many youths start on drugs at an early age and advance from marijuana to hard narcotics within one year. In an effort to combat the drug problem, the SEED was founded approximately four years ago. The basic model for the program is the general treatment program developed by Alcoholics Anonymous, with some very important modifications.

The counselors or staff members are rehabilitated drug offenders. After having gone through the program themselves, they have been judged to have the necessary skills and motivation to assist in helping others. These skills consist basically of the ability to develop an empathic relationship with others, the presence of strong desires and a dedication to help others and themselves, and finally, the ability to become skillful and successful group leaders.

The group sessions may be categorized loosely with the more formal Guided Group Interaction and Transactional Analysis-type groups. In the sessions of the SEED, both formal and informal group pressures are brought to bear upon the individual members by other members and leaders. As may be expected, it takes a very skillful leader to know when and how to apply pressure to any particular member or any particular segment of the group. This leader also must know how to channel the group's pressures to effective and fruitful endeavors. The group leaders are extremely adept at reading the character of each member and then applying or halting the pressures. Having once been drug offenders themselves, they are able to pierce the protective shell which each drug offender throws about himself. The group leaders refuse to fall into the verbal and the cognitive traps which the drug offender erects. In the language of *Transactional Analysis,* the leaders see the games drug abusers may be playing and refuse to play them. They then point out to the individual how false ideas have led him to his present state of affairs.

The atmosphere where the guided group interaction takes place contains simply *affection, empathy, discipline* and *love.* This *love* is a powerful tool in the hands of skilled leaders. In social power terms, the leader has been endowed referent power by the other members of the group. While at no time will he deny any group member, he does, however, skillfully manage the application of power. He uses his power to maintain motivation by reassuring those members who may have just received the brunt of a group session.

The above-described atmosphere of love has been coupled with the skillful handling of guided group interactions to form the SEED's unique and highly successful program. A new member attends two full weeks of twelve-hour sessions. If he has not made adequate progress, he may continue for two more weeks. Once a member has shown that he is responding, he is then allowed to return home. Prior to this he has stayed in the home of another participant and has gone to school or work from that home. After finishing this period, he returns to SEED for further group sessions every night for three hours and all day Saturday. This process lasts for three months. The member is then *straight* and attends only once or twice a week from then on.

During the day, there are two separate groups: one for males, the other for females. Particular problems are discussed and solutions found. In the evening, there is a general session which every member attends. The staff members take turns leading the discussion and help each other whenever necessary. Twice a week there is an open session in which parents, friends, teachers, probation and parole officers, and concerned others participate. At the open meetings, there are usually about 250 members and up to four hundred visitors.

An essential element in the success of the SEED is the amount of community participation and aid. Referrals to the SEED program come through many channels. Some are self-referrals, others come because of parental or peer pressure. The various courts are probating individuals to the SEED and sometimes send an individual to it for a presentence diagnostic-type study. Many individuals, of course, come because of the attention of concerned adults such as relatives, teachers and police officials. The SEED, because of its unique method and unequaled success ratio (now claimed to be over 90%), has managed to gather full community support.

Summary

In summary, the SEED is an organization of former drug offenders who are dedicated to helping others. Its program of guided group interaction, honesty, concern, and understanding seems to have meshed into a workable method. The testimony of parents, doctors, friends, teachers, prison officials, members of school boards, and others all point to the fact that the SEED is a viable, dynamic program.

Major questions relating to overall long-term effectiveness are: (1) what happens when the dominant peer group dissolves and (2) what is the future result of resolving drug dependency through strong reliance on individuals and groups or peers assuming such associations could be maintained.

REFERENCES

Berne, Eric: *Transactional Analysis in Psychotherapy.* New York, Grove, 1961.

Cull, J. G.: Age as a factor in achieving conformity behavior. *J Ind Gerontol 5*:28-35, Spring, 1970.

Cull, J. G.: Conformity behavior in schizophrenics. *J Soc Psychol, 117,* 1971.

Hardy, R. E., and Cull, J. G.: Language of the drug abuser. In Hardy, R. E. and Cull, J. G. (Eds.): *Drug Dependence and Rehabilitation Approaches.* Springfield, Thomas, 1973.

Urbanik, Richard: Report on the SEED: A working drug treatment program in Fort Lauderdale, Florida. Department of Correction, State of North Carolina, 1971 (unpublished).

CHAPTER 19

CASE STUDY DESCRIPTIONS OF REHABILITATION COUNSELING SERVICES IN DRUG ABUSE AND DELINQUENCY

A LL COUNSELORS WORKING with drug abusers, regardless of their specialty, are certainly rehabilitation counselors in the broad sense. Rehabilitation work with the drug abuser has developed rapidly as a major professional area of concern. No field is fraught with more problems for the helpee and the helper. The purpose of including case studies is to offer information on the problems which the counselors face. Whether or not the counselor reading this material considers himself a rehabilitation counselor, he may be interested in the service system which is available through state agency rehabilitation approaches.

Accomplishment of rehabilitation broadly defined is in such great demand throughout the country especially in schools, colleges, clinics, community agencies and hospitals that every effort must be made in order to bind together and integrate the work of counselors in various settings in order to enhance rehabilitation efforts. The reader of the case material will rapidly get a "feel" for some of the types of problems, failures and successes which certainly make up the picture of rehabilitation of persons who are experiencing difficulty in adjusting.

The cases which follow offer information concerning some general descriptions of human behavior which are attempted by professional persons in an almost desperate effort to be of help. Material is also given on referral sources, social data, medical information, educational and psychological data including the vocational plan and overall financial cost to a state rehabilitation agency. The cases reflect the efforts of agency personnel to work

276

with clients who are attempting to adjust to drug related problems. In some cases information concerning services is scarce and no doubt services themselves are scarce.

In few instances is group work being utilized although it is one of the more effective methods of working with drug abusing individuals (both juvenile and adult).

In cases where services must be resumed after a person is "rehabilitated," information generally is to the effect that clients have not been effectively rehabilitated. Certainly, it is not only the responsibility of vocational rehabilitation counselors to locate and provide rehabilitation resources. This is the job of all counselors. All counselors should recognize that the state vocational rehabilitation agency is a major resource to complement the work which they are already doing. Cooperation and team work is a must among counselors if these problem areas are to be attacked with any substantial degree of success.

C. W. B.
Black—Male—18
Married
9th Grade Education
Drug abuse characterized by an inability to adjust vocationally and socially. Character disorder (inadequate personality).

Referral Source

Mr. B was referred to the Department of Vocational Rehabilitation by the prenatal clinic at City Hospital. He and his wife currently are undergoing family counseling prior to the birth of their child. Previously he had been a client of DVR but was closed from a referred status for failing to respond to attempts of counseling or evaluation. He has been in the city's methadone treatment program for the last three years for his heroin addiction.

Social Data

Mr. B is an eighteen-year-old male. He is married and is expecting his first child. He and his nineteen-year-old wife are presently living with his uncle in center city. They have been drawing general relief for the last year.

Mr. B became addicted to heroin at the age of fourteen. His drug abuse began with the use of marijuana at the age of thirteen. He graduated to heroin and after three years his maximum usage was three bags a day. When he was fourteen he lost his mother upon whom he was extremely dependent and was virtually on his own. His father separated from his mother when he was very young. He remembers nothing about his father. It was at this time he began experimenting with drugs.

Mr. B presents a pleasant, neat appearance. His dress reflects his constricting economic circumstances. His social life is quite limited, partly due to economic circumstances and his rather narrow range of interests.

Medical Data

Mr. B stated that his health is good. While he was on drugs, he suffered from malnutrition, but since he has been on the methadone program he has regained his health.

The local physician found Mr. B to be well developed and well nourished and in no apparent distress. He is oriented in all spheres. On the basis of the general medical examination Mr. B seems to have no overt physical or emotional problems. His drug seeking behavior is apparently under control by methadone.

General Medical Examination

General Appearance—This is an eighteen-year-old black male who is well developed and well nourished with no acute distress.

Pulse: 78
Respiration: 18
Blood Pressure: 115/75
Skin and Hair: Normal
Head: Normal in size and shape
   Eyes: brown
   Teeth: good
Neck: Normal
Spine: No deformity
Chest: Lungs are clear
Heart: Normal
Abdomen: Negative

Extremities: No gross physical abnormalities
Neurological: No gross physical abnormalities
Reflexes: Present
Weight: 142 lbs.   Height: 5'7"
Impressions: This individual is in normal health.

Educational Data

Mr. B dropped out of high school after the ninth grade. He stated that his grades while in school were average and below C's and D's. His major reason for leaving school was financial—being on his own, he felt that he needed to make some money. While in school he did not participate in any extracurricular activity. Overall, he found school to be of little interest or value to him.

Psychiatric Evaluation

The psychiatrist found Mr. B evasive about his psychiatric history and drug history. He presents overt symptoms of anxiety and tenseness in normal situations. Episodes of depression were noted but were not considered extremely significant. This particular individual is characterized as having an inadequate personality. It is my impression that Mr. B is a young man not greatly endowed intellectually. On top of this, he is passive, inadequate, dependent, and lacking drive and energy. Certainly a training program within his limits of intellect and emotional stability is in order. However, Mr. B should not be placed in a situation which would cause frustration. He fears failure a great deal and will take it rather badly.

I would suggest that he has developed sufficient obsessive defenses that will enable him to make a reasonably good employee once he can settle down into a semi-skilled "rut."

He has a tremendous amount invested, from an emotional point of view, in his present marriage. He will work hard to achieve stability in this situation.

Psychological Data

A battery of tests consisting of the Wechsler Adult Intelligence Scale (WAIS), Graves Design Judgment Test, Minnesota

Clerical Test, The Crawford Small Parts Dexterity Test, Wide Range Achievement Test, the Thurston Interest Schedule, the Incomplete Sentence Blank, Draw a Person and the Cornell Index —Form N2. The results are indicated below:

WAIS: Norms 18-year-old group

Verbal Subtest	*Scaled Scores*
Information—7	Arithmetic—6
Similarities—9	Digit Span—9
Comprehension—6	Vocabulary—5

Performance Subtest	*Scaled Scores*
Digit Symbol—12	Picture Design—6
Picture Comp.—8	Object Assembly—10
Block Design—11	

Verbal Scale IQ—83
Performance Scale IQ—95
Full Scale IQ—87

Graves Design Judgment Test
Raw score—56—85th percentile

Minnesota Clerical Test
Raw score—149—93rd percentile

Crawford Small Parts Dexterity Test
Pins and Collar subtest—40%
Screws subtest—73%

Wide Range Achievement Test

Reading	3.9 grade	2%
Spelling	3.7 grade	2%
Arithmetic	4.9 grade	4%

Thurston Interest Schedule

Highest interest was the physical science, art, and business areas. Areas of least interest was computational.

Mr. B is a person in the mid-range of dull normal verbal intellectual ability and in the middle average on the performance scale. His full scale score places him in the upper range of dull normal intelligence. He possesses good skills in the areas of abstract reasoning and short-term memory. Hampered by poor vocabulary and limited information fund, Mr. B lacks the ability to deal with tasks requiring social knowledge.

The results of the tests indicated that he possesses adequate manual skills to function in construction areas. He would be hampered in training that required reading skills such as heavy equipment operations.

Personality

Responses on the Incomplete Sentence Blank suggests an immature individual. He has feelings of hostility directed toward his father. He prizes work highly and is very concerned about his ability to function in competitive physical tasks. Also of great concern to him is his present unemployment situation.

The Cornell Index revealed that Mr. B has little trouble in relating to those around him. He is troubled about unemployment which affects his feelings of adequacy and self-worth.

It is recommended that Mr. B avoid any training programs that require a classroom situation. He could function in an on-the-job program in the construction area.

Vocational History

Mr. B is presently unemployed. His longest period of employment was as a longshoreman. This job lasted for two years. He left because of an apparent lack of demand for his services. He then went to work for a trucking company as a packer. He left this job because of poor pay. The last job he held was as a metal cutter for a bathtub company. This job lasted for a month. He was fired because of absenteeism. Mr. B stated that his absenteeism was due to his involvement with drugs.

Mr. B functions at the dull normal intelligence level and has no salable job skills. He has been addicted to heroin and is currently under treatment for his addiction. His previous employment has been sporadic and without any skill value. His inability to obtain stable employment and support his family has caused depression and anxiety. With his inadequate personality and lack of training, he has been unable to maintain permanent employment. His frustration tolerance and self-image are low. He also has difficulty in relating to authority figures. These conditions constitute an employment handicap.

Vocational Objective

Carpenter's Helper—Mr. B has had some previous experience in carpentry handiwork and with some success. He wishes to be trained as a carpenter's helper and eventually will advance to apprentice or master carpenter.

This goal is within his capabilities, provided he is adequately prepared for the work task. In order to gain the necessary training and skills, the client will have to be helped to prepare for interviews, situations and questioning by prospective union apprenticeship programs.

Plans

The client will be provided counseling and guidance and given help in preparing for apprenticeship program interviews and for training.

R. E. M.
White—Male—18
Single
10th Grade Education
Inadequate personality with paranoid tendencies due to drug intoxication

Referral Source

Mr. M was referred to the Veterans' Hospital (VA) by his parents, who were very concerned about their son's drug addiction. Mr. M began using drugs while in the Army and has continued to use drugs since his discharge two months ago. He recently lost a job as a salesman with a major tire company, which may or may not be related to drug use. Mr. M says he realizes the fatal prognosis and wants to get off drugs so he can go to work and make a fresh start.

Social Data

Mr. M is an eighteen-year-old man who was admitted to a VA Hospital for drug misuse. His parents are a very pleasant and neatly attired couple. His father is in his early forties, his mother is in her late thirties. He was their first child. There are six other children in the family. The parents describe Mr. M's early childhood as a very emotional one. He had temper tantrums frequently and often passed out from crying so hard that he stopped breathing. During his adolescent and teenage years he was always quiet and had only a few friends. He also never has been too comfortable with girls. His parents made a point of saying that he did not "run around" with the "hell raisers" and seemed to think that this was one of the important factors in his favor. Mr. and Mrs. M feel their son is not a "bad boy."

Mr. M's parents related some of their son's guilt feelings over problems with their younger son, Jim. It seems Jim ran away from home just two days before Mr. M returned home from the service. Jim ran away with a thirty-five-year-old woman who Mr. and Mrs. M feel was manipulating and using him.

He now feels that Jim ran away because of him, although he had been quite close to his younger brother. Jim is still away from the home although his parents have heard that he is well. There are six other siblings in the family, sisters aged eighteen, fourteen, eight and five, and brothers aged sixteen and eleven. Mr. M comes from a family that is described as comfortable with the necessities of life but never an overabundance of money. His father works regularly and is very strongly committed to the value of work; "the necessity for hard work to get anywhere in life." His mother is a warm supportive person who is greatly distressed over her son's use of drugs and weeps easily on discussing this.

Both parents claim that they knew nothing of his taking drugs until recently when they first noticed a gross change in the patient's behavior. They described him as being normal, outgoing and happy when he first came home and then overnight he became very depressed and very frightened. Mr. M's rapid decompensation was followed by:

1. paranoid feelings in regard to people in the backyard laughing at him;
2. paranoid feeling regarding attempts made by neighbors to harm his family physically and their reputation;

3. his reluctance to get off the bus when he was going down-
town to the employment office. This caused him to stay on
the bus the entire route and go right back home. He stayed
in the house, totally afraid to leave.

At this point, Mr. M and his parents felt the need for hospital-
ization and he very anxiously presented himself to the VA office.

He dropped out of school in the tenth grade because he was in
constant trouble with the teachers. He enlisted in the Army,
thinking that the Army life would be nice. When he was disappointed and frustrated in the Army, he began taking drugs in
order to relieve his depression while in Vietnam. He was taking
speed, grass, and LSD. He has had thirty trips on LSD in the last
two years. Mr. M, a Vietnam veteran, was discharged from the
Army with a general discharge under honorable conditions. He
continued to take drugs until one week prior to being admitted
to the VA Hospital.

His girlfriend left him because he was "on drugs" but since he
sought treatment, she returned to him.

Educational History

Mr. M completed ten years of school and was described as an
average student. He did not participate in extracurricular activities in school. He did enjoy playing basketball around the house
but never played it in school. Once he got into high school he
could not adjust to the high school routine. His parents were not
really sure what it was, if it was that he could not grasp the material or if the classes were too competitive with the other students. During his stay in the VA Hospital, Mr. M took and passed
his General Educational Development (GED) test.

Psychological Data

Mr. M was referred for psychological evaluation in order to
assess possible organic impairment caused by his drug usage. He
was administered a battery of tests consisting of the Wechsler
Adult Intelligence Test, Bender-Gestalt, Projective Drawings and
the Rorschach.

Test Behavior

He was cooperative, coherent, and relevant throughout the interview and testing. He manifested some interest in and motivation to succeed on the tasks. The major clinical impression of this young man was that of a beaten individual. Although he was quiet, soft-spoken and self-denigrating generally, there were occasional sparks of animation.

Test Findings

The measures related to intellectual functioning suggest that this veteran has not suffered organic impairment due to the drug use. His Full Scale IQ on the WAIS was 105 indicating that he is currently functioning in the normal range. (Verbal IQ—106, Performance IW—103) While Mr. M seems to have the potential for bright normal functioning there are indications that emotional and environmental factors have interfered with his developing adequately. He performs well on tasks that require nonverbal skill, demonstrating moderately above average ability to concentrate and attend freely to noninterpersonal tasks. His performance decreases on the more academic, verbal and interpersonal tasks.

Mr. M's performance on the projective measures indicates some of the likely sources of his emotional and intellectual difficulties. These are quite consistent with the veteran's description of his family relationships and his schooling.

He has apparently employed denial as a major defense against strong feelings of inadequacy. These inadequate feelings seem to stem from the relationship Mr. M had with his father. His father is seen as a strong masculine figure who apparently thought little of his son and at least unconsciously made that quite clear. Unable to deal with these feelings and resolve this relationship, Mr. M, as he entered adolescence, apparently took the "easy way out." "If I am nothing, I'll flunk out of school, etc.," at the same time he was a "man" in this flunking subgroup.

Mr. M appears basically to be a bright and sensitive young man. He seems aware of the raw deal he dealt himself in order to cope with his emotional stress. This has apparently heightened his feelings of inadequacy and lack of self-worth and through the denial there is a fairly strong feeling of depression. In efforts to combat these unacceptable feelings of inadequacy, Mr. M at times comes across as hostile and aggressive. This dynamic picture may help to explain his choice of "uppers" rather than "downers" or any other drugs.

At the present time Mr. M's use or denial is sufficiently intact to interfere with his adequately grappling with and resolving these inter- and intrapersonal difficulties himself. It is the clinical psychologist's opinion that, if Mr. M is, or can be, convinced to enter individual psychotherapy or intensive counseling, he has the capacity for insight and growth from this experience. Additionally, when such counseling is undertaken, Mr. M seems quite capable of furthering his education vocationally, and perhaps, even academically.

Summary

Mr. M's current performance indicates that he is in the normal range of intellectual functioning. There is no evidence in the protocol to suggest organic impairment or psychosis. At the present time he may be considered an Inadequate Personality with paranoid tendencies due to drug intoxication. The records suggest that attitudes within his family have fostered this self-perception. Therapy could prove beneficial and is recommended.

Medical History

Mr. M has a history of drug usage which led to his military discharge and subsequent admission to the VA Hospital. He has been hearing voices and is panicked by thoughts that someone is going to hurt him, although he doesn't know who this someone is.

Mr. M's mental and physical status reveal an eighteen-year-old male, thin, looking utterly panicked, eyes red from tears, claiming that he does not trust anybody and is afraid to be in the building because "the whole world is crazy."

Mr. M states that he has been in good general health except for these feelings. Smoking, occasionally drinking, and use of

LSD, speed, and marijuana are Mr. M's habits. He has had none of the childhood or adult illnesses and is sensitive to poison oak.

Because he is afraid, **Mr. M** claims that "they" think he is a queer, and an addict, and so on. . . . The physician felt that the client was inadequate, immature, and withdrawn, with a flat affect.

Physical Examination

Patient is in no distress, well oriented.
Eyes: Negative
Throat: Negative
Neck: No adenopathy
Lungs: Clear to A and P
Heart: Negative
Abdomen: Soft, no masses, no area of tenderness
Reflexes: Patellar—o.k.
Diagnosis: Acute psychosis, paranoid type

Vocational History: Testing and Counseling

Prior to enlisting in the Army Mr. M worked as an inspector for nine months at D&H, a screw machine company in his hometown. After his discharge from the Army, he worked for a major tire company as a salesman. Mr. M lost this job due to his drug misuse.

A battery of vocational and interest tests consisting of the Lee Thorpe Occupational Interest Inventory, Minnesota Vocational Interest Inventory, and the Edwards Personal Preference Schedule were administered by a counseling psychologist. According to the Lee Thorpe Occupational Interest Inventory, Mr. M showed interest in the mechanical field, and he would be satisfied in being an electronic pressman, or a stock clerk. He also stated that he would like to be trained as a steam fitter.

According to the Edwards Personal Preference Schedule, he sees himself as being an aggressive, exhibiting, showing off person. In reality, he is only eighteen. He could be given some allowance to be immature. We are glad that he now realizes that he can get along so much better without the effect of drugs.

Mr. James Smith, Mr. M's former employer at D&H, was approached about Mr. M's reemployment. Information was made concerning Mr. M's reemployment with D&H Company, upon Mr. M's release from the hospital.

Hospital Summary

Mr. M on admission was markedly frightened and suspicious. He stated that the whole world looked crazy to him. On the admission ward, he presented himself as a hostile and negative person. He requested his discharge against medical advice. After being coaxed by the staff, he "opened up" and admitted his paranoid feelings and suicidal ideas. While in the hospital Mr. M continued to suffer from ideas of reference and persecution for quite awhile. He is uncooperative and angry, claiming that he was not sick. A urine test proved that he was not taking his medication. He was confronted about this and he agreed to take his medication provided that it would not make him drowsy. Mellaril, 50 mg. q.i.d., was prescribed. Once this medication was increased, Mr. M's condition began to improve.

Mr. M has shown quite a bit of improvement in his condition since being admitted. His affect now seems more appropriate and he is showing more spontaneity. He seems free from psychosis but could have flashbacks in the future from his past experiments with LSD. Mr. M has been on several passes home and has apparently refrained from taking drugs while there. The hospital staff feels that Mr. M is ready to go back and resume working as an inspector at D&H Company. This will place him back in a familiar place where he feels he is wanted. And, he knows too where to go and what to do when he is ready for the GI bill training as a steam fitter. He also agreed with us that he will seek supportive therapy and counseling at a mental hygiene clinic. Upon discharge Mr. M was given a twenty-one-day supply of Mellaril®.

J. A. S.
White—Female—18
Single
High School Graduate

Drug abuse characterized by an inability to adjust vocationally and socially.

Referral Source

Miss S was referred to the Department of Vocational Rehabilitation by Dr. B of the Adolescent Clinic in the City Hospital. She is presently being followed at the Adolescent Clinic. Miss S has been diagnosed as having an adjustment reaction to adolescence, characterized by drug abuse. She has been in the methadone program and has received guidance and counseling.

Social Data

Miss S is an eighteen-year-old white female. Her family background is less than ideal. Her parents recently have divorced and since then she has been on her own a great deal. Her father is an alcoholic now living out of this state. She is the youngest of three children all of whom have experienced problems. She feels that her mother is not very concerned about her actions and cares very little about her. She and her mother argue almost constantly.

Miss S was arrested for drug abuse. She was caught using heroin. She is presently out on bond and was referred for a physical examination and an evaluation of her drug dependence before she went to court. She was placed on probation with the stipulation that she enter a drug treatment program. Before the arrest, she had used heroin regularly for the previous six months. She has used a variety of drugs including cocaine, marijuana, LSD, heroin. She was exposed to hepatitis two weeks before her arrest. One of the boys she and her friend were sharing their "works" unit with had hepatitis. In spite of all her troubles, she did manage to graduate from high school by going to summer school.

Medical Data

Miss S was seen by a clinic physician for a general examination and for determination of a physical addiction. She states that she feels fine with no physical complaints. Since she has been exposed to hepatitis through the use of a friend's dirty needle, ten cc. of gamma globulin were given as a prophylaxis. Her general appearance is that of a thin, healthy, adolescent female.

General Physical Examination

Height: 64″   Weight: 117½ lbs.
Vision: Normal
Skin
    Color—normal   Pallor—no
    Eruptions—mild   Icterus—no
Hair: Oily
Eyes: Normal
Nose: Obstruction—no   Sinus Tenderness—no
Mouth and Throat: Oral Hygiene—poor
    Gums—caries present
    Tonsils—normal
Lymph Glands: Normal
Thorax: Normal
Lungs: Clear to auscultation
Hearing: O.K.
Epistaxis: No
Hay Fever: No
Toothache: No
Chest Pain: No
Cough: Mild
Appetite: Fair
Abdominal pain: No
Dysuria: No
Blood Pressure: 120/70
Heart: RSR—normal
Abdomen: Soft
Genitalia: Stage of development, stage V
Neurological:
    Gait—good   Pilonidal Sinus—normal
    Strength—good   Coordination—good
    Balance—good   Reflexes—normal
Feet: normal
Femininity
Personality Traits: Tense, restless

Positive findings revealed needle scars on both arms. It is the opinion of this physician that she is physically addicted, needs psychiatric referral and at some time gamma globulin as a prophylaxis for possible hepatitis. The physical impression is that of a young, healthy female with the exception of needle marks. It is also recommended that she be placed in the methadone program.

Educational Data

Miss S has not done well in school, especially in high school. Her grades were below average—D's and F's; however, she did manage to graduate from high school by attending summer school to make up for credits lost during the regular year. A transcript of her high school performance indicated that Miss S was not involved in any extracurricular activities.

Psychological Data

Upon completion of the medical, Miss S was referred to the Guidance Clinic for psychiatric therapy. A battery of tests consisting of the Wechsler Adult Intelligence Scale, Bender-Visual-Motor Gestalt Test, Wide Range Achievement Test-Reading Section, House-Tree-Person, and the Roschach Test were given.

Miss S is a thin, brown-haired, brown-eyed girl who was pleasant and responsive and who had a tendency to talk in a dunning fashion and to play with her rather greasy, straight hair. She seemed rather dull and uninteresting in physical appearance in that she was dressed somewhat sloppily in brown, short culottes, a short brown suede jacket and loafers. However, she was actually a rather pretty girl with pretty eyes and a pleasant smile which was seen all too infrequently. Miss S sat sprawled in her chair and seemed unaware of her bare thighs being exposed, yet she was overly anxious to keep her chest covered with her jacket; she almost seemed to make a "thing" out of keeping her jacket closed. She appeared to enjoy the testing, and as time went on became more comfortable and was able to laugh; at such times her eyes sparkled and she was a very attractive girl. She talked at length about wanting to leave her mother and go out on her own but at the same time feeling guilty since she was the last child. She thinks her father is a "nice guy" but does not like living with him. She snickered and became evasive while talking about her father; and gave the impression that there is far more involved here than meets the eye. She spoke of her feelings of depression, her having been caught and her sexual experiences with various boys in a curiously detached, depersonalized way. She rationalized having been caught as "the vice squad is corrupt," and that "this city is too big and unfeeling." She considers the people where her father lives as being "warm," "friendly, loving and judging people for their inner self." She further says that people who take drugs because of nothing better to do are much like her.

Miss S is able to function on the bright normal level of general intelligence according to her full scale IQ of 117; her verbal score of 114 and her performance scale of 122. She has difficulty in those areas which require concentration and synthetic ability on visual-motor tasks; her concentration has a tendency to come and go with the results that the quality of her performance fluctuates. On the other hand, she was able to demonstrate superior social comprehension and judgment in a hypothetical situation. Her "gifted" score on the subtest which involved attention to environmental essentials suggests that she is overly concerned with things rather than people. Other areas tested generally fell in the bright normal range. Certainly this is a very bright girl whose intellectual functioning tends to be somewhat erratic because her intellectual energies are being dissipated by emotional concerns. Miss S is presently reading on the 10.2 grade level, which gives her a standard score of 103 and places her in the 58th percentile for one of her age group. This is considerably below her level of intellectual functioning and is an example of her problem with utilizing her intellectual ability in everyday living situations. At this time there does not seem to be any indication of a central nervous system dysfunction. Her test results are those of a bright, sensitive, withdrawn, immature, and somewhat regressed individual who is maintaining a passive-feminine orientation in her approach to her world as a defense against inward strivings toward destructive fighting and sadistic impulses which actually terrify her. She is one who feels depressed, constrained, and trapped and has a sense of not being alive and of watching life pass her by at this time. Actually, she feels unable to participate in life and goes to great lengths to project the blame on others, circumstances, places, etc. so that she will not be forced to recognize her depressed, inadequate state. She entertains many feelings of inner emptiness and futility.

This is a girl who has much sex role confusion and who appears to be experiencing panic over a sexual identity crisis. She is confused about who and what she is, is frightened and feels guilty because of her narcissistic and autoerotic urges. She often provokes situations such as seducing the male in order to resent and blame him later for the predicament in which she finds herself. When she deals with the male, it is in terms of her feelings of intense hostility, and her tendency to deal with males as well as people in general in a sneaky, self-centered and manipulatory way. She does have some feelings of panic concerning the male inasmuch as she has a tendency to project on to him her intense sadistic, destructive, aggressive and annihilating impulses.

Miss S views the female with a sense of anxiety; she feels erratic about the female and has a tendency to be evasive and avoidant when she deals with the female. She attempts to defend against her sensual impulses toward the female by projecting them onto others. Actually, she remains at the narcissistic level and attempts to cope with her homosexual urges by fleeing to heterosexual involvement in the way of defense. She is one who has intense dependency and oral needs, who is weak and passive, yet who has feelings and impulses which threaten to be out of control. This is a girl who wants and needs controls and who is presently experiencing panic over an imminent loss of control. She identifies with people on an immature, self-centered level but has little real sensitivity to and concern about people.

It is recommended that she be placed in a living situation which imposes strict controls such as a school away from home, or if this is not feasible, that she be hospitalized. In any event she should be involved in psychotherapy (which will be intensive), preferably of a group therapy nature. It is felt that this girl is experiencing an identity crisis and is fence-sitting at this time; thus, which way she moves will depend upon the treatment and living situation which she experiences within the next year or two.

Vocational Data

Miss S has never been employed, full-time or during the summers. She has expressed an interest in pursuing a career as a social worker and would like to go to college.

Miss S received a medical evaluation in December, 1973 and was found to be within normal physical limits with no physical restrictions or activities to be avoided. Client was noted to be on the methadone program due to drug abuse. Based on a psychiatric and psychological evaluation this client is seen currently as demonstrating numerous characteristics of a behavioral disorder. Client has been involved in drug abuse, drop-out behavior, and has experienced anxiety and depression due to her condition. This condition constitutes a substantial handicap to employment. With the provision of appropriate vocational rehabilitation services a favorable outcome is anticipated for this rehabilitation plan.

Vocational Objective

Social Worker—Since that date of the initial interview this client has received counseling and guidance. Based on the diagnostic information obtained in this rehabilitation program, this client has been receiving attention from the Adolescent Clinic at City Hospital and the Guidance Clinic. These institutions have provided the diagnostic information which indicates at the current time that this individual is ready for the provision of appropriate rehabilitation services toward the above indicated vocational objective. In order to achieve this goal, she must receive formal vocational academic training within a local facility, tuition, necessary fees, and books, psychotherapy, medication, maintenance, clothes, and transportation will be provided by the rehabilitation program. At the appropriate time in this individual's rehabilitation plan, she will be placed within competitive employment and follow-up provided in order to insure an adequate vocational adjustment. The estimated duration of this plan at the current time is five years.

Overall Plan and Financing for One Semester:

Tuition—one semester	$ 235.00
Activity Fee—one semester	12.00
Health Fee—one semester	20.00
Books—one semester	50.00
Psychotherapy—15 sessions @ $30.00	450.00
Maintenance—4 months @ $80.00	320.00
Clothes	75.00
Transportation	45.00
Methadone—5 months @ $47.00	235.00
TOTAL	$1,442.00

R. G. L.
Black—Female—20
Single
High School Graduate (Two Years College)
Drug abuse characterized by an inability to adjust vocationally and socially. Character disorder with aggressive and infantile manifestations.

Referral Source

Miss L's initial referral to vocational rehabilitation was by Dr. Wood of the drug addiction clinic of City Hospital where she was a patient from an overdose attempt. The referral was made for purposes of counseling and support. Miss L has been unable to adjust due to drug abuse. Drug misuse has handicapped Miss L both educationally and vocationally. At the time of the suicide attempt it was felt that further treatment was needed and presently it would be unfeasible for Miss L to receive vocational rehabilitation services. Miss L was later referred by Mr. Trice of a local drug treatment program.

Social History

Miss L is a twenty-year-old, single, black, female from the Bronx, New York. She has a three year history of heroin abuse along with a potpourri of other drugs including cocaine, barbiturates, LSD and methadone. She graduated from Thomas Jefferson High School in New York, where she was in the top quarter of her class. After graduation, she came to this city and attended City University for two years before dropping out and going back to New York.

Both of Miss L's parents are living and other significant family members include her older sister, C, who lives in Washington and her younger sister, J, a graduate of a local drug treatment program and currently a staff member.

Miss L was recently detoxified from heroin addiction in New York via Methadone. She then came to this city to visit her sister. On the third day of her visit, she left her sister's home in an apparent daze. She was later found by her sister walking the street in a confused and disorganized state. Miss L entered her sister's car and within five minutes had a major motor seizure. She was brought to the emergency room with a history of having taken ten to twelve grams of Isoniazid in a suicide attempt. In the emergency room, she had four more major motor seizures, poorly controlled with ten milligrams i.v. Valium® does.

Miss L was first introduced to drugs while a senior in high school. She stated that her reasons for using drugs was to become part of the "in" crowd at school. Her first experience was with soft drugs (marijuana). She gradually progressed to LSD and finally heroin.

Medical History

Miss L stated that she has been in good health since she detoxified from heroin in New York. There is no history of hepatitis or abscess due to her drug use. Physical examination at the time of Miss L's suicide attempt revealed a well-developed, well-nourished, black female who was agitated, tachypneic but awake and responding to commands. Her blood pressure was 140/90; pulse, 98; temperature, 101.3; respirations, 28. The pupils were equal and reactive to light. The examination of the heart showed a normal sinus rhythm without murmurs or gallops at a rate of ninety-five beats per minute. The neurological examination was given. Miss L responded to commands and appeared to realize what was going on about her. Her sensory and motor systems were intact. No pathological reflexes were present. She had hyperactive deep tendon reflexes bilaterally. No muscle weakness was evident.

Thirty-six hours after ingestion, the patient was awake and oriented, breathing normally off the nasal oxygen with normal vital signs. At the time of discharge, the patient was alert and oriented.

Discharge Diagnoses:
1. Isoniazid toxicity
2. Seizures secondary to No. 1
3. Metabolic acidosis secondary to No. 1, resolved

Disposition:
1. Appointment in medical follow-up clinic at which time a lateral chest will be done.
2. Appointment in the psychiatry clinic.

Physical examination was given after client recovered from her overdose.

General Medical Examination Record

R. G. L.   Age 20   Female   Single
Height: 5'5"   Weight: 105 lbs.
Eyes: Normal   Conals
Ears: Hearing—good
Nose: Normal
Mouth: Normal
Throat: Normal
Lungs: Chest films show no evidence of aspiration pneumonia
Abdomen: Normal
Sclerae: Not icteric
Circulatory System: Normal
Nervous System: Normal
Skin: Clear and normal
Orthopedic Impairment: None
Laboratory Data:
Blood gases on the Bennett respirator showed a PO_2 of 108, pCO_2—25, pH 7.20 and a bicarbonate of 9

Blood sugar—.199
White blood count was 16,900
Sodium—150
Potassium—4.2
Chloride—102
CO_2—12
Chest films revealed a right hilar density with no evidence of
  pneumonia
Extremities:
No cyanoses, clubbing or edema
Good peripheral pulses

Educational History

Miss L was graduated in the top quarter of her class at school.
While there she was especially interested in the arts, i.e. music
and painting. Although actively involved in the academics, she
did not participate in extracurricular activities. She stated that
she was a "loner" and had few friends. There was no indication
that school authorities knew of her drug addiction.

After graduation from high school, Miss L came to this city
and attended City University for two years. This was due in part
to the fact that her sister lived there. Her curriculum area was liberal arts with emphasis in music. During her two college years, she
became more involved with drugs especially heroin. Her grades
began to drop and Miss L finally withdrew after her second year
and went back to New York

Vocational Data

Miss L's work experience has been limited to the summer
months between school years. Her principal employment for her
summers was a waitress for a nationally-known restaurant chain.
This job was temporary in nature. The client has no interest in
this area as far as permanent employment is concerned.

Psychological Data

Due to her suicide attempt, Miss L was referred for psychiatric
evaluation. The report stated that this client has no prior history
of overt psychiatric systems. Over the past two weeks, Miss L has

had suicidal ruminations, insomnia, sadness or crying. She describes her life as one of loneliness and sadness. She indicated that she was unable to form close relationships with others. It was also felt by the psychiatrist that Miss L had occasional blurring of ability to organize thinking. With this wild uncontrolled thinking, her affect is flattened. She denied depressive systems at present.

Miss L's history suggests early signs of schizophrenia. The possibility exists that the central nervous system stimulating inclination of the Isoniazid may be exposing an otherwise subclinical thought disorder.

When Miss L was asked to reconstruct the night of the suicidal attempt, she was unable to remember any of the night's experiences. She stated that when she recovered from the effects of the drug, she did not realize why she was in the hospital.

Miss L was seen as an above average person in general ability. The fact that she was a good student in school is indicative of her ability. It was felt that she could best benefit from an intensive drug treatment program. In such a program support and counseling could provide her with the needed tools enabling her to make an adequate adjustment. She will also be provided with constant supervision. The rehabilitation counselor concurred with these recommendations. Due to drug addiction and misuse, she has been functionally limited in that she has been unable to adjust socially and vocationally. In order to learn to live free of drugs in our society, she became an inpatient at a local drug halfway house. It was the opinion of the rehabilitation counselor that Miss L's disabling condition presented a definite vocational handicap in that she was unable to maintain herself in society, unable to continue in college and unable to obtain and maintain employment.

The final clinical impression was that she had a definite character disorder with aggressive and infantile manifestations.

Report From the Drug Treatment Center

Upon first entering the program, Miss L displayed an over-evaluation of herself in terms of an attitude of superiority. She was condescending, arrogant, uncooperative and cynical. She listened to no one and chronically alienated others around her. It was felt that this infantile behavior was a manifestation of severe feelings of inadequacy. She exhibited a rather cavalier attitude toward her own life when she first entered the program. One week prior to coming in as a program participant she attempted suicide by taking a large number of Isoniazid tablets. When this was discussed with her, she reacted with unrealistic good humor as if it were some kind of a joke.

After not being able to be worked with effectively in several of the local drug facilities, she was assigned to the North Street Halfway House where she finally responded. The staff members began to see the development of positive attitudes in relationships with others, a friendliness and a development of a definite warmth which was not present before. She also accepts criticism without becoming antagonistic and hostile.

Her improvement was to such a point that it was felt she could stabilize in a work situation. There has not been, on the other hand, a complete resolution of the conflicts she brought with her upon entering the program. With positive support, she has responded greatly and if this is continued in the program and on the job, more growth can be expected. Miss L's vocational rehabilitation counselor was notified as to her improvement and her readiness to work.

Miss L's primary disability has been diagnosed as drug abuse characterized by an inability to adjust vocationally and socially. A character disorder characterized by aggressive and infantile behavior has been diagnosed as the secondary disability. Due to drug addiction, she has been functionally limited in that she has been unable to adjust socially and vocationally. In order for her to live free of drugs in society it was necessary for her to become an inpatient at a drug treatment halfway house. It is felt that through the services and support of the drug treatment program, this client will be rendered fixed to return to gainful employment.

Plan and Summary

A rehabilitation plan was written with detective (private investigator) as the vocational objective. This vocational objective was felt to be reasonable and attainable in that this client is well-qualified based on her varied drug experience to work in undercover work to help in identifying drug "pushers." This position will be an on-the-job training situation in which she will receive training and experience as an undercover agent.

Summary of Services

Miss L will enter an on-the-job training situation at no cost to DVR. She will have the transportation needed to begin this employment. She will also receive follow-up services to assure satisfactory adjustment to the job. While involved in the training and employment, she will continue as a halfway house resident where she will receive continued treatment and support. The estimated length of service is four months.

B. T. S.
White—Male—19
Single
High School Graduate
Drug abuse characterized by an inability to adjust vocationally and socially

Referral Source

Mr. S is a nineteen-year-old white male. Two years ago, this client was in a vocational rehabilitation school unit. During his senior year he dropped out of school and left town. Recently he returned to Richmond and was referred to this vocational rehabilitation counselor by his former school unit counselor as a client in need of services due to residuals of drug addiction.

Social History

Mr. S comes from a disrupted family background. This client's mother died when he was very young and he was raised and cared for by various women within the family (2 sisters and an aunt). The client remembers being extremely effeminate and afraid of his peers. His father has been a disabled alcoholic for a long period of time. Mr. S had interrupted relationships with his father and received no financial support or guidance while growing up. The client stated that he separated completely from his father when he was fifteen years old. Ever since he has been on his own, searching for his identity and attempting to cope with his emotional problems.

Mr. S has been a drug user since his high school years. This client was a heavy user of amphetamines and eventually became dependent upon these drugs. He also had used LSD and speed. His leaving high school during his senior year was due primarily to drug abuse. After Mr. S dropped out of school, he went to Canada, gradually working his way across the states and finally became a "speed freak" in San Francisco's Haight-Ashbury. He lived with a couple and their child. During his stay in Haight-Ashbury, Mr. S was seen by a psychiatrist in a free clinic where he was found to be an extremely depressed youth with homosexual drives and a drug dependency (see psychological). He was placed in a drug treatment center and withdrew from drug use.

Mr. S is a seemingly bright young man who is attempting to work out his problems and his loneliness without family guidance and support. He has been living with friends and acquaintances for the past two years. He is seen by the vocational rehabilitation counselor as being cooperative, alert, and quite willing to bend to survive.

Educational History

Mr. S completed eleven and one-half years of school before dropping out and going to San Francisco. While there he did manage to finish his remaining course work and graduated from a local San Francisco high school. Also while in California, Mr. S qualified for a civil service appointment by passing the Civil Service Examination. He is an intelligent individual who expresses a desire to go to college or to learn a skill or trade.

Vocational History

Mr. S's vocational experiences are limited due to his home environment, drug abuse, and age. He has not worked while living in this city. While in San Francisco he did qualify and passed the Civil Service Examination. He then secured a job with the postal department as a clerk in the concentration center. He earned three dollars per hour. He held this job for two weeks before he was forced to quit due to drugs. This client managed to find odd jobs and eventually worked his way back to this city. He has since been unemployed receiving support from his friends and relatives.

Psychological Data

Psychiatric Abstract From the Haight-Ashbury Free Clinic

Mr. S presents symptoms of anxiety and depression. He is a highly dependent youth and has been placed in a situation with which he is unable to cope, following a failure of a mother substitute relationship. He has been clinging to this relationship for some time as a defense against his very strong homosexual drives. However, he recently entered into a homosexual relationship with another young man, and as a consequence feels that he has achieved some resolution of his identity conflicts.

This client has been a drug user for many years and recently became dependent upon amphetamines. It is quite probable that his present emotional state is in part due to wasting effects of continued use of amphetamines, LSD and other psychedelic drugs.

In summary, Mr. S is unable to function in the appropriate masculine roles and has resolved his psychosexual conflict through a homosexual adjustment.

Since data was not obtained in regard to Mr. S's school cumulative record, the Revised Beta and Kuder Preference Test were administered by the vocational rehabilitation counselor. Revised Beta results revealed a score of 120 placing Mr. S well above the upper limits of average intelligence. The Kuder Preference Test indicated this client's interests are in the fields of literature and art.

These findings were discussed with Mr. S. He stated he has done considerable writing of poetry and prose and apparently has talents in those areas. Mr. S intends to further develop these talents in college, but at the present time he wants to become self-supporting, preferably through sales or clerical work. These are his stated goals at the present.

Medical istory

Mr. S's medical history reveals that he has had no systematic difficulties or apparent illness except the residuals of drug abuse. Mr. S was sent to a local physician for his general medical examination. On the basis of the following report no further recommendations were made.

General Basic Medical Examination Record

Frequent Headaches: No
Hearing: No
Extreme Fatigue: Yes
Nervous System: Normal
Persistent Cough: No
Pain in Chest: No
Unusual Irritability: Yes
Swollen Ankles: No
Loss of Appetite: No
Difficulty in Memory: No
TB: No
Hernia: No
Operation: No
Hemorrhoid: No
Diarrhea or Constipation: No
Eyes: 20/20—left; 20/20—right
Nose Thorax: Negative
Lymphatic: Normal
Heart and Circulation: Normal
Abdomen: Normal
Ano-rectal: Normal
Difficult Vision: Yes

Fainting: No
Asthma: No
Unusual Gain or Loss of
    Weight: No
Cough Producing Blood: No
Short Breath: No
Fever: No
Difficulty in Thinking: No
Frequent Indigestion: No
Rheumatism: No
Convulsions: No
Varicose Veins: No
Accident: No
Burning in Urine: No
Height: 73"   Weight: 129 lbs
Hearing: O.K.
Mouth or Teeth: Normal
Chest and Lungs: Normal
Blood Pressure: 100/50
Genito-Urinary System: Normal
Skin: Normal

Mr. S's primary disability has been diagnosed as an emotional disorder characterized by an inability to stabilize in work. A secondary disability has been diagnosed as residuals to drug abuse. Mr. S expects to complete his education in college but at this time he needs to gain his independence and self-esteem. Due to his exceptional intellectual talents and personal insights into his problems along with his withdrawal from drug usage, there is reasonable expectation that he can be gainfully employed.

Plan

A vocational rehabilitation plan was written with sales clerk as the vocational objective. This vocational choice was based on the client's intellectual ability, experience, and interests. It was felt by the counselor and the client that time was needed for the client to plan his future. A stock clerk position was found with a local department store. The client will earn $50/week.

Services Rendered

Guidance and Counseling
General Medical Examination
Transportation
Rent for a month
Food bills for a month
Clothing
Job Placement
Follow-up

Cost to Vocational Rehabilitation—$250.00
Client was closed rehabilitated

Case Reopened

Six months later, Mr. S came and told his rehabilitation counselor he quit his job after six weeks. The position as a stock clerk was not challenging enough for Mr. S. He stated that he needed to be more deeply involved in some occupation more in line with his self-image.

Mr. S appeared to be hostile, depressed and lonely to the vocational rehabilitation counselor. He blurted out his feelings in a somewhat philosophical manner. He spoke of moving many times in the past six months. He wanted to talk about the state of the economy and he didn't believe there was a job "out there for him." He has been disappointed in not getting a job as a mail clerk.

His Kuder Performance Record Vocational (KPRV) was again interpreted for him. Some effort was made to explore which move would be more in the direction of his long-range goals.

"Library Assistant" and "Proofreader" seemed to be appropriate jobs for consideration. Local opportunities might include copy editing with a newspaper. Literary and musical interest were suggested by the KPRV. An appointment was made for Mr. S to take the General Aptitude Test Battery (GATB).

It was felt that Mr. S may have real potential as a composer and arranger if he is willing to go through formal training. At this time he frowns upon formal education and wants to get a job. He doesn't feel academic discipline is that important since he picks up things very quickly on his own, including some composing of music.

GATB scores indicate Mr. S has good general capacity:

General Intelligence (G)—133   Clerical Perception (Q)—154
Verbal Aptitude (V)—145   Motor Coordination (K)—140
Numerical Aptitude (N)—130   Finger Dexterity (F)—106
Spatial Aptitude (S)—107   Manual Dexterity (M)—91
Form Perception (P)—121

Mr. S was informed of the results. The conversation tended to center around music as his long-range area of interest. He has considered music school. The vocational rehabilitation counselor stressed the importance of some concrete long-range planning and the use of his talents. An appointment was made with the chairman of the music department of City University.

Mr. S would first like to work in the post office to prove to himself that he can hold a job for at least one half year. An appointment was made with the post office about a job as a clerk.

In his interview with the chairman of the music department, Mr. S played some of his original compositions. The chairman felt Mr. S has good potential in the area of music and persuaded him to apply for admission as a music student.

Mr. S then talked to the personnel director at the post office concerning employment. He trimmed his hair and presented a neat appearance for the interview. He mentioned his prior use of drugs to the personnel director. The vocational rehabilitation counselor felt this probably "killed" any chances of him getting a job. The client was then urged to search for jobs in the city. He found a job in a medical lab and was hired by Dr. H. Mr. S discussed the possibility of on-the-job training as a lab assistant under Dr. H's direction. It is a thirteen-month training program.

Mr. S's GATB reveals that for the vocational profile of the medical lab assistant, he has more than sufficient scores to qualify him for this work (requirements G—110; S—95; P—110; client has G—133; S—107; and P—121).

The Kuder Performance Test did show a correlation of 79 percent in scientific computation and the clerical field. He is well motivated to pursue this goal having had discussed this with Dr. H of the department of anatomy under whom he will be working.

This program offers ample opportunities for future employment since a local hospital expects to hire all of these trainees. The client will learn to dissect and prepare specimens for slides and to do all the jobs related there to and to operate completely with full responsibilities as a medical lab assistant. Tuition will be payable to the Department of Anatomy for this training at a rate of $86/month. Maintenance to be sought through the Department of Public Welfare and the Training Services Project at a rehabilitation center. Total Cost of Services—$2,318.

Dr. H will be supervising training and totally responsible for all of Mr. S's weekly hours, progress and reporting to the counselor.

Job duties:

1. Learn the preparation of tissue and various techniques.
2. Learn how to assist in surgical operation of animals.
3. Learn the ordering and caring of equipment.
4. Learn the care and treatment of animals for research.
5. Learn to use all equipment.
6. Learn the proper method of mixing and using stain chemicals and dyes.

Mr. S received a Training Service Project stipend with the stipulation that the money will not be paid if the student:

1. has three absences in a week
2. is placed on leave for more than one week
3. shows unsatisfactory progress
4. leaves training program

Client entered the training program in April. After the first month, Mr. S was doing a moderately good job. Dr. H felt his main problem was that of being easily offended by any types of critical opinion related to work. Mr. S knows the techniques on paper but occasionally has a little trouble transposing this knowledge to practices. He attempts to do some things without really thinking carefully about them before doing the task. Dr. H has stressed the importance of his appearance and communications with his fellow workers.

The vocational rehabilitation counselor feels that the client is having difficulty in regulating himself to work but is making progress and is "sticking with it."

Several months later, Mr. S was again evaluated. Dr. H indicated that Mr. S is learning the proper skills well and does a good job when told what to do. Dr. H senses a feeling of importance to the functioning of the lab by Mr. S. Progress is being made both in technical skills and fellow relationships. The vocational rehabilitation counselor counseled his client about his appearance. He accepted this and changed it sufficiently.

In the last progress report received, Dr. H indicated Mr. S is increasing in skill proficiency. Client is still having trouble in the area of properly conceiving what is to be done. The rehabilitation counselor felt Mr. S was improving in this motivation, acceptance of responsibility and initiative. He has come a long way from "wandering in the streets."

During the fourth month of on-the-job training, Mr. S began experiencing peculiar sensations which he described very vividly as the sensation of "drifting away or being associated with reality." He is also aware of occasional hallucinatory experiences especially of visual and especially when looking at a blank wall or into a clear sky.

Mr. S was sent to Dr. O, a neurologist. In addition to the above sensations the client has had on occasion some olfactory hallucinations with varying and differing odors each time. He denies headaches, diplopia, tinnitus and peripheral paresthesias. The neurological examination is entirely within normal limits except for a very slight difficulty walking a tandem.

The EEG is abnormal showing some spontaneous paroxysmal dysrhythmic slowing occurring at frequent intervals lasting one to three seconds. These changes are consistent with this symptomatology and as his history might suggest. It is difficult to know the etiology of this abnormal EEG. It is likely that this is a residual of some recurrent toxia or anoxic cerebral manifestations occurring in the past.

Interpretation

Paroxysmal dysrhythmic slowing. This change suggests a diffuse corticoid dysfunction of a chronic nature and the possibility of a lowered seizure threshold to generalize nonconvulsive and/or convulsive seizures without aura. These recommendations and changes should be improved with Valium.

Summary

After six months in the training program Mr. S terminated himself by leaving and going on the "road" again. It was felt by the rehabilitation counselor that the client had begun to take drugs again.

Vocational rehabilitation could not accept him for services again unless he went to a drug treatment halfway house for therapy. He refused to do this. This case was then closed—reason—failure to cooperate.

Case Reopened

After a month, Mr. S contacted his vocational rehabilitation counselor and asked for drug therapy and a chance to continue in his training. After a month in a drug treatment halfway house, client left. The vocational rehabilitation counselor was unable to locate Mr. S.

NOTE: The vocational rehabilitation counselor last heard that Mr. S is in Belgium traveling from place to place.

CHAPTER 20

LANGUAGE OF THE DRUG ABUSER

THIS SECTION OFFERS a glossary of the language of the drug user. The glossary is in no way complete, but every effort has been made to select those words and terms which may be used most frequently. The reader should remember that the use of these words varies dramatically among geographic regions. A word which is popular in one area may be used very seldom in another.

These words represent the word usage of many addicts throughout the country; however, it is doubtful that any one addict would be familiar with all the included terms.

The argot which addicts use gives a clear description of their way of life. From the terms the reader will be able to discern the compensatory use of drugs by the individual with an inadequate personality and the necessity for many users for escape from reality. Many of the words of the language of the addict are words or modifications used originally by opium smokers, and a number of these words are Oriental in origin.

If professionals are to be of help to members of the drug culture, they not only must understand the language of the drug abuser but also must have a feeling for the differences in his perceptions of words and his use of language. Work done by the authors (Cull and Hardy, 1973a; Cull and Hardy, 1973b; and Hardy and Cull, 1973) indicate subcultural groups use language in decidedly different fashions. Racial differences and differences in physical capacities cause individuals to use and perceive everyday language in an altered fashion. Consequently, professionals who work with drug abusers must understand the jargon of this group. This glossary is only the first step in developing this understanding.

LANGUAGE OF THE DRUG ABUSER

A

Abe—A five-dollar bill.

Acapulco Gold—A high quality of marijuana.

Acid—LSD (Lysergic Acid Diethylamide). Hallucinogen.

Acid Dropper—One who uses LSD.

Acid Freak—A habitual user of LSD; cube head.

Acid Head—LSD user.

Action—The selling of narcotics. Anything pertaining to criminal activities.

Amp—A 1-cc methedrine ampule, legitimate.

Amphetamines—Stimulants which are generally Dexedrine®, Benzedrine®, Methedrine®, or Biphetamine®. Bambita, bennies, bottles, browns, cartwheels, chick power, copilots, dexies, eye openers, footballs, greenies, hearts, jolly beans, jugs, LA turnabouts, lid proppers, orangies, peaches pep pills, roses, speed, truck drivers, ups, wake ups, whites.

Amys—Amyl nitrate, stimulant.

Angel Dust—PCP, an animal tranquilizer.

Artillery—Equipment for injecting drugs.

Away—In jail.

Axe—Musical instrument.

B

Back up—A condition in which blood backs up into the syringe while injecting a drug into the vein.

Backtrack—To make sure a needle is in proper position when mainlining by withdrawing the plunger of the syringe before actually injecting the drugs.

Bad Trip—Bummer.

Bag—Situation; category.

Bag—An envelope of heroin (see nickel bag and dime bag).

Bagman—An individual who sells drugs.

Bambita—Desoxyn® or amphetamine derivative.

Bambs—Barbiturates.

Band House—Jail.

Bang—Fix, shot; injection of narcotics.

Barbiturates—Sedatives, usually Seconal, Nembutal, Amutal®, Luminal®, Tuinal®, Barbs, blue heavens, double trouble, nimbie, peanuts, purple hearts, rainbows, red devils, sleeping pills, yellow jackets.

Barbs—Barbiturates.

Bay State—A standard medical hypodermic syringe, usually made of glass with metal reinforcement, using a plunger and screw-type needle.

Bean Trip—Intoxication from ingesting Benzedrine; a benny jag.

Beat—To cheat or out-bargain.

Bee That Stings—A drug habit, especially one coming on; "a monkey on my back."

Belt—The euphoria following an injection of narcotics. A shot or a quantity of drugs to be injected.

Bennies—Benzedrine.

Benny jag—Intoxication from ingesting Benzedrine.

Bernice—Cocaine.

Bhang—Marijuana. See *Cannabis.*

Big C—Cocaine.

Big D—LSD.

Big John—The police or any law enforcement officer.

Bindle—A small package of narcotics.

Bit—A prison sentence.

Black and White—A policeman.

Black Beauty—Speed in a black capsule.

Blackjack—Paregoric which has been cooked down to be injected in a concentrated form.

Blank—Bag of nonnarcotic power sold as a regular bag (also dummy, turkey).

Blanks—Gelatin capsules supposedly filled with a drug which are actually filled only with milk powder or sugar powder or sugar cubes supposedly saturated with LSD which have only food color.

Blasted—Under the influence of drugs.

Blast Party—Group gathered to smoke marijuana.

Blotter—A piece of absorbent paper on which LSD has been absorbed.

Blow—To lose something—to smoke marijuana.

Blow a Pill—To smoke opium.

Blow a Stick—To smoke a marijuana cigarette.

Blow Snow—To sniff cocaine.

Blow Weed—To smoke marijuana.

Blue Birds—Blues, barbiturates.

Blue Devil—Amobarbital sodium in solid blue form.

Blue Heavens—Barbiturates.

Blue Mist—A sugar cube colored blue by an LSD preparation.

Blues—Barbiturate.

Blue Velvet—Sodium amytal®, Pyribenzamine®.

Bombido—Injectible amphetamine (also jugs, bottles).

Boost—Steal.

Booster—A professional shoplifter, male or female.

Boot—Pushing and pulling the plunger of a syringe to cause a "rush."

Booze—Alcohol.

Bottles—Injectible amphetamines.

Boy—Heroin.

Bread—Money.

Brick—A kilogram of marijuana compressed under pressure to retain the shape of a brick.

Browns—Long-acting amphetamine sulfate (capsules, many colors, mainly brown).

Buffotenine—A drug chemically related to DMT derived from dried glandular secretions of certain toads as well as from the *amanita* fungus.

Bug—To annoy.

Bum Beef—False complaint or information which usually is given deliberately to the police.

Bum Kick—Boring, unpleasant.

Bum Rap—An arrest or conviction for a crime the man acually did not commit, as distinguished from denying it.

Bum Steer—See bum beef.

Bum Trip or Bummer—A bad trip on LSD.

Bundle—Twenty-five $5 bags of heroin.

Burned—Rendered useless or vulnerable by recognition; e.g. "A narcotic agent was burned and unable to continue surveillance." Also, to receive nonnarcotic or highly diluted drugs.

Bust or Busted—Arrested; broke.

Buttons—*See mescaline.*

Buy—A narcotic peddler; a purchase of narcotics.

C

Caballo—Heroin.

Cactus—See *peyote.*

Cactus Buttons—See *mescaline.*

Can—A car; A city jail.

Candy—Barbiturates.

Cannabis—Known variously as bhang, charas, dagga, ganja, kif, macoha, and marijuana.

Cap—A person, especially a young Black, who has to hustle to support his habit. Also, a gelatine capsule or a capsule of drugs.

Cartwheels—Amphetamine sulphate in round, white, double-scored tablets.

Cat Nap—To get small (and very welcome) snatches of sleep during the withdrawal period.

Chalk—Methedrine.

Charas—Marijuana. See *Cannabis.*

Charged Up—Under the influence of drugs.

Charley—Cocaine.

Charley Coke—A cocaine addict (restricted to New York and New England).

Chicago Leprosy—Multiple abscesses.

Chicken Out—Cop out.

Chicken Powder—Amphetamine powder.

Chip—Heroin.

Chipping—Taking narcotics occasionally.

Chippy—Nice-looking girl.

Chloral Hydrate—Joy juice.

Clear up—To withdraw from drugs.

Clout—To steal, especially as a shoplifter.

Coasting—The sensation of euphoria following the use of a drug. Used of all drugs except cocaine. Serving an easy prison sentence.

Coast-to-Coast—Long-acting amphetamine sulphate in round forms in many colors. Also LA turnabouts, copilots, browns.

Cocaine—Bernice, big C, charley, coke, corine, dust, flake, girl, gold dust, happy dust, heaven dust, her, ice, snow, star dust, white nurse.

Codeine—School boy.

Cohoba—Powdered seeds used as snuff.

Coke—Cocaine.

Coked Up—Under the influence of cocaine.

Cold Turkey—Sudden withdrawal without any alleviating drugs.

Come Down—The end of a trip; the depressed feeling when the drug effects are fading.

Connection—A drug supplier.

Contact—A person who has a connection or who knows a supplier of drugs.

Cooker—Bottle top or spoon used for dissolving heroin in water over flame.

Cook-It-Up—To prepare heroin (or other opiates) for injection by heating it in a cooking spoon.

Cool— (adj.) In complete control.

Cool— (v) To wait.

Cop a Fix—To obtain a ration of narcotics.

Copilots—Amphetamines. Also truck drivers, bennies.

Cop or Connect—To buy or get; to purchase drugs.

Cop-out—To inform; to pull out or chicken out; to confess; to alibi.

Cop to—Admit to stealing.

Corine—Cocaine.

Cotton—The small wisp of cotton placed in the cooking spoon and used as a filter when the solution is drawn up into the needle.

Cotton Head—A narcotics abuser who depletes his supply of narcotics and attempts to secure one more injection by recooking the cotton used from previous fixes.

Crackling Shorts—Breaking into cars.

Crank—Methedrine; stimulant.

Crash—An unpleasant ending of a trip.

Crash Pad—Apartment set up specifically for people to sleep in.

Crib—One's home or apartment. A house of prostitution. A hypochondriac with many persistent symptoms.

Croaker—Unscrupulous doctor who sells drugs or prescriptions to illicit drug users.

Crutch—Device used for holding shortened butt of Marijuana cigarette. See *Roach Clip.*

Crystal—Methedrine. See *Speed.*

Cube—LSD on sugar cubes.

Cube Head—See *Acid Freak.*

Cut—The dilution of a narcotic with substances like lactose (milk sugar) or quinine, strychnine, etc., in order to increase the profit of the drug trafficker.

Cut Out—To leave a certain place.

D

"D"—LSD.

Dagga—See *Cannabis.*

Daisy—A male homosexual. Also sissy, queen, sex punk.

Dead—No action.

Deal—Sell narcotics to addicts.

Dealer—Anyone who buys or sells stolen goods. A peddler.

Dealing—Keep on with whatever one is doing; selling dope.

Deck—Several bags of drugs.

Desoxyn—Amphetamine derivative.

DET—A chemically developed hallucinogenic drug—it has not been found occurring in nature.

Deuce—Two-dollar package of heroin.

Dexies—Dexedrine, stimulant.

Dig—To understand; to follow.

Dime Bag—A ten dollar purchase of narcotics.

Dirty—Possessing drugs, liable to arrest.

DMT—A hallucinogen found in the seeds of certain plants native to parts of South America and the West Indies. The powdered seeds have been used for centuries as a snuff, "Cohoba."

Dollies—Dolophine®; synthetic heroin.

Dolly—Methadone.

Dolophine—Dollies, synthetic heroin.

DOM or STP— (4-Methyl-2, 5-Dimethoxyamphetamine) An hallucinogenic drug produced in the laboratory which induces euphoria and other hallucinogenic effects.

Doo Jee—Heroin.

Dope—Narcotics. Information. To drug. This term, like "dope fiend," tends to be taboo among addicts, though they use both perjuratively.

Dope Hop—A prison term for drug addicts, mostly used by guards, turn-keys, and police.

Double Trouble—Amobarbital sodium combined with secobarbital sodium in red and blue capsules.

Down—Basic; depressed.

Downer Freak—A habitual user of "downers."

Downers—Sedatives, alcohol, tranquilizers and narcotics.

Dragged—A post-marijuana state of anxiety.

Drop—Swallow a drug.

Dropped—Taken orally.

Dry—Without drugs.

Dummy—A bag of nonnarcotic powder sold as a regular bag. Also blank, turkey.

Dust—Cocaine.

Dynamite—Something extra special or good.

E

Echos—See *Flashback*.

Eighth—Eighth of an ounce of heroin.

Electric—Overpowering, this is a positive statement.

Eye Dropper—Medicine dropper used with hypodermic needle as makeshift syringe. Most addicts actually prefer it to a syringe.

Eye Opener—Amphetamines.

F

Fag—A pimp. Not to be confused with the general slang *fag* (a homosexual) clipped from faggot.

Fall—To be arrested. To receive a prison sentence. See *Bust*.

Fat Jay—A marijuana cigarette approaching the size of a commercial cigarette or larger. They are made large to compensate for weaker types of marijuana.

Fed—A federal agent, usually a narcotics agent. Also, The Man, narco.

Finger—Stool pigeon.

Finger Gee—Stool pigeon.

Finger Wave—A rectal examination for contraband narcotics.

Finif or Finski—A five dollar bill.

Fink—A stool pigeon; an untrustworthy person. Also wrong, no good, rat.

Five-cent Bag—A five dollar Heroin Fix.

Fix—Injection of narcotics.

Flake—Cocaine.

Flash—A quick jolt of high in abdomen or across chest from heroin shot.

Flashback—Partial reoccurrence of an LSD trip.

Flea Powder—Grossly inferior heroin.

Flipped—Becoming psychotic after an overdose of drugs.

Floating—To be high on drugs.

Fly—Sophisticated yet carefree; wise in the ways of the underworld.

Flying—See *Floating.*

Footballs—Amphetamine sulphate in oval-shaped tablets of various colors. Also greenies.

Fox—Good-looking girl.

Freak—An individual who is excessive in some area; for example, "acid freak" or "speed freak."

Freak-out—Bad experience with hallucinogenic drugs.

Fuzz—Policeman or detective.

G

Gal Head—Narcotics addict.

Ganja—Marijuana. See *Cannabis.*

Garbage—See *Flea Powder.*

Gee Stick—An opium pipe. Obsolescent.

George—Very good.

Get a Finger Wave—The process of having the rectum searched for drugs.

Gig—Job.

Girl—Cocaine.

Give Wings—To start someone else on narcotics.

Going Up—Taking drugs, particularly "uppers."

Gold Dust—Cocaine.

Gold Leaf Special—A marijuana cigarette which is thought to be very potent.

Goods—Narcotics, especially as they are bought and sold. Used by addicts or dealers in letters, phone calls, or telegrams.

Goof Balls—Barbiturates.

Goofers—See *Goof Balls*.

Gow—Narcotics in general, especially those used hypodermically.

Grapes—Wine.

Grass—Marijuana.

Greenies—Amphetamine sulphate (oval-shaped tablets).

Green Score—Profit made by passing counterfeit money.

Gun—Hypodermic needle for injecting heroin.

H

"H"—Heroin.

Hack—A physician.

Hairy—Heroin.

Hang Tough—Take it easy, quiet down, stop.

Hang Up—A problem, generally a personal problem or a psychological problem.

Happy Dust—Cocaine.

Hard Stuff—Narcotics.

Harpoon—The hollow needle used with a joint. Also spike, silver serpent, pin, machine, tom cat.

Harry—Heroin.

Hashish or Hash—Marijuana.

Hawk—LSD.

Hay—Marijuana.

Head—A user of drugs. Usually a user of LSD.

Hearts—Dextoamphetamine sulphate in orange-colored, heart-shaped tablets. Also orangies, dexies, peaches, bennies, roses.
Heat—Police or detective.
Heaven Dust—Cocaine.
Heavy—Deep or profound.
Heeled—See *Dirty*.
Hemp—Marijuana.
Henry—Heroin.
Her—Cocaine.
Heroin—Boy, caballo, doo jee, "H," hairy, harry, henry, horse, joy powder, junk, scag, scat, skit, smack, stuff, tecata, white lady, white nurse.
High—Under the influence of drugs.
Hip—Aware.
Hit—To shoot a narcotic.
Hit On—To ask for.
Hog—PCP.
Holding—See *Dirty*.
Holding—Having drugs in one's possession.
Hooked—Addicted.
Hooker—Hustler, a prostitute.
Hop—Opium for smoking. Narcotics for injection or inhalation.
Hophead—Hype; a drug addict.
Hopped Up—Under the influence of narcotics.
Horse—Heroin.
Hot Shot—Cyanide or other poison concealed in narcotics to kill a troublesome addict.
Hump—To work.
Hustling—Activities involved in obtaining money to buy drugs.
Hype—Drug addict; hophead.

I

Ibogaine—Derived from the roots, bark, stem, and leaves of an African shrub.
Ice—Cocaine.
Ice Cream Habit—See *Chipping*.

Idiot Juice—Nutmeg and water mixed for intoxication, largely used in prisons.

Indian Hay—Marijuana.

Informer—Stool; an addict assisting police in arresting peddlers.

Iron Horse—A city jail. Most other underworld terms (can, joint, band house, etc.) are also used by addicts.

J

"J"—A joint of marijuana.

Jag—Under the influence of amphetamines.

Jailhouse High—A high obtained from eating nutmeg.

Jeff—To be obsequious, especially Negroes in relation to whites.

Jive— (adj.) Worthless.

Jive— (n) Marijuana.

Joint—A marijuana cigarette. The prison.

Jolly Beans—Amphetamines.

Joy Juice—Chloral hydrate.

Joy Pop—Use of heroin in small amounts occasionally.

Joy Powder—Heroin.

Jugs—Injectible amphetamines.

Juice—Alcohol.

Juice Head—An alcoholic.

Junk—Narcotics, usually heroin.

Junker—A narcotic addict.

Junkie—Narcotic addict.

K

Key—One kilo of marijuana.

Kick—Stop using narcotics through complete withdrawal.

Kick Back—The addict's almost inevitable return to narcotics after having kicked the habit.

Kick Cold—Treatment in which the addict is taken off drugs suddenly.

Kif—See *Cannabis.*

Kilo—A large amount of narcotics from a pusher's point of view; technically 2.2 pounds. See *Key.*

Knockers—The testicles. A woman's breast.
Knock Out Drops—Chloral hydrate.

L

LA Turnabouts—See *Coast-to-Coast*.
Lamb—The passive receptor in a homosexual relationship.
Lame—Square.
Laughing Grass—Marijuana.
Lay Dead—To do nothing.
Lemonade—See *Flea Powder*.
Lettuce—Money.
Lid—A small quantity of marijuana, usually about one ounce.
Lid Proppers—Amphetamines.
Lipton Tea—See *Mickey Finn*.
Lit—Under the influence of drugs.
Lit Up—Under the influence of drugs.
Load—See *Deck*.
Loco Weed—Marijuana.
Long-tailed Rat—Stool pigeon.
Louse—A stool pigeon. (Also finger, finger gee, long-tailed rat, mouse, rat).
LSD—Acid, sugar cubes, trips, Lysergic Acid Diethylamide, Big "D," Hawk.
Luminal—A barbiturate.

M

"M"—Morphine.
Machine—See *Harpoon*.
Macoha—See *Cannabis*.
MDA—Synthetic stimulant and hallucinogen.
Made—Recognized for what you are.
Mainline— (n) The vein, usually in the crook of the elbow, into which the needle addict injects narcotics.
Mainline— (v) To inject narcotics directly into a vein.
Maintain—Keeping your head during a difficult situation.
Maintaining—Injecting a narcotic directly into a vein.
Mandrix—See *Methaqualone*.

Manicure—Marijuana with everything removed except the leaves.

Marijane—Marijuana.

Marijuana—Bahang, cannabis, charas, ganja, grass, hash, hashish, hay, hemp, Indian hay, jive, laughing grass, loco weed, jarijane, pot, railroad, weed, reefer, rope, tea, Texas tea, weed.

McCoy—Medicinal drugs in contrast to bootleg drugs.

Medical Hype—A person who has become accidentally addicted during medical treatment for illness or disease; one who obtains bona fide drugs through doctors or hospitals.

Mellowing—The period of a crash when a person is on speed.

Melsedin (In England)—See *Methaqualone.*

Mesc—Mescaline; hallucinogenic drug derived from the bottoms of the peyote cactus plant native to Central America and Southwestern United States. (Also peyote.)

Meth—Methedrine or Methadone.

Methadone—Dolly, dolophine amidone.

Methaqualone—An addictive, sedative, hypnotic drug. See *Mandrix, Melsedin* (in England), optimil, parest, Quaalude®, "soapers," Sopor, Strasenburgh's Tuazole (in England).

Mickey—Chloral hydrate.

Mickey Finn or Mickey—Chloral hydrate in a drink to knock out a victim. Also euphemistically, "Lipton Tea." A powerful physic such as croton oil, slipped into a whiskey to make the victim sick or to drive him away from a hangout.

Mike—A microgram.

Miss Emma—Morphine.

Mojo—Narcotics of any kind in a contraband trade; but usually morphine, heroin, or cocaine.

Monkey—A drug habit involving physical dependence.

Monkey on my back—Early abstinence symptoms. A drug habit.

Morphine—Hard stuff, "M," Miss Emma, morpho, white nurse, white stuff, unkie.

Morpho—Morphine.

Mother—An individual's drug peddler.

Mouse—A stool pigeon.

Mr. Twenty-Six—A needle (refers to the gauge of the needle).

N

Nailed—To be arrested.

Narc or Narcos—The law; narcotic agent.

Needle Fiend—An addict who gets pleasure from playing with the needle by inserting an empty needle for the psychological effect.

Needle Freak—One who enjoys using the needle. See *Needle Fiend.*

Needle Habit—A habit which is satisfied by hypodermic injections.

Needle Park—To New York addicts, upper Broadway and Sherman Square.

Needle Yen—A desire for narcotics taken hypodermically. A masochistic desire to mainline.

Nembies—Nembutal.

Nemmies—Nembutal.

Nickel—A five dollar bag of narcotics or marijuana; also a five-year sentence.

Nickel Deck—Five-dollar package of Heroin.

Nimble—Nembutal.

Nimbies—Nembutal (Pentobarbital).

Nimby—Nembutal (Pentobarbital).

Nod—To be sleepy from a dose of drugs.

Nut City—A mythical place in which anyone feigning insanity is said to live.

O

OD—An overdose of narcotics.

Off—Off of drugs, not to be taking drugs at the present time.

Off Someone—To kill someone or to beat someone up.

On Ice—In jail. To lie low or go out of sight temporarily. Wanted by the law.

On the Nod—Sleep from narcotics.

OP—Opium.

Opiates—Narcotics. Generally either opium, morphine or heroin.

Opium—OP.

Optimil—See *Methaqualone.*

Orange Owsley—See *Owsley Acid.*

Orangies—Dexedrine (Dextroamphetamine, orange colored, heart-shaped tablets).

Out-of-it—Confused, disoriented, unknowing; also, an outside person who is not part of the drug culture.

Out There—Confused.

Overjolt—Overdose of heroin.

Owsley's Acid—LSD (West Coast slang after the illegal manufacturer, Augustus Owsley Stanley, III).

Owsley's Blue Dot—See *Owsley's Acid.*

O.Z.—One ounce of marijuana.

P

Pack Heat—To carry a gun.

Pad—User's home; place where he shoots up.

Paid off in gold—Arrested by a federal officer who flashes his gold badge.

Panic—Shortage of narcotics on the market.

Paper—A legal prescription for drugs.

Parest—See *Methaqualone.*

PCP—Angel dust. Peace pill. Hog.

Peace Pill—PCP.

Peaches—Amphetamine sulphate in rose-colored, heart-shaped tablets. (Also roses, hearts, bennies, orangies).

Peanuts—Barbiturates.

Peddler—A seller of narcotics.

Pep Pills—Amphetamines. Also, wake-ups, eye openers.

Pet—The police.

Peter—Chloral hydrate.

Petes—Chloral hydrate.

Peyote—Mescaline.

P.G.—Paregoric.

Phat—Well put together.

Piece—One ounce of heroin; a gun.

Pill Head—Addict on pills.

Pin—See *Harpoon.*

Pink Owsleys—See *Owsley's Acid.*

Pinks—Seconal (Secobarbital sodium).

Pipe—An opium smoker.

Plant—Stash-cache of narcotics.

Pluck—Wine.

P.O.—A parole or probation officer.

P.O.—Paregoric.

Pot—Marijuana.

Pratt or Prat—A hip pocket.

Psilocybin or Psilocyn—Hallucinogenic drugs derived from certain mushrooms generally grown in Mexico.

Purple Hearts—A barbiturate.

Purple Owsley—See *Owsley's Acid.*

Pusher—Seller or dealer of drugs.

Put On—To deceive by design; to make fun of or to mislead someone.

Put the bee on—The act of begging narcotics.

Put the croaker on the send—A "fit" or spasm staged by an addict to elicit sympathy.

Q

Quaalude—See *Methaqualone.*

Queen—Male homosexual.

Quill—Matchbook cover used to inhale narcotics. Powdered drug is placed in fold.

R

Rags—Clothes.

Railroad Weed—Marijuana of poor quality.

Rainbow Roll—An assortment of vari-colored barbiturates, popular among addicts on the West Coast.

Rainbows—Amobarbital sodium combined with secobarbital sodium in red and blue capsules. Also, red and blues and double trouble.

Rap—Talk.

Rat—Stool pigeon.

R.D.—A red devil.

Red and Blues—See *Rainbows.*

Red Devils—See *Reds.*

Reds—Seconal, secobarbital sodium.

Reefer—Marijuana cigarette.

Riff—Train of thought.

Right On—Affirmation of a truth; encouragement or support.

Rip Off—Steal or purchase of false narcotics.

Roach—Butt of a marijuana cigarette.

Roach Clip—A device used to hold the butt of a marijuana cigarette.

Rope—Marijuana. So called because when smoked it smells of burning hemp.

Roses—Benzedrine (Amphetamine Sulphate), rose-colored, heart-shaped tablets.

Rosy—Wine.

Run—Period of addiction.

Rush—The intense orgasm-like euphoria experienced immediately after injecting a drug. Also, flash.

S

Sam—Federal narcotic agents.

Satch—A method of concealing or smuggling drugs into jails.

Satchel—A girl.

Scag—Heroin.

Scat—Heroin.

Scene—Where something is happening.

Schmeck—Heroin.

School Boy—Codeine.

Scorch—To abuse someone verbally and very severely.

Score—To find a source of drugs.

Script—A prescription written by a physician to obtain drugs.

Script Writer—A sympathetic physician; someone who forges prescriptions.

Seccy—Seconal (Secobarbital sodium).

Seconal—Sleeping pill; depressant, pinks.

Send it home—To inject narcotics intravenously.

Serpent—See *Harpoon*.

Sewer—The vein into which drugs are injected.

Sex Punk—A male homosexual.

Shakedown—To be arrested or held without charges in order to persuade the addict to supply information to police.

Shank—Knife.

Shit—Heroin.

Shoot—See *Maintaining*.

Shooting Gallery—Place where several addicts gather to shoot dope.

Shoot Up—See *Mainlining*.

Short—Car.

Short Go—A small or weak shot.

Shrink—A psychiatrist or psychologist.

Shucking—Wasting time.

Shy—To prepare a pill of opium for smoking.

Silver—See *Harpoon*.

Silver Serpent—See *Harpoon*.

Sissy—A male homosexual.

Sitter—An individual who is sophisticated in the use of drugs, who will oversee others who are on LSD to make sure they don't harm themselves.

Sixteenth Spoon—Sixteenth of an ounce of heroin.

Skin—Cigarette paper used for a marijuana cigarette.

Skin Popping—Injecting drugs under the skin.

Sleeping Pills—Barbiturates.

Smack—Heroin.

Smashed—High on drugs.

Sneaky Pete—Wine.

Sniff—To sniff narcotics (usually heroin, cocaine, or glue).

Snort—To sniff powdered narcotics.

Snow—Cocaine.

Snowbird—A cocaine user.

Soapers—See *Methaqualone*.

Sopor—See *Methaqualone*.

Sound Someone—To feel someone out.

Speed—Methamphetamine; any stimulant, especially amphetamines.

Speedball—A cocaine-heroin combination.

Speeder—A user of methamphetamine.

Speed Freak—An excessive user of methamphetamine.

Speeding—Using methamphetamine.

Spike—See *Harpoon.*

Splash—Methamphetamine.

Split—To leave a place, sometimes in haste.

Spot Habit—See *Ice Cream Habit.*

Square—Lame.

Stable—The community of girls who prostitute for one pimp.

Star Dust—Cocaine.

Stash—A place to hide drugs or money; generally a place well-hidden but readily available.

Steam Boat—A tube such as an empty toilet tissue roll which is used to increase the amount of smoke from a marijuana cigarete going into the lungs in order to increase the effectiveness of the cigarette.

Steam Roller—See *Steam Boat.*

Stick—A marijuana cigarette.

Stir—Prison.

Stoned—High on drugs.

STP—Hallucinogen; lasts for seventy-two hours.

Straight—An addict's feeling of well-being after taking drugs.

Strasenburgh's Tuazole (in England)—See *Methaqualone.*

Strawberries—An LSD preparation.

Strung-out—Confused.

Stuff—Heroin.

Sugar—Narcotics, generally heroin.

Sugar Cube—This is quite often a vehicle for LSD, a drop of LSD is absorbed by the sugar cube before being taken.

Sunshine—An orange or yellow tablet of LSD reputedly to be of a very potent strength.

Swingman—A drug peddler.

T

T or T Man—A big man. A federal agent, especially a "narco."

Take a Trip—Using LSD.

Take Off—To smoke. To rob a place, especially of narcotics.

Taste—Small quantity of narcotics usually given as a reward or favor.

Tea—Marijuana.

Tea Man—A marijuana user.

Tecata—Heroin.

Ten-cent Pistol—Bag containing poison.

Texas Tea—Marijuana.

THC—Synthetic hallucinogen; produces same effect as marijuana. Tetra Hydro Cannabinol. The active ingredients in marijuana.

The Man—Policeman or detective.

Ticket—A dose of LSD.

Tie Off—Stopping circulation in order for veins to rise.

Tight—Close.

Tinge—See *Flash*.

Tired—Old or worn out.

Tom Cat—See *Harpoon*.

Tooies—Tuinal capsules. See *Double Trouble*.

Tracks—Scars along the veins after many injections.

Trap—Prison.

Travel Agent—A person who sells LSD.

Trey—Three-dollar bag of narcotics; generally heroin.

Tripping—Taking a hallucinating drug.

Tripping Out—Same as tripping.

Truck Drivers—Amphetamines.

Tuanol—Sleeping pill; depressant.

Tuinal—A barbiturate. Also called rainbows or double trouble.

Turkey—Clod or square. A bag of nonnarcotic powder sold as a regular bag.

Turn On—To be excited by; to get high on drugs.

TV Action—Euphoria from drugs.

U

Unkie—Morphine.

Uppers—Stimulants; cocaine, speed and psychedelics.

V

Vegetable—A person who has lost all contact with reality due to drugs.

Very Outside—Extremely far out or weird.

Vet—A prison or jail physician.

Vines—Clothes.

Vipe—To smoke marijuana.

Viper—A marijuana smoker.

W

Wake Up—Morning shot.

Wake-ups—Amphetamines.

Wasted—Stoned or drunk.

Way Out—Incomprehensible. The best.

Weed—Marijuana.

Wheels—Car.

White Cross—A white tablet of speed which is sectioned with a cross.

White Lady—Heroin.

White Nurse—A term used to cover cocaine, morphine or heroin; but more often morphine.

White Owsley's—See *Owsley's Acid.*

Whites—Amphetamine Sulphate in round, white double-scored tablets.

White Stuff—"M," hard stuff, morphine.

Wig—Head, hair.

Wig Out—To become psychotic as a result of narcotics.

Wine—Grapes, pluck, rosy, sneaky pete.

Wired—Addicted on a narcotic drug.

Works—Equipment for injection of drugs.

Y

Yellow Jackets—Nembutal, barb, depressant. Phenobarbital Sodium in yellow capsule form.

Yellows—Nembutal.

Z

Zonked—Under the influence of narcotics.

REFERENCES

Cull, J. G., and Hardy, R. E.: A study of language meaning (gender shaping) among deaf and hearing subjects. *J Perceptual and Motor Skills, 36:* 98, 1973a.

Cull, J. G. and Hardy, R. E.: Language meaning (gender shaping among blind and sighted students). *J Psychol, 83:*333-334, 1973b.

Hardy, R. E. and Cull, J. G.: Verbal dissimilarity among black and white subjects: A prime concern in counseling and communication. *J Negro Educ, 42*(1):67-70, 1973.

Hardy, R. E. and Cull, J. G.: *Drug Language and Lore.* Springfield, Thomas, 1975.

INDEX

A

Acceptance, 9
Activities of Daily Work Scale, 206, 208
Addiction
    drug, 180, 282, 298, 299, 301
    withdrawal, 267
Adjustment
    psychological, 1-2, 80, 118, 139, 265
    training, 264
    work, 208, 264
Adler, Alfred, 86, 194
Administrative responsibility, 153
Age discrimination, 255
Agency
    coordination, 110
    responsibilities, 154
    roles, 154
Aggressor, 220
Aging
    emotional aspects, 256
    process, 264
    psychological adjustment, 265
    psychological aspects, 257
    social needs, 260
Alexander, M., 184, 189
Allan, W. S., 34, 36
Allport, G., 96, 104
Ambrosia, Lillian, 248, 253
American Association of Marriage and
    Family Counselors, 218
American Mutual Insurance Alliance, 43
American Psychiatric Association (APA),
    179
American Psychological Association, 26,
    31, 218
Amphetamines, 302, 303
Antisocial reaction, 180
Architectural barriers, 45, 125
Arrest record, 192
Artificiality, 229
Association of Volunteer Bureaus, 62
Auditory clues, 113

Auerbach, A. H., 105
Axelrod, S., 245

B

Bachrach, H., 105
Barker, R., 89, 104
Barrett, A., 55
Bauman, Mary K., 46, 53, 54, 104, 112,
    114, 127
Baumeister, Alfred A., 209
Beard, Bruce, 117, 123
Beers, Clifford W., 61, 72
Behavior
    conformity, 256, 272
    group, 226, 231
    impulsive, 200
    maladaptive, 207
    modeling, 228
    non-verbal, 13
    runaway, 248-250, 252
    socially responsible, 252
    test, 285
    vocational, 38, 239
Behavioral patterns, 21, 140, 165
Berne, Eric, 274
*Blindness, What It Is, What It Does and
    How to Live With It,* 111
Body image, 87, 91, 95, 137
Borderline retarded persons, 205
Bors, E., 104
Bozarth, J. D., 18
Brammer, Lawrence M., 18
Bridges, C. C., 48, 54, 115
Brill, A. A., 238, 245
Brown, H. R., 124, 127
Bruebacher, John, 127
Byrne, R. A., 243, 245
Byrne, Richard H., 127

C

Caplow, T., 238, 245
Career planning, 235, 236

333

Williamson, E. G., 127
Wilson, W. D., 117, 123
Withdrawal, 98, 103
  symptoms, 267
Work adjustment, 208, 264
  training, 264
Work evaluation, 38
Work evaluators, 206, 208
Work orientation, 235
Work personality profile, 38

Work release program, 167, 185
Work training, 48
Workers Worth Their Hire, 41
Working relationship, 6
Wrenn, C. Gilbert, 127
Wright, B., 87, 89, 104, 106
Wright, K. C., 36, 55, 116

Y

Yoder, N. M., 46, 53, 104, 112, 114, 127